CONVERSATIONS
ON *Success*

To Your Great Success!!

Pat Mayfield

INSIGHT PUBLISHING
SEVIERVILLE, TENNESSEE

Published by Insight Publishing Company
P.O. Box 4189
Sevierville, Tennessee 37864

10 9 8 7 6 5 4 3 2

Printed in The United States

ISBN: 1-932863-78-8

Table Of Contents

A Message From The Publisher

Some of my most rewarding experiences in business, and for that matter in my personal life, have been at meetings, conventions, or gatherings after the formal events have concluded. Inevitably, small groups of ten to fifteen men and women gather together to rehash the happenings of the day and to exchange war stories, recently heard jokes, or the latest gossip from their industry. It is in these informal gatherings where some of the best lessons can be learned.

Usually, in informal groups of professionals, there are those who clearly have lived through more battles and learned more lessons than the others. These are the men and women who are really getting the job done and everyone around the room knows it. When they comment on the topic of the moment, they don't just spout the latest hot theory or trend, and they don't ramble on and on without a relevant point. These battle scarred warriors have lessons to share that everyone senses are just a little more real, more relevant, and therefore worthy of more attention.

These are the kind of people we have recruited to offer their insights and expertise for *Conversations On Success*. The book is filled with frank and powerful discussions with men and women who are making a significant impact on their culture, in their field, and on their colleagues and clients. It is ripe with "the good stuff," as an old friend of mine used to always say. Inside these pages you'll find ideas, insights, strategies, and philosophies that are working with real people, in real companies, and under real circumstances.

It is our hope that you keep this book with you until you've dog-eared every chapter and made so many notes in the margins that you have trouble seeing the original words on the pages. There is treasure here. Enjoy digging!

Interviews conducted by:

David E. Wright
President, International Speakers Network

Chapter 1

TERRY STROM

THE INTERVIEW

David E. Wright (Wright)
Today we are talking to Terry Strom. Terry started his career as an engineer with an MBA from the University of Southern California. He then moved into sales has been the Vice President of Sales and Business Development for a software development firm and a technical consulting company. He has been a Vice President/Director of Sales for an international medical service firm, and created a large international direct sales company. He has spoken to over 250,000 sales professionals on stages with Tom Landry, Rudy Rutiger, Charlie "Tremendous" Jones, Oliver North, Wes Bevis, Tim Timmons, Willie Jollie and many others. He does training, motivational keynote addresses, and breakout sessions in the areas of motivation, sales skills, and communication skills. Also as a sales coach/consultant he helps businesses create and improve their sales process, develop successful sales teams, develop sales training systems, and most importantly increase their sales. Terry welcome to *Conversations on Success.*

Terry Strom (Strom)
Hello David, how are you?

1

Wright

Terry, why do you say everyone sells and that you believe that the sales vocation is the highest calling of a profession, if done properly?

Strom

First of all, everyone is involved in sales. When we look for a spouse we're selling, when we look for a job we're selling, when we're trying to convince a friend to do something our way, we're selling. What I mean when I say selling can be the highest calling of a profession if done properly is; if you are truly doing a good job in sales, you are not a salesperson - you are a trusted advisor. You are someone your clients are looking to for help with finding a solution to their problems.

Sales is not just selling a product or service, but determining what the needs, desires, and wants of your clients are, and then giving them a solution to those problems. Over time, if you are a trusted advisor, you clients actually come to you not just for products or services, but for ideas and solutions - they come to trust your knowledge and wisdom because you are the person who's brought solutions to them in the past. That's really what selling done properly is - determining the need and then finding a solution to take care of that need. If you are a trusted advisor, you become someone who has much more value to your clients than just that of a salesperson. This is true whether you are selling for a company in a paid position, you're the owner of a company, you are selling directly to the general public, or you're selling to other businesses. The idea here is that you are bringing solutions to them that make their lives better, you're bringing more income into their businesses, your bringing more income and/or time into their lives, and ultimately you are bringing a higher lifestyle to them. This is what you are providing by being a trusted advisor. That's what I mean when I say selling can be the highest calling of a profession if done properly.

Wright

You have said in the past that commitment and focus are really important to a sales career. Could you tell our readers why you feel that way?

Strom

To explain this, I will give you this example: think of a man walking across a freshly watered lawn in his flat loafers and the water is squishing under his feet. Then think of his wife, who may be half as heavy as him, walking across the same freshly watered lawn wearing her pointiest high heeled pumps. Then visualize her falling backwards as those pointy high heeled pumps sink deeply into the soil. Those pointy high heeled pumps will have much deeper penetration into the wet soil because all of her weight is concentrated in a small targeted area. Meaning that where you have maximum focus, pressure, and force in a small area, you will have maximum penetration into that area. It's the same for sales, where you focus with a lot of effort in a very targeted market, you will have higher penetration into that market.

Therefore, whatever you do in sales you need to focus on your target market, and most importantly on the specific needs of that target market. That's where you're going to get the maximum penetration and best results. I give the same example of the high-heel pumps with defining a target market. A lot of people in business, including salespeople, go after a broad spectrum of potential clients. However, If you can narrow your potential clients down to a very specific target market that has a very specific need for what you offer, and you learn what that need is, then when you sell to that market you're going to have much more penetration (and success) in that market.

Additionally, if you're going to be successful in any endeavor you have to be committed, and this is particularly true in sales because it's an occupation where you can make a lot of money, but you have be committed and persistent to make it work successfully. Therefore, understand that in sales you can make a lot of money and succeed or make very little money and fail based upon whether or not you are committed to your plan.

I think of the example of the Greek sea captain who took all of his warriors across the Mediterranean Sea to fight a war against an enemy. He dropped off all of his soldiers onto the foreign soil and then he ordered all the ships to be burned. Then as the soldiers were watching their ships burning, they said "Oh my gosh we're going to die here!" What they realized very quickly was that they either win the battle or they die, and as a result they had a much more focused and committed attitude towards winning that battle, and therefore they did. It's the same thing with sales. If you're going to be successful, you need to make a commitment that you're going to focus all of your energy and stay committed in a long-term persistent manner on developing your sales cycle, developing your clientele, following through, closing deals, and bringing in the sales.

The number one rule in sales is you have to get started and stay persistent and consistent to create momentum and sales. For example, there are a lot of people who do a lot of jogging. However, before they started jogging they really didn't want to jog, and the night before they started jogging they made the decision that they were going to start the next morning. That night, they set the alarm clock for five in the morning; the alarm clock goes off and the bed feels very comfortable and they hit the snooze button. They sleep a little bit longer and they hit the snooze button again and again. Pretty soon it's too late to go jogging and they get up and think, "Oh well, I can't go jogging today because its too late – Oh well." Then they are frustrated because they didn't go jogging, however, the next night they make a new decision and say, "I'm going to get up tomorrow morning and I'm going to go jogging." Again, the alarm goes off and they hit the snooze button, but they think, "You know what, I need to get up, and I need to jog." Therefore they get up and go jogging, and man it's cold out there and it's not fun. They don't feel good, its cold and dark, they haven't jogged in a long time or ever, and they're out of shape and really hurting. Then the next morning they do it again, and the next morning again, and over time, even though at the beginning it was extremely hard to get started, it's now actually easy to get up. In fact, it's starting to get fun because they're starting to see some results. Now they start to jog and don't get so out of breath, and all of a sudden they start to get that little euphoric feeling of getting into shape. The endorphins start popping when the jog is finished, and they really start feeling good about what they just did. In fact, now it's easy to get up in the morning because they're starting to get in shape, and it's starting to work, and they are creating momentum.

It's the same with sales, in the beginning you're making the cold calls, you're getting out to those clients through mailers, and calling and dropping in at their offices, etc. At first it doesn't seem like anything's happening, it's painful to make the cold calls, but you've got to get it started. After a while you're starting to prime the pump. You're starting to develop relationships. People start calling you back. You start making and going to the appointments, then you start to close a few deals. All of a sudden it starts to get exciting, the momentum is starting to grow, and your sales are starting to close and become profitable for you. But, before you can create momentum and have success, you have got to get started.

Wright

What do you mean that in sales you must learn from every situation, whether it is good or bad?

Strom

I look at sales as a learning process, where you learn by actual experience. I have a term I use called "verbal sparring" (I'm kind of a connoisseur of martial arts). I've done a couple of different styles, some were full contact where you actually make contact with the person and the other was where you pull your punches. What I realized is that in the martial arts style where you pulled your punches and you don't really hit your opponent and they don't really hit you, I never really got good at it. I didn't learn how to take a punch or to balance myself when I took a kick, a punch, or a block. My body did not learn how to stay centered and balanced when I was actually in a fighting situation. I found I learned best when I was in the actual environment that required full contact, where I was in the real situation with a real combatant. It was in these situations where I learned to take a punch or a kick properly and not get off balance or get un-centered.

It's the same with sales, the best way to get good at sales is to learn while you are in the actual process with real people, experiencing real challenges, and real objections, and learning from everything you do. I remember when I first started in sales and I'd go do a follow-up appointment and I wasn't able to close the sale, then I'd be driving away and I'd have a case of what I call "delayed intelligence," where I forgot what might have been the most important thing I should have said, which could of closed the sale. But I'd already driven away, and as a result I would become very frustrated and mad at myself. I would say to myself, if I would have just said this or that I would have closed the sale. But I didn't, instead I forgot and so I beat myself up as I was driving down the road. However, I realized that getting mad at myself was not helping me move forward in my sales career, but backwards because it was de-motivating me. Therefore, from then on I decided that I was only going to do what was going to move me forward and not backwards, and from that day on I learned to learn from every experience good or bad. Therefore after that point, each time I made a mistake after I left an appointment, I'd be driving down the road yelling at myself. saying, "Terry, did you learn something from the mistake you just made?" I'd yell back to myself, "Yes!" Then I'd say, "Terry, are you going to do something different in the future as a result of what you just learned?" I'd say. "Yes," Then I would say: "Ok Terry, now that you have learned something from that mistake, it was a positive experience, therefore learn from it and move on."

As a result, from then on when I make a mistake or an error and thought I should have done something differently, I would learn from it and implement it correctly the next time, therefore making it a positive experience. Then, if I forgot again, I would go through that same process. What I learned from this is that you can read about something one time, five times, or ten times and you may still not learn it, but when you make a mistake, there is a much higher probability that you will learn from it.

Additionally, there are three types of people in the buying/selling process. First there are "no/no's," those are the people who will never buy from you. Then there are "yes/no's," who are people who could buy from you under the right situation if you handle their objections properly. Lastly, there are "yes/yes's"—which are that small 3 to 4 percent of people who at any one time are always ready to buy what you have. However if you practice on the no/no's, who are never going to buy from you (so there is nothing to lose by practicing on them), you will get better at dealing with objections, giving your sales presentation, and going through the sales process. Therefore if you practice with the no/no's, when you get in front of a yes/no, there is a very high probability that you can turn them into a yes/yes.

Wright

You have said that great sales people develop a strong sense of intuition, what do you mean?

Strom

I remember after spending several years in sales and getting very good at it, I would go on a follow-up appointments with one of my sales people as a sales manager. They may have been working with this client for days, weeks, months, or longer. I would walk into the room, talk to the client for a few minutes, close the deal, and walk out. Then my sales people would look at me and say, "How did you do that?"

Each time you are in a sales situation and learn from it, as I said earlier through verbal sparring, a new file was put into your brain. Therefore, each and every time you go to do a follow up or to do a sales presentation another file is inputted. Then after a while when you have been through so many different experiences you can walk into a room and in a nanosecond your brain looks for the file closest to that situation and pulls out that file. You then start to go in that direction, and sometimes it's right and you just close the deal right then. However, it's not the right situation your brain will create a new file combining the initial information with the new information; and then sticks it back into your brain as a new file for future reference. Then your brain takes this new information into account and goes looking for the next closest file to that and brings it out to guide you.

What actually happened is that by going through so many different sales experiences, I developed an intuition because I had actually been there before (through the brain-file process I described in the paragraph above); and was therefore able to develop a "feel" for the situation just by walking into the room that made me so much more effective. This is what I mean by intuition and anyone can develop it by verbal sparing and learning from each and every sales experience.

Wright

What do you mean when you tell a new salesperson to "live in the land of uncomfortable?"

Strom

To most people sales can be an uncomfortable endeavor, especially when prospecting and cold calling. I teach new salespeople that once you have done your prospecting, made your cold contacts, people are starting to call you back, and started to develop a base of clients and customers; that's when it gets fun; because now you're just following up with people, taking orders, and closing sales. However, at the very beginning, as you're establishing your base, I tell new sales people that for that first several months (six months to a year) that they are going to live in the land of uncomfortable if they want to be successful. During that time you need to do what most people don't want to do such as prospecting and cold calling. However, I have a saying, "I will do today what other people will not do, so I can live a lifestyle tomorrow that other people will never live."

Understand that the most successful people in the world have learned to do the things that they don't want to do for a period of time; and when you think about it, there are a lot of people in this world who don't make a lot of money, who aren't successful, and who have never pushed themselves to do what's uncomfortable. They may be in a job where they're bored and not happy, but they are comfortable, and they have never pushed themselves to do the uncomfortable. To be successful in sales you need to push yourself to do what is not comfortable for a period of time, and if you think about it, how many people are successful compared to how many people are not, and I can guarantee that the majority of people who are successful have done uncomfortable things that unsuccessful people were not willing to do. Therefore I encourage you to be willing to live in the land of uncomfortable and do what you don't want to do for a while to establish your sales business.

Wright

Let's talk about the different sales postures; specifically passive, assertive, and aggressive.

Strom

In sales there are three ways that sales people deal with their clients and customers. One is called passive, meaning "your rights are important but mine are not." People may like these kinds of salespeople, but they may not respect them or buy from them; and many passive people get pushed around and walked on by others. Secondly, there's what I call aggressive sales people, where they run under the mindset "my rights are important, but your rights are not." These salespeople are what I call "drivers," and they tend to run over people. They may get things done and people may respect them, but they don't like them and don't build long term profitable relationships with them. Lastly, there's the assertive sales person, who runs under the mindset "my rights are important and your rights are important." People generally respect and like this type of salesperson, and this mindset is the best for establishing long term profitable relationships that continue for many years.

Therefore, the most successful mindset for sales is the assertive mindset. Let me give you an example of why this is so. Let's say your setting up a follow-up appointment with one of your clients and you don't want a no-show or last minute cancellation that wastes your time. Therefore, you should be thinking in your mind as you're setting up that appointment, "John, you have the right to say no to meeting with me, but John if you say yes, I have the right to expect you to be there when you said you were going to be there." Then in real time, as you're working with John to set up the appointment, you can actually say to him, "John are you sure you going to be at your office at 3:00 pm on Thursday to meet with me?." Then if John says "yes," I further lock in John by taking it away from him and making him take it back from me. I do this by saying "great John, therefore are you sure you're going to be there outside of a major emergency, because if your not, then we have to reschedule for another time when you are sure, because I can't afford to waste that appointment time". Now if John says "well if that is it case maybe we should reschedule," he was going to cancel and not be there any way, in which case you would of wasted your time. However, if says "yes, I will be there," then he has taken it back from you and there is much higher chance of him actually following through with the appointment. This is the assertive way of doing business where your rights are important and my rights are important. This shows your clients that you respect both their time and your time. However, and most importantly, you must always show your clients that you respect your time, because if you don't then your clients will not respect your time either. Understand that when you act in the assertive area where you expect others to follow through with what they say they're going to do; there's a much higher chance that they will.

Wright

What is the assertive/aggressive boundary?

Strom

I find that there's an area between being assertive and being aggressive where people need to be pushed a little bit. Let me give you an example. This will also involve what I call "no one buys in the land of polite." I'm going to be able to teach this by actually giving an example. I remember early on in my career when things were really starting to take off, and I had just finished my MBA from USC, I decided I needed to get myself a stockbroker or investment counselor. I started by calling on different stockbrokers and there was an investment counselor who worked with one of our family members. They put him in touch with me and he came over to our house, and let's say his name was Joe. Anyway, Joe came over and he gave me a great presentation on flip chart with shiny, glossy pages. He told me a little about his background, and that he had a degree in divinity (I have nothing against a degree in divinity but he just didn't seem like he was a business oriented type of person). I had just finished my MBA and I actually felt I knew more about the stock market than he did. He set up a follow-up appointment for me the next week and I said fine, let's get together then. I then told him, "Joe I'm going to be meeting with other stock brokers and investment counselors in the interim, and by the time we get together I may have already picked someone else." He said, "no problem, but here's some information, check it out and let's get back together next week." So we set the appointment.

The following day or two I meet with a stockbroker who I was very impressed with. This guy was sharp,, he was talking MBA talk, I could tell he knew his stuff, he was already very successful, he lived in a very successful area, he had done well, and I was excited - he was my guy.

Joe then came over the next week for the follow-up appointment. I already knew that I was not going to work with him. This is where my saying "nothing happens in the land of polite" comes in. Right then, because I knew he was wasting his time, I was very polite. I just wanted to get him out of my home as soon as possible so he wouldn't waste any more of his time. I felt uncomfortable because I knew I was not buying from him. Joe went through his follow-up and at the end he attempted to close the sale with me.

I said, "Well Joe, I'm really not interested right now."

He said, "Okay, not a problem, I really appreciate your time. Here's my information. If you ever change your mind, please give me a call," and he left.

The problem was, did he have any idea why I said no? No he didn't. We have a saying in engineering that fifty percent of the problem is solved once you know what the problem is. Joe had no idea what the problem was and why I wasn't buying, so he could not deal with any objections because he didn't know anything about why I was not interested.

What Joe should have done is pushed me past the assertive/aggressive boundary. That means he should have put me on the spot, taken me a little out of my comfort zone, been a little aggressive with me, and made me give him the real reason why I was not buying. He should have said something like, "Terry, last week when we got together you said you really were interested in getting an investment counselor or stockbroker, and is that still true?" I would of said "Yes."

"Then Terry, if that's still true, why aren't we doing business right now?" Well now I would have to say something I didn't want to say when I was in the land of polite, Then I didn't want to hurt his feelings, but now that he pushed me, we were no longer in the land of polite, Therefore, I'd say, "Joe, I saw your presentation and it was nice and everything, but I felt having an MBA myself that I had more experience with stocks and business than you did with your degree in divinity. I felt that you really did not know that much about stocks and that you used your flip chart as a crutch, and therefore I wasn't impressed and I felt that I knew more about stocks than you did."

Now that we were no longer living in the land of polite because Joe pushed me past the assertive-aggressive boundary, he had gotten my objection out of me, and because I wasn't being polite anymore, I had given him the real reason I was not buying. When I was in the land of polite, I didn't want to hurt his feelings so I wasn't going to tell him that I didn't think he was qualified. But now that he had pushed me passed the assertive/aggressive boundary, I had told him the truth, and now he had something to work with. He now had an idea of why I was not buying from him and he could work on overcoming my objection.

So, at that point, what could he have done? He could have told me that his partner had a Ph.D. from Berkeley or Harvard in Finance. . He could have told me that he had additional training that I didn't know about. He could have told me about a great program they had for people like me, and that he could give me the kind of support I needed or that there was an associate of his whom I could work with who could give me the support I needed. At least now that he knew what my objection was, he could do something. But until he pushed me out of the land of polite and pushed me across the assertive/aggressive boundary to give him my real objections and maybe hurt his feelings, he had nothing to work with in order to try and overcome my objections and close the sale. So that's what I mean by "no one buys in the land of polite" and that sometimes you need to push people past the assertive/aggressive boundary to get to the real issue so you can overcome their objections and close the sale"

Wright

Let's talk about why you say sales is a numbers game, and explain the concept of a sales funnel.

Strom

If, you look at a funnel, it's wide at the top and very narrow at the bottom. For sales to come out of the bottom as closed sales you need to put a lot of potential, prospective, or possible sales leads in at the top. To start the process you do cold-calling, prospecting, direct mail, etc (wide funnel at the top). Then you set up presentations where fewer people follow through (the funnel starts to get narrower). Then you show your presentation to a smaller number of people (the funnel gets even narrower). Then you have the follow-up appointments with even fewer potential clients (the funnel gets even narrower). You now go through the follow-up process, doing one or more follow-up appointments, perhaps even bringing someone to help you make the close. You continue this until you're finally down to the very narrow part of the funnel where the closed sales come out of the bottom of the funnel.

The problem is that if you don't keep putting in prospects at the top of the funnel when your getting started (at the widest part of the funnel), then closed sales are going to stop coming out of the bottom of that funnel. Additionally, if you start and stop, and don't stay persistent and consistent, you are going to wear yourself out and never get closed sales.

I am going to explain this by going through my "Don't Drop the Clutch too Soon" story. When I was sixteen years old my first car was a 1971 yellow Pinto. I was very proud of that car. It was a very inexpensive car and it had a lot of mechanical and electrical problems; but that was the only car I could afford at the time - I was a broke teenager. Anyway, my Pinto had some electrical problems and I could not afford to get the electrical problems fixed by a mechanic, Therefore, Many times it would not start on its own, and I ended up having to push-start it a lot.

Now there's a technique to push-starting a car, and you've got to build up enough speed and momentum so that when you drop the clutch the car comes to life and the engine starts. For example, I'd put my little brother Mike in the front seat and say, "okay Mike, what I want you to do is hold the steering wheel straight and put your foot on the clutch, and don't let the clutch come back up until I yell, 'drop the clutch'," I would then go around to the back of the car and start pushing. (Where's the hardest part of push-starting a car? It's at the very beginning when it's at a dead stop.) I then began pushing, pushing, pushing, and I was getting the momentum up and I was just about ready to yell to my brother to drop the clutch. But then he dropped the clutch before I yelled and the car came to a dead stop. I then smacked right into the back of the car and. I was not happy. By now I was hurting and mad at Mike, and I ran around to the front of the car and said, "Mike, you dropped the clutch too soon - you can't do that. You've got to wait until there's enough momentum and speed to drop the clutch and I yell drop the clutch."

I then gave Mike a little more training, and again I went to the back of the car and started pushing it again. Remember, the hardest part of push starting a car is the very beginning when its at a dead stop. I began pushing again and I was just about ready to yell drop the clutch, and he dropped the clutch too soon again... Wham! I ran right into the back of that car again. I hit my knee on the bumper and my nose on the back windshield. I was not happy. I ran around to the front of the car and yelled, "Michael, do *not* drop the clutch too soon."

If I wanted to get from one end of the block to the other end of the block and I had to push-start my car ten times, starting and stopping, starting and stopping, starting and stopping, I would be completely worn out before I got to the end of the block. Whereas if my brother would have not dropped the clutch too soon and I would have pushed long enough and hard enough, it would not have been hard to push start my car and get it to the end of the block with one push start instead of many. But for it to be easier, I would have had to stay persistent and consistent and not of backed off pushing the car hard enough and long enough, and not drop the clutch too soon. Then when Mike finally dropped the clutch and the car came to life I could jump in the car and drive it to the end of the block with very little energy expended, compared to push-starting it ten times within the same block.

It's the same with sales, the hardest part of the sales process is at the very beginning when your doing the cold contacts, the cold calling, etc. If you keep pushing hard enough and long enough so that you start putting prospective sales in at the top of the funnel and follow through with them to the presentation, the follow-up, and the follow-through, and you keep doing it and you don't stop early, then you're going to start getting closed sales dropping out of the bottom of your funnel. If you become frustrated because you're not getting any closed sales or very few closed sales and you "drop the clutch too soon" at any point, you go back to ground zero. Perhaps you back off for a few days or a few weeks and then you meet with your sales manager or you go to a motivational seminar. You get re-inspired and you go back and start again, but now you have to start all over again.

It's just like dropping the clutch too soon with the car. By the time you get to the end of the block with the car you're worn out. By the time you get to the end of the first six months in your sales position you're wiped out and the sales aren't happening because you didn't hang in there long enough to build momentum, and therefore closed sales never start to come through the bottom of the funnel on an automatic regular basis. However, if you would of actually push-started your system long enough to get to the point where your sales process would begin working on it own, you would start to be successful. Therefore In sales don't drop the clutch too soon!

Wright

So tell me, why is momentum so important in successful sales?

Strom

Having four kids I have managed several different soccer teams. I found the teams that take more shots on goals end up getting more goals. The idea is to take as many shots as you can to succeed. You miss 100 percent of the shots you don't take.

In momentum what happens is: 1) The more you do, the better you get at what you do, 2) The more you do the more probability you are going to have success because of the many shots you're taking, 3) The more you do the more confidence you're going to get as you're getting better and as sales start to follow through. Again, the more you do, the better your posture will be when you're talking to people and prospective clients. People don't buy from needy sales people; they buy from confident sales people. If you build momentum by putting in the numbers you'll get better at what you do, you'll have a better posture, you'll get more confidence, and you'll have a higher probability of closing sales. You need to build momentum in your sales process.

Wright

What an interesting conversation. I think our readers are going to get a lot out of this. I know I have. Not only food for thought but some changes that I might want to put into my own life from some of the things that you've said. I really do appreciate you taking this much time with me Terry to discuss this important chapter of *Conversations on Success*. And I really do appreciate all that you've shared with me here today.

Strom

   Thank you David, its been great talking with you.

About The Author

Terry Strom is an sales process consultant, executive business coach, author, and professional speaker in the areas of motivation, sales, and communication skills. He has spoken in front of over 250,000 sales professionals. He has been the Vice President/Director of three different corporations. Terry has an MBA from USC, is a Certified Guerrilla Marketing Coach, and is a member of the National Speakers Association.

Terry Strom

Phone: 951.695.0192

Email: terrystrom@stromint.com

www.terrystrom.com

Chapter 2

DR. DENIS WAITLEY

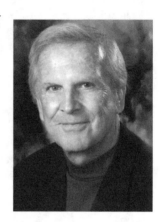

THE INTERVIEW

David Wright (Wright)

Today we are talking with Dr. Denis Waitley. Denis is one of America's most respected authors, keynote lecturers, and productivity consultants on high performance human achievement. He has inspired, informed, challenged, and entertained audiences for more than twenty-five years from the boardrooms of multi-national corporations to control rooms of NASA's space program, from the locker rooms of world-class athletes to the meeting rooms of thousands of conventioneers throughout the world.

With more than ten million audio programs sold in fourteen languages, Denis Waitley is the most listened-to voice on personal and career success. He is the author of twelve non-fiction books, including several international bestsellers. His audio album, "The Psychology of Winning," is the all-time best selling program on self-mastery. Dr. Waitley is a founding director of the National Council on Self-Esteem and the President's Council on Vocational Education. He recently received the "Youth Flame Award" from the National Council on Youth Leadership for his outstanding contribution to high school youth leadership.

A graduate of the U.S. Naval Academy Annapolis and former Navy pilot, he holds a doctorate degree in human behavior.

Denis, it is my sincere pleasure to welcome you to *Conversations on Success!* Thank you for being with us today.

Denis Waitley (Waitley)

David, it's great to be with you again. It's been too long. I always get excited when I know you're going to call, maybe we can make some good things happen for those who are really interested in getting ahead and moving forward with their own careers in their lives.

Wright

I know our readers would enjoy hearing you talk about your formative years. Will you tell us a little about your life growing up in the context of what you've achieved and what shaped you into the person you are today? Do you remember one or two pivotal experiences that propelled you on the path you eventually chose?

Waitley

I believe many of us are redwood trees in a flowerpot. We've become root bound by our earlier environment and it's up to each of us to realize that and break out of our flower pot if we're going to grow to our full potential.

I remember my father left our home when I was a little boy. He said goodnight and goodbye and suddenly I became the man of the family at age nine. My little brother was only two, so I had to carry him around as my little shadow for the ensuing years. To this day my kid brother has always looked at me as his dad, even though there are only seven years difference between us. He'll phone me and ask what he should do and I'll tell him, "I'm your brother, not your father!"

Our dad was a great guy but he drank too much and had some habits that took a firm hold on him. He never abused me and always expected more from me than he did from himself. I had a push-pull—on the one hand I felt inadequate and guilty when I would go to succeed but on the other hand he kept feeding me the idea that he missed his ship and I'd catch mine. The only thing I could do to get out of that roller coaster impact was to ride my bicycle twenty miles every Saturday over to my grandmother's house. She was my escape. I would mow her lawn and she would give me such great feedback and reinforcement. She told me to plant the seeds of greatness as she and I planted our "victory garden" during World War II. She told me that weeds would come unannounced and uninvited—I didn't need to worry about weeds coming into my life, they didn't even need to be watered.

I said, "Wow! You don't have to water weeds?"

And she said, "No, they'll show up in your life and what you need to do, my grandson, is model your life after people who've been consistent and real in their contribution as role models and mentors."

She also told me that a library card would eventually be much more valuable than a Master Card. Because of my grandmother reading biographies of people who'd overcome so much more than I was going through, I thought, "Wow! I don't have any problems compared to some of these great people in history who really came from behind to get ahead." I think that was my start in life.

I went to the Naval Academy because the Korean War was in force and you had to serve your country, so the best way was to run and hide in an academy. If you earned enough good grades you were put through without a scholarship or without money from your parents. Since my parents didn't have any money it was a great way to get a college education.

I became a Navy pilot after that and learned that if you simulate and rehearse properly you'll probably learn to fly that machine. But much of it has to do with the amount of practice you put into ground school and into going through the paces. As I gained experience being a Navy pilot I eventually decided to go on and get my advanced degree in psychology because I wanted to develop people rather than stay in the military. I pursued a program where I could take my military and more disciplined background and put it into human development. That's basically the story.

I earned my doctorate, I met Jonas Salk and Dr. Salk introduced me to some pioneers in the behavioral field and then along came Earl Nightingale who heard just a simple evening taped speech of mine and decided that maybe my voice was good enough, even though I was a "new kid on the block" to maybe do an album on personal development which I did in 1978. It surprised me the most and everyone else also that it became one of the bestsellers of all time.

Wright

Being a graduate of Annapolis and having been a Navy pilot, to what degree did your experience in the Navy shape your life and your ideas about productivity and performance?

Waitley

David, I think those experiences shaped my life and ideas a great deal. I was an original surfer boy from California and when I entered the Naval Academy I found that surfer boys had their heads shaved and were told to go stand in line—everyone's successful so you're nothing special. I found myself on a team that was very competitive but at the same time had good camaraderie.

I realized that I didn't have the kind of discipline structure in my life that I needed. I also discovered that all these other guys were as talented or more talented than I was. What that shaped for me was realizing the effort required to become successful is habit-forming. I think I learned healthy habits at the Academy and as a Navy pilot just to stay alive. To perform these kinds of functions I really had to have a more disciplined life. That set me on my stage for working more on a daily basis at habit formation than just being a positive thinker only.

Wright

In our book, *Conversations On Success!* we're exploring a variety of issues related to human nature and the quest to succeed. In your best-selling program, *The Psychology of Winning*, you focus on building self-esteem, motivation, and self-discipline. Why are these so crucial to winning and success?

Waitley

They're so crucial they're misunderstood. I think especially the term "self-esteem" is misunderstood. We've spent a fortune and we had a California committee on it, we formed the National Council on Self-Esteem. What has happened, in my opinion, is that self-esteem has been misused and misjudged as being self-indulgence, self-gratification—a celebrity kind of mentality. We've put too much emphasis on the wrong idea about self-esteem.

Self-esteem is actually the deep down, inside the skin feeling of your own worth regardless of your age, ethnicity, gender or level of current performance. It's really a belief that you're good enough to invest in education and effort and you believe some kind of dream when that's all you have to hang onto.

What's happened, unfortunately, is that we've paid so much attention to self-esteem it's become a celebrity and an arena mentality kind of concept. Most people are "struttin' their stuff" and they're celebrating after every good play on the athletic field whereas if you're a *real* professional, that's what you do anyway. A real professional is humble, gracious, and understands fans. I think that what we've done is put too much emphasis on asserting one's self and believing that you're the greatest and then talking about it too much or showing off too much in order to make that self-esteem public.

The real self-esteem has two aspects: 1) Believing that you deserve as much as anyone else and that you're worthy. Someone may look at you and tell you they see real potential in you. If you can feel that you have potential and you're worth the effort, that's the first step. 2) The second step is to start doing things to give you confidence so that when you do something and learn something it works out and you'll get the self-confidence that comes from reinforcing small successes. That combination of expectation and reinforcement is fundamental to anyone who wants to be a high achiever. That's what self-esteem is really all about—deserving on the one hand and reinforcing success in small ways to get your motor running and feel the confidence that you can do better than you have been.

Fears crop up and get in the way of our motivation. In my case I was afraid of success. Nobody had ever succeeded in our family and because they hadn't I felt inadequate to be able to succeed. Whenever it would show up around the corner I would think, "Well, this is too good to be true for me, you don't deserve that." So I would feel a little bit doubtful of my abilities. When I would succeed there would be an attendant, "Yelp!" I would feel because I would not believe I deserved what I had achieved.

I think fear is the thing that gets in the way of our motivation because we're all motivated by inhibitions and compulsions. You should be motivated more by the result you want rather than the penalty. That's why I've always said that winners are motivated by reward of success rather than inhibited or compelled by the penalty of failure. If you get this conviction that you're as good as the best but no better than the rest—I'm worth the effort, I'm not Mr. Wonderful, I'm not the center of the universe but I can do some things that I haven't done yet—and then apply this motivation to desire rather than fear, that is when self-discipline comes into play.

I'd have to say, David, I could spend the entire interview on self-discipline because I missed it as one of the most important ingredients in success. I've always been a belief guy, an optimism guy, a faith guy, and all the self-esteem things but I think, as time went on, I forgot the amount of discipline it takes for anyone who is a champion in any endeavor and I think I'm back on that track now.

Wright

I can really appreciate this Flame Award you won from the National Council on Youth Leadership for helping high school leaders. I've got a sixteen-year-old daughter and I know how difficult and important it is. But in some circles self-esteem has gotten a bad reputation. For example, in many schools, teachers won't reward high achievers for fear of hurting the self-esteem of others in the classroom. Many people feel this is not helpful to these children. In your opinion, where is the balance between building healthy self-esteem and preparing kids and adults to cope and succeed in a competitive world?

Waitley

I think that there has to be first of all some kind of performance standard. A good example is the Olympic Games. The idea of the Olympic Games is to set a standard that you've tried to live up to in your own way as a world-class person, realizing that there can only be so many Olympians and so many gold medallists and so on. I think, on the one hand, it's really important to have standards because if you have a standard, then you have something tangible to shoot for or to measure against.

I think there's a problem, however, in that only so many people can be medallists and win medals at the Olympics. One of the reasons that the high jump bar, for example, is set so that everyone can jump over it the first time, is to experience the feeling of success that first jump produces. The feeling of success is working in the competitor before the bar gets raised to world record height and to much higher standards than even the normal Olympian.

I'm one who believes in testing. It's difficult when you have a "No Child Left Behind" concept because many times today we're going pass/fail. We're moving people up through the grades regardless of their performance simply because we don't want them left behind and therefore feeling that they're not able to function simply because they can't compete with student who've been given many more opportunities to succeed than others.

Having said that, I'd say that healthy self-esteem is gained by giving specific stair-step, incremental, bite-sized pieces and perhaps there needs to be several different standards set. Usually the grading system does that and the point system does that where you have someone who has a four point three grade average because of all the extra credits they're taking. Then you have those with a three point eight and then those who are just barely passing. Unfortunately then, what that does is enable only a few people to get into universities and the others have to go to community colleges.

What I will have to say, however, is that we in the U.S. have to be very careful that we don't dumb down or lower our standards for excellence in our schools. Traveling as much as I do, I have discovered information such as there are 300 universities in Beijing alone, just in one city in China. The way it goes internationally is the public schools in Japan, for example, are much more competitive than the private schools. If you're in Japan going to a public school, you have to really perform up to the highest standards in order to ever think of qualifying for any kind of university. You'd have to go into a vocational school if you didn't compete in higher standards in public schools in Japan. The same thing is true in Singapore, China, and in the developing nations.

We have a situation brewing here where we've got global developing countries with really high standards in English, mathematics, engineering, and science. And we have educators in the U.S. who are more concerned making sure that the self-esteem of an individual doesn't get damaged by this competitive standard. I think we have to maintain standards of excellence.

I wish we had kept dress codes in schools. I have found schools that have marching bands and a certain amount of uniformity not only have greater athletic performance but they also have higher academic standards. The same is true globally. There's an argument that if you put kids in uniforms, you're going to limit their creative thinking. The truth is, if you can standardize the way people appear in their style, then you can focus more on substance—their experience, imagination, contribution, and their study—the core of an individual rather than the surface of an individual can be developed much better. If we can combine the more disciplined aspects of the developing countries with the more entrepreneurial, creative, free-thinking aspects of our society, which means we're critical thinkers (i.e., you throw us a problem and we'll try everything we can possibly think of to solve it), whereas in the developing countries they'll use a textbook or an older person's experience.

We're very entrepreneurial here in America but I'm very much concerned that our standards are being lowered too much and if we're not careful we're going to take our place in the future as a second-rate educational country and therefore forfeit the idea of being a technological and market leader.

Wright

I also hear grumbling about motivation. I'm sure you've seen business people roll their eyes a bit at the mention of listening to "motivational tapes" or CDs. Some tire of getting all hyped up about change or sales goals for example, only to lose their excitement and fail to reach their goals. Are they missing something critical about the nature or application of motivation?

Waitley

I really believe they are, David. I think they're missing the idea that what you *want* in life turns you on much more than what you *need* in life. Too often business managers even today focus on the hard skills because they say that the other skills are "soft skills." Well, there's no such thing as a hard or soft skill because you can't separate your personal from your professional life anymore. You get fired more for personal reasons—for being late, for your habits, for you hygiene, your behavior, your anger. This idea that technical training as opposed to motivation is the way to go is misguided. I have found that employees are excited and are full of desire and energy because management listens to them, reinforces them, is interested in their personal goals, and is interested in keeping them inspired. That inspiration is what we remember. So, when we go to a meeting we remember how we felt about the meeting, not the specifics of the meeting. I think this emotional component—keeping people's energy and desires foremost and doing a desire analysis of employees rather than just a needs analysis—is very, very important. I often think this is lost in the idea that we're giving a pep talk, or a quick fix, or a band aid when, as Zig Ziglar has mentioned so many times, "Motivation is like taking a bath. You take a bath every day and you might say why take a bath, you're going to get dirty anyway." But the very nature of doing it, and doing it on a habitual basis makes this positive energy continue to flow and motivation becomes habit-forming. I think you need a lot of it to keep these habits of excellence or else you'll just be running scared—you'll be afraid not to do well because you'll lose your job. Believe it or not, we have a lot of employees in America who are working harder than they ever have before so they won't be fired. That's not really the way to go after a goal, constantly looking through the rear view mirror trying to cover your behind.

Wright

If you don't mind, I'd like to change the focus a little to the topic of self-discipline. Everyone seems to know what they should do and how they should change but they just can't discipline themselves to take the necessary steps to do so. What is the secret to becoming a disciplined person?

Waitley

I think the secret is to get a team, a support group, a mastermind group because not only is there safety in numbers but there's accountability in numbers. When we are accountable to one another to maintain a certain standard of discipline, it's much easier to work out if someone else is getting up at six-thirty in the morning with you. It's much easier to have a support group if you're interested in maintaining a healthier diet, for example, because the temptations are irresistible to procrastinate and to fall off the wagon. That's why I believe you need a team effort.

It also has to be understood in an immediate gratification society that there is no success pill that you can swallow. There is no quick way to get rich and get to the top. There is this steady ratcheting to the top and that's why I think leaders need to say it's going to take us about a year to get any permanent change going. So, I think we should all understand there may be a little dip in productivity as we start this new program of ours—a little dip at first and a little uncertainty—but over time, over about a year, we're going to become like an astronaut or an Olympian. We need to engrain these ideas so they become reflexive and it takes about a year for an idea or a habit to become a reflex. This idea of being able to do it in twenty-one days is misguided. I don't think it takes twenty-one days to learn a skill, it may take twenty-one days to learn to type, it may take twenty-one days to begin to learn a skill, but it takes a year for it to get into the subconscious and take hold.

I think we have to learn that discipline is practicing on a daily basis for about a year so that it will become a habit—a pattern—that will override the old inner software program.

Wright

I'm a big believer in the greater potential of the individual. I remember a fellow—Paul Myer—helped me a lot when I was a young guy. He was in Waco, Texas, with a company called Success Motivation Institute. You may know him.

Waitley

I know him very well. Actually, he's one of the icons and pioneers in this whole field. He and Earl Nightingale were the first ones to ever have a recorded speaking message other than music. Earl and Paul were pioneers in audio recording and I have still a great respect for Paul. I just spoke for his organization about a month ago.

Wright

He personally helped me a lot when I was younger and I just really appreciated him. In your program, *Seeds of Greatness*, you outline a system for nurturing greatness. Will you give us a brief overview of this program?

Waitley

It's taken me thirty years to get this thing to where I want it. I wrote the book twenty years ago titled, *Seeds of Greatness*, and sure, it became a bestseller but so did *One Minute Manager*, *In Search of Excellence*, *Iacocca*, and every other book at that time. I have trouble keeping that thing pumped up.

Over the years I've found that *Seeds of Greatness* for me, has been a system. What I've had to do is go back through all the mistakes I've made as a family leader. I knew I was a father and not a mother *and* father so I had to find a mother who was also a good clinical psychologist who had worked with every form of behavioral problem and put our efforts together so that we had a man and a woman as family leaders with clinical and other experience who could give parents or leaders of the day a certain track to run on where they could coach their small children and adolescents on a daily basis. I provided a perpetual calendar that gives coaching tips of the day— what I call "sign on the day" and "sign off the day"—for parents to use to communicate with their kids. Then I had to put nineteen CDs together—audio tracks—that covered these "roots and wings," which I would call the "core values" and the more motivational or, if you will, ways to set your kids free. The idea of parenthood should be to lay the groundwork, make it safe to fail an experiment and then send them off on their own as independent, not codependent, young adults so they can reach own destiny. I divided it into "roots of core values" and "wings of self-motivation and self-direction" and tried to balance the two so that whether you're from a blended family, or a single parent, and whether you're structurally religious or whether you're spiritually religious, it would work regardless of your personal core belief system.

I'm very happy that we've finally put together a self-study program that can be taught by the authors or by people who are licensed facilitators. It's something that a family leadership group could take and work on their own at their own speed by watching, listening, interacting with their kids, and using a combination of a written book, the audios, the DVDs, and this coaching calendar to maybe put it all together so that over a period of six months to a year they might be able to effect some changes in the way they interact with their kids.

Wright

Sounds great! Before our time runs out, would you share a story or two about your real life coaching and consulting experiences? I know you've coached astronauts and Super Bowl champions as well, haven't you?

Waitley

Well, I have. I've been lucky to work within the Apollo program in the simulation area. I found that simulation prevents failure of the first attempt. In other words, if you're going to go to the moon and they're going to shoot you up a quarter of a million miles up and back in a government vehicle, you had better have your rehearsal down and really pat. The astronauts teach you that the dress rehearsal is life or death. The Olympians teach you that at the moment you go to perform, you need to clear your mind so you can remember everything you learned without trying—you develop muscle memory and reflex.

Twenty-one years ago when Mary Lou Retton was doing the vault and she needed a nine point nine five to tie the Romanian for the gold medal in women's all around gymnastics. I asked her what she was thinking about when she went to vault and said, "Oh gosh, I guess what everyone thinks about—speed, power, explode, extend, rotate, plant your feet at the end. When the pressure is on I get better just like drill. Come on, Mary Lou, this is your moment in history."

I thought, "Wow! That's not what everyone thinks. What everyone thinks is, 'Thank God it's Friday,' 'Why me?' 'Don't work too hard,' 'Countin' down to Friday,' 'Looking to five P.M.,' 'Romanians are better trained, probably on steroids,' " So I get these stories of Olympians who have internalized this wonderful running the race in advance and simulating as well.

I guess the one story that I'll share is about a ten-year-old boy. In about 1980 this boy came to a goal-setting seminar. He told me that none of the people who had paid their money were really working on their goals. They were really thinking about what they were going to eat and golf. I gave him a work book and told him to go back and do what they were supposed to do and write down his abilities and liabilities, what he was going to do this year and next year and five years from now and twenty years from now. He got all excited because he thought it was this wonderful game that you can play called, Write the Future, or Describe the Future. So he ran back and worked on the project and forty-five minutes later he astounded the adults in the audience by saying he was earning money mowing lawns and shoveling snow so he could go to Hawaii on the fourteenth of July so that he could snorkel on the big island of Hawaii's Kona Coast. Then he said next year he'd be eleven going into the fifth grade and he was going to models of what was going to be a space shuttle and he was going to begin to learn more about numbers and math. In five years he'd be fifteen and as a tenth-grader he said he would study math and science because he wanted to go to the Air Force academy—he was all excited about that. I asked him what he was going to be doing in twenty years and he said he'd be an astronaut delivering UPS packages in space.

I forgot all about him and twenty years later, sure enough, I saw him on the Today Show as they showed a picture of an astronaut on a tether line pulling the satellite into the bay of the space shuttle. I thought, "My gosh! This kid did what I only talk about in the seminars." He was a living, breathing example of someone who was focused on this. I said to my family, "Look what he did!" And they said, "What have *you* been doing for the last twenty years?" I said I was a goal tender. They told me I should be a goal achiever too.

Wright

What a great conversation. I always enjoy talking with you. It's not just uplifting—I always learn a lot when I talk with you.

Waitley

Well, David, I do with you as well. You've got a great program and you do a lot of good for people who read and watch and listen. I think you give them insights that otherwise they would never get and I'm just grateful to be one of the contributors and one of the members of your global team.

Wright

It has been my sincere pleasure today to visit with a truly great American, Dr. Denis Waitley. Denis, thank you for taking so much of your time to share your insights and inspirations for us her on *Conversations On Success!*

Waitley

Thank you very much, David.

About The Author

Denis Waitley is one of America's most respected authors, keynote lecturers and productivity consultants on high performance human achievement. He has inspired, informed, challenged and entertained audiences for over 25 years from the board rooms of multi-national corporations to the control rooms of NASA's space program; from the locker rooms of world-class athletes to the meeting rooms of thousands of conventioneers throughout the world. Recently, he was voted business speaker of the year by the Sales and Marketing Executives' Association and by Toastmasters' International and inducted into the International Speakers' Hall of Fame. With over 10 million audio programs sold in 14 languages, Denis Waitley is the most listened-to voice on personal and career success. He is the author of 12 non-fiction books, including several international best sellers, *Seeds of Greatness, Being the Best, The Winner's Edge, The Joy of Working*, and *Empires of the Mind*. His audio album, "The Psychology of Winning," is the all-time best selling program on self-mastery.

Dr. Waitley has counseled winners in every field from Apollo astronauts to Superbowl champions, from sales achievers to government leaders and youth groups. During the past decade, he served as Chairman of Psychology on the U. S. Olympic Committee's Sports Medicine Council, responsible for performance enhancement of all U. S. Olympic athletes. Dr. Waitley is a founding director of the National Council on Self-Esteem and the President's Council on Vocational Education, and recently received the "Youth Flame Award" from the National Council on Youth Leadership for his outstanding contribution to high school youth leadership. As president of the International Society for Advanced Education, inspired by Dr. Jonas Salk, he counseled returning POWs from Viet Nam and conducted simulation and stress management seminars for Apollo astronauts. A graduate of the U. S. Naval Academy at Annapolis, and former Navy pilot, he holds a doctorate degree in human behavior.

Dr. Denis Waitley

The Waitley Institute

P.O. Box 197

Rancho Santa Fe, CA 92067

www.waitley.com

Chapter 3

JIM CARTMILL

THE INTERVIEW

David Wright (Wright)

Today we are talking with Jim Cartmill. Jim is an accomplished speaker and author with a mission to see people bring their lives into focus and balance. He has brought his transformational message of hope, humor, and encouragement to over one million people coast-to-coast and around the world. His years of experience as a nationally recognized expert on generational trends, a high performance coach, an elected official, and a successful CEO of Let's Talk Health, Inc., a multi-million dollar nutritional supplement company, give him unique insight into building a mission-driven life focused on balance and relationships.

Acclaimed for both his content and delivery, Jim can capture a crowd and make them laugh and send them home motivated to create positive change and get the results they want. That is why internationally acclaimed speaker and best-selling author Dr. Denis Waitley calls Jim Cartmill "a rising star on the national speaking platform." Jim, welcome to *Conversations on Success*.

Wright

Is it possible in the society where we live to create balance?

Cartmill

When I talk about balance, what I am really talking about is the behavioral choices we make in our daily lives. We need to live our lives with intentionality as it relates to the expenditure of our time and resources toward those key slices of the pie chart we call our lives. The problem is, in today's society we have more choices than ever; but they still revolve around central key values that we have determined are important to us.

We can talk about the many obstacles and problems in our world, but that does not take away our responsibility to make right choices to create a sense of balance between the many competing opportunities that daily vie for our attention. Many people talk about living balanced lives, but the data tends to validate the fact that there is a serious disconnect between the time and attention we give to areas of our lives that we say are important and what we really focus on in our lives. Our approach has become what I call the "More, Better, Different World." We believe that if we somehow do more things either better or different, our lives will fall into balance. The reality is, we need to do less activity and more reflection on what is most important to us. "More, Better, Different" is not the path toward transformation. This mantra has caused us to be perhaps the most unbalanced generation in the history of our nation.

Wright

What are some societal barriers to living balanced lives?

Cartmill

There are three areas of our lives that prevent us from living a balanced life: Habits, Attitudes, and Relationships. Habits relate to our behaviors, attitudes relate to our perception of life, and relationships are the glue that makes it all come together.

The problem is our society is changing faster than at any other time in history. The original Chaos Theory postulated that our society had short periods of chaos with long periods of stability. The rapidity of change we see today has flipped that theory on its head—we now have long periods of chaos with short periods of stability.

Just 100 years ago the average life expectancy was forty-seven, only eight percent of homes in America had a telephone (in stark contrast to elementary school kids who now bring cell phones to school) and there were only 8,000 cars in the U.S. with only 144 miles of paved roads. With these facts in mind you can begin to see a picture of a world that is changing exponentially. Technology alone has forever changed the way we live, creating what I call an "information-rich / relationship-poor" world. We are more connected than ever, but our communication is often superficial and does not provide the accountability and coaching necessary to live a balanced life. As a result of this, even our children are growing up in a society that is so over-scheduled they need a Personal Digital Assistant to keep themselves on track.

We are literally raising a generation of kids who are growing up fast on the outside, without giving them the tools necessary to deal with life on the inside. This overextension of activity and information-overload literally paralyzes us from developing consistency in our daily lives. *This consistency can only be established though the development of strong relationships.*

This information-rich / relationship-poor world evidences itself in the media bombardment we experience today. The saturation of media in our society is an overwhelming and unprecedented phenomenon in our history. I'm not talking just about television. The whole spectrum of media includes television, radio, Internet, cell phones, iPods, and the many other devices and outlets that push information to us in a fashion that is often inescapable and all consuming. In fact, television is becoming almost outmoded as the media king. Recent Nielsen polls indicate that adults fifty years old and older watch almost double the amount of television than young people ages twelve to seventeen.

The media onslaught has also caused us to become a niche society that prevents us from experiencing common threads among our neighbors and friends. Consider the fact that in the late 1950s and early 1960s there were less than ten nationally circulated publications. We remember *Life, Look,* and *Newsweek* that communicated much of what we as a society agreed with and very little of that which was subject to debate and argument. Today, there are more than 50,000 national magazines, many of which seek to exploit our differences rather than reinforce key principles and values that unite us as people.

Wright
So what then does it take to create this balance?

Cartmill

The first step toward creating this balance is recognizing that we cannot live life to its fullest in a vacuum. As human beings we were hard-wired for relationships that create purpose in our lives. As a result of being uniquely designed for relationships with each other, we have the ability to develop the accountability necessary to live our lives in balance.

We have the unique opportunity to be dream-makers rather than dream-takers. It is crucial for us to build a dream team around us that will encourage us in our vision for life. It was Benjamin Franklin who had a group of friends he called, "My Most Amazing Friends Group." They met together on a weekly basis for forty years exchanging ideas and encouragement to each other. Thomas Edison had a similar group he met with on Friday nights for seven years called the "Mastermind Alliance." Out of that group of individuals more than 300 patents and forty inventions were created that literally changed our world.

It was Jean Nidet, founder of Weight Watchers who said that her ability to help so many people around the world came from a simple act she learned as a teenager. During walks through the park she would see mothers talking among themselves while their toddlers sat on swings with no one to give them a push. Her response: "I'd give them a push...and you know what happens when you push a kid on a swing? Pretty soon they are pumping themselves." She then went on to share that this is her role in life: "I'm here to give others a push."

Because we are designed for relationships with people, we all need a dream team around us to "give us a little push" when we need it.

Wright

So how does your perception of life affect the behavioral choices you make in your day-to-day living?

Cartmill

I currently serve as the President of the Sweetwater School District Board of Trustees, the largest secondary school district in the nation. During one of my campaigns I heard of a sign that hung over the desk of a political consultant in town that simply read: "perception is the only reality." It is sad, but true, that often we let perception get in the way of making wise choices in our lives. When we look at our lives through the lens of negative perceptions, the reality of life can overwhelm us. Many of the positive and negative perceptions we have of ourselves are based on a lifetime of experiences.

Wright

So what role does your personal history play in your present and future life as it relates to balance and change?

Cartmill

As we reflect on our lives and choose a course of action that will require change, we need to understand the role our history has in living our life both in the present and in the future. Each of us brings a unique history to our daily lives. History is something that shapes us, but it need not define us. Key truths that are relevant to the impact our history has in our lives include the fact that if I am not able to share my history with the people on my dream team, it's going to be very difficult for them to help me. In *Alice in Wonderland* the statement is made, "If you don't know where you are going, any path will do." I would suggest that if those closest to me don't know where I have come from, it's going to be very difficult for them to help me get to where I need to be.

When I get on a plane to go speak somewhere, I actually dread the almost obligatory question, "What do you do for a living?" It tends to be such a positional question, as if being a corporate executive is somehow superior to being a waiter or a taxi driver. My first response to this question is to share with my seatmate that I am a televangelist (I tend to travel quietly after that). If that doesn't scare them off, I then proceed to flip the question in a different direction by asking them where they grew up and what they did for fun as a kid.

You see, we all grew up somewhere and depending on our generation, we share commons experiences of growing up. This is a great starting point to understand what motivates a person and allows us to see that who we are as an individual is much more important that what we do. Stephen Covey states it so eloquently when he says we are human beings, not human doings.

Our history also reveals our scars. A famous pastor and speaker, Dick Foth, has said, "Scars aren't bad; they just tell us where we don't want to go again." Many of us can point to physical scars on our body from a lifetime of mishaps. But the emotional scars are the ones that often take their toll on our ability to create balance and positive change in our lives.

I was at a conference several years ago where the speaker separated everyone into small groups. He then asked each individual to share the time in his or her life that he or she felt most victimized. Well, I'm not much for looking at the negative side of life, but I sure was able to share a laundry list of events that I felt garnered me the title of "most victimized." I thought I had that title in the bag until a lady in her mid-sixties began to speak. She spoke in a hushed tone as she remembered a time in her life when she was four years old. Her mom had just returned home from the hospital after undergoing back surgery. She went on to share that she was playing on the top bunk of her bunk bed as her mom entered the room.

Her mom looked up at her and said, "Honey, I want you to stand up and jump to Mommy."

Knowing that her mom had just been in the hospital and that her back was in pain the little girl said she didn't want to jump to her because it might hurt her back.

Her mom responded by saying, "It's okay, just trust Mommy. Stand up on your bed and jump into my arms."

The little girl obeyed her mom, stood up on her bed, and jumped toward her mom's outstretched arms. As she jumped, her mom took two steps back as the little girl went crashing toward the floor.

When she landed, she looked up at her mother, tears streaming down her face, and heard her mother say, "Don't you ever trust anybody in this world, not even your own mother."

This lady, now more than sixty years old, had been literally paralyzed by fear of trusting others throughout her entire life. Her perception of life, filtered through deep emotional scars that were garnered from a difficult relationship with her mother, prevented her from building positive relationships into her life to overcome those obstacles.

UCLA recently released a study indicating that emotional scars are registered in the brain in the same way that physical pain is registered. We need to be aware of the scars in our life, but use them in a way that changes our future behavior. Understanding our history and the role it has played in shaping our lives will help us to build key individuals into our lives who will enable us to define a future that more truly reflects our dreams and aspirations.

Wright

So how do you implement change in your life to create the kind of balance that you're talking about?

Cartmill

We first need to determine what it is we want to change. Too many people change things in their life just for the sake of change without really considering their own value system and what the change communicates to others. What we value is demonstrated by our observable behavior and we need to be honest in determining whether our lives are aligned with what we see as our mission in life.

I served more than twenty years as a domestic missionary so I always tell people that when they seek change in their lives, they need to develop a missionary mindset. One of the ways I do this with organizations and individuals is to take them through my comprehensive Mission-Driven Life Planning™ process. The first step toward developing this mindset is to spend time reflecting personally and with your dream team. Be brutally honest in how you see yourself now and what your dream is for the future. It was Leo Tolstoy who once said, "Everyone thinks of changing humanity, but nobody ever thinks of changing themselves." It is easy to talk about the global change we would like to see in our world, but much more difficult to see it in our own lives.

The second step in the process is to learn the fine art of keeping things simple. A cookbook was recently found in South Dakota from the late 1800s and inside was a recipe for rabbit stew. The first step of the recipe was: 1. Catch the rabbit. Sometimes we make ourselves crazy by over-scheduling meetings and events and under-scheduling time for reflection and contemplation. Morris Adler made this observation, "We visit others as a matter of social obligation. How long has it been since we have visited with ourselves?" When we talk about the subject of change, the best way to keep it simple is by narrowing our focus to broaden our vision.

The third component to this change process in our life is learning to not become comfortable and complacent. A five-year-old was being tucked into bed by his mom. After a kiss on the forehead and a hug good night, the mom began to make her way toward the master bedroom. As she walked down the hall, she heard a loud thud coming from her son's bedroom. Running back into the room she saw her son lying on the floor disoriented and confused. When she asked him what had happened, her son simply replied, "I don't know mom—I think I stayed too close to where I got in."

As living, breathing human beings, we are a lot like that little boy. Sometimes we choose to stay too close to where we go in. We love our comfort. In fact, the best selling chair in America is still the Lazy-boy.

You never hear a competitor come up with the "Risker-boy" chair or the "I'm going to work harder-boy chair."

Tragically, the warp speed in which our society is changing sometimes stymies our ability to function at full capacity. The intense compression of change literally collides with our own sense of history and we are unable to make crucial steps toward the future. The only way to combat this comfort factor is to build growth into your dream team to hold you accountable.

The last component of the change process is understanding the importance of focusing on behavioral change rather than just attitudinal change. I tend to be a cheerleader by nature. I always seek to build up and encourage, but every major study that has ever been conducted on the subject of change both personally and in the workplace clearly indicates that behavioral change is the real catalyst for sustained change. You can have all the positive thoughts you want—and I believe they are important—but true change comes through our willingness to change our behavior.

Many will remember the now infamous warning from the Surgeon General in 1964 that cigarette smoking is hazardous for your health. The problem is, even with that warning, the smoking rates in America continued to climb. How many of us have ever started a diet or exercise regimen that fizzled out after a couple of days? We had great intentions and probably even felt good about our new found enthusiasm. The problem occurred when we didn't internalize the behavior and make it a habit. We literally need to inculcate ourselves with the behavioral changes we seek. Webster's definition of inculcate is as follows: "to teach and impress by frequent repetitions or admonitions; to set permanently in the consciousness or habit patterns."

At a minimum, it takes thirty days to produce a habit that has any type of sustainability. Part of my Mission-Driven Life Planning™ process includes exercises and worksheets to chart your progress toward making behavioral goals a habit rather than just a good idea. It has been said, "It is better to act your way into a new way of thinking, rather than to think your way into a new way of acting." This is backed by years of study and should be heeded by those seeking positive, demonstrable change in their lives.

My wake-up call for change came in the year 2000 when I went in for a routine physical. After the examination the doctor concluded our time together by stating, "Congratulations, you are now clinically obese." What a wake up call! I determined that I needed to get serious about behavioral changes in the physical area of my life. I set a goal to run the San Diego Rock 'n' Roll Marathon within the year. To make sure I had a large dream team around me, I announced the goal at our annual back-to-school day in front of 3,000 employees! From that point forward, there was no turning back. There was no event or school I could visit where someone didn't ask me how my training was going for the big race. In June of 2001, I ran the entire 26.2 miles of the marathon and lost fifty pounds through the yearlong process of training. Why? Because I was able to internalize behavioral change that I intuitively already knew I needed by publicly broadcasting my goals and inculcating myself through months of training by acting on my beliefs.

Wright

I've heard that you say one should live their life as a testimony rather than a title. How do you do that?

Cartmill

We first need to recognize that behavior is much more important than the title on our business card. Who you are is much more important than what you do in life. We have all had people in our lives who, because of their position in life, feel they are superior or better than we are. Choosing testimony over title means understanding the contrast between making a difference in our personal lives and in the lives of others and the position or title that we hold.

Before Mother Teresa passed away, Dan Rather interviewed her on national television. She described in great detail the way she would serve the poor on a daily basis and how she would cradle in her small arms those who were stricken with leprosy and other diseases common to the region where she lived in Calcutta.

As she was sharing this with Dan Rather, he paused and said to her, "Mother Teresa, I don't think I could do what you do for all the money in the world."

She reflected for a moment and responded, "Well Mr. Rather, neither could I, neither could I."

You see, Mother Teresa's life was truly a testimony. Because she followed her calling, she knew from experience that who she was—her testimony—was much more important than her position in life. Here was a diminutive little lady who had kings and queens, presidents, and heads of state come to visit her because of the difference she was making in lives. So her testimony was much more important than just her title.

Wright

You've mentioned "dream team" two or three times in our conversation. Would you further explain this concept?

Cartmill

Your dream team is the group of individuals you build into your life who are able to speak the truth in love (even when it doesn't feel good), who truly desire the best for you, and who are willing to help you achieve that best. We all have an ongoing need to be counseled and sometimes preached to when we are moving in a direction diametrically opposed to what we say we desire in our lives.

There are four characteristics I look for in a dream team member. The first characteristic is **someone who demonstrates priority in his or her relationships.** He or she understands that people are more important than prestige, power, or popularity. There was a time in our society when you used things and loved people. Now the message seems to be that it is all right to use people and love things.

When I talk about priorities, I am really talking about values. You can easily see a person's priorities by looking at only two things: their calendar and their checkbook. The calendar on my Apple computer has color-coding for the different categories in my life, so I decided to assign the deep purple color for any events that relate to my family. I intentionally put my family events in my calendar, big or small, so that I can easily see if I am honoring my commitment to spend time with my family. It is a visual and sometimes very humbling perspective on how my behaviors line up with my desires regarding how I show priority to my family.

The second characteristic I seek in members of my dream team are people who **create a climate of transparency**. In the business world, transparency seems to be the new buzzword. Business transactions need to be "transparent," meetings are "in the open," and financial accounting is "visible" to all. How much more should we be transparent to those who are a part of our dream team? It is vital that we have the ability to share with those closest to us what's on the inside versus the image we sometimes portray on the outside. We have a tremendous capacity to mask very real pain and struggle in our lives.

One of my former students was great at being transparent. Roger served as a waiter for a restaurant as a senior in high school, trying to save some money for college. One night he was serving a lady who was complaining about everything Roger did. There was nothing he could do right. (Maybe you can relate to this scenario.) Finally, for the fourth time, the lady called Roger over to her table. He begrudgingly walked over to the table thinking to himself, "What can this lady possibly want now? I've done everything I possibly can to make her happy."

Arriving at her table, she cast a steely gaze on him. "Waiter, this potato you gave me is a bad potato. I don't like this potato," she bellowed.

Roger began thinking to himself, "I didn't cook the potato—what does she want me to do about it?" As various thoughts raced through his head, he came up with a plan of action, as smart, intelligent high school seniors are apt to do. Roger looked down at the lady's plate, reached down to grab her potato, picked it up off of her plate and proceeded to spank it, saying "Bad potato, bad, bad potato!"

The lady went into a state of shock as Roger ever so gently put the potato back on the lady's plate and said, "Now if that potato gives you any more problems, you let me know."

The amazing part was that Roger received one of the biggest tips of his life. He was able to take a negative, critical situation and turn it into something positive by being transparent. Your dream team needs to be made up of people who don't take themselves so seriously and who provide an environment where you can be yourself.

The third area that I think is important in this dream team is the ability to create a **climate where mistakes are permitted.** Let's face it—none of us are perfect people. We all make mistakes and hopefully learn valuable life lessons. The point is, if we are not making mistakes we're not taking risks toward moving forward in our lives. We need to have people in our lives who will embrace us for our good traits and work with us in the areas we need help. It is so easy in this world to have a negative, critical spirit. Often times the very things we criticize in others, we ourselves deal with in our lives.

In my college days I went to a conference where the facilitator got on the microphone and announced to the 200 people gathered in a hotel ballroom that he wanted us to look around the room and find the person we disliked the most. Now most of us had been together for just that week so you can imagine this was not going to be an easy task. He then went on to give a few more ground rules. We were also to look for three of four alternate people (just in case somebody picked our number one choice first!). He then said that when he counted to three, he wanted us to get out of our seats and go to that person. His last stipulation before the countdown was that the person we picked had to also agree that *we* were the person *they* disliked the most also (or at least be one of their alternates).

Now here I am, a gentle soul who was serving in the ministry at the time and I was supposed to pick someone I disliked the most? I thought I was supposed to like everybody. Evidently that was not the case. The facilitator counted to three and I was on the hunt! I figured I needed to find someone first before they found me. And then it happened. Over in the corner of the room I saw a woman who reminded me of a recent relationship that broke my heart.

I made a beeline toward her and almost proudly stated, "You're it! You're the person I dislike the most!"

Without hesitation, she responded, "You're it also and you're not even one of my alternates!"

We were now facing each other, as were hundreds of other people who had picked each other as the person they disliked the most. The facilitator said, "Pick a person A and a person B. Person A, you go first and tell person B why you dislike them so much."

I chose to be person A so that I could spew out my venom first. I looked at her and said, "You look really superficial and stuck up to me. You look like someone who is afraid of relationships and doesn't care about anybody but yourself!"

I was really getting into this until the facilitator cut us off. Then he said, now person B, tell person A why you dislike them so much.

When she got done dressing me down, I'll never forget what the facilitator told us as we finished the exercise. Before I share what he said, I want you to visualize the person in your life you would have chosen that you dislike the most. The facilitator said, "The person across from you who you chose because you disliked them the most, may or may not have some of the bad traits and characteristics that you pointed out." He then proceeded to drop the bombshell, saying, "But I guarantee you one thing—you do have some of those traits in your life and you are dealing with them right now." Ouch! That didn't feel so good. I had just called myself stuck up and superficial— someone afraid of relationships. I was literally blaming events and relationships in my past for my present behavior. I was using the very behaviors I disliked in others to protect myself from being hurt.

As a child of the 1970s I grew up with the television as my babysitter after school. *Gilligan's Island, The Brady Bunch* and The L.A. Thunderbirds of *Roller Derby* fame were my favorites. On occasion, those old-time southern preachers would also mesmerize me.

I'll never forget one night, flipping through the channels and pausing at a station where a preacher was saying something that profoundly changed the way I looked at myself and what I perceived to be my imperfections. He said, "When a dog plays checkers, you don't criticize his game, you're just surprised and pleased that he is playing at all." You see, we are all like that dog trying to play checkers, we're all going to make mistakes, but we need to create a climate where mistakes are permitted in order for us to grow.

Fourth on my list for dream team material is a commitment to be **intentional in our behaviors**. A story in the *San Francisco Chronicle* described an automobile accident that was experienced by a couple driving a 1960s death trap of a vehicle—the infamous VW van. They were so light on top that even mild gusts of wind were enough to knock them off course. As they were driving their van and approaching a bridge, a huge gust of wind literally flipped the van over two times. The wife, who was driving the van and was not wearing a seat belt, was thrown from the vehicle as it flipped over. As the van stopped rolling, the woman got up from where she landed and saw her husband who was now pinned underneath the van. The man in the car behind them, who had witnessed the accident, pulled over and observed something medical doctors will tell us is possible, but still hard to believe. The wife got up, ran over to the van that was now lying on top of her husband and with one arm lifted the vehicle up and with the other arm, grabbed her husband and pulled him out to safety.

The question for us regarding our own ability to be intentional in our behaviors is this: Do you think this woman would have been able to accomplish this great feat if she had doubted her own ability? What if she would have said, "Maybe I should see if the man following behind us will get out and help," or, "I'm sure someone has called an ambulance from their car and help is on the way." No, this loving wife saw what needed to be done and she did it, forsaking all doubt regarding her strength, her ability, or her will. We need to have the same type of intentionality in the members of our dream team.

The last characteristic for an effective dream team member is someone who demonstrates through their actions **a commitment to**

compassion and caring. The word "care" comes from the Gothic root *kara* which means "to lament." To care is to grieve, to experience sorrow, to cry out with, to enter deeply into human suffering, and become present to another's pain.

In fact, I believe a good dream team member excludes the word sympathy from their vocabulary. Sympathy says, "I feel sorry for you because of your circumstances." Rather, we should replace sympathy with empathy. Empathy says, "I hurt with you and understand your pain. I will be with you through the good and bad times in your life."

Tony Campolo, the noted sociologist from Eastern College, cited an interesting study of people who were ninety-five years old and older. The study asked them a simple question, "If you had your life to live all over again, what would you do differently?" The top three responses vividly demonstrate the concept of compassion and care. These seasoned citizens concluded that if they had their life to live all over again, they would first take more time to reflect.

Reflection is a lost art in our society and it prevents us from fully appreciating the relationships that matter most in our lives. Reflection really is all about building memories with those you love and taking time for self-examination. At the end of my life, I want to remember those special moments with my wife, Cindy, making up games with my little girl, Blythe, and even those challenging teen years of my stepson, Jason, who allowed plenty of opportunities for growth as he became a man.

The second observation the researchers made was that they would want to take more risks in their life on their do-over. David Livingstone, the infamous missionary who gave us the Henry Stanley quote, "Dr. Livingstone, I presume?" after being lost in the interior of Africa for a year, was a classic risk-taker. He had a missionary mindset and sacrificed time with his family, was taken ill on numerous occasions, and was even vilified by people who didn't like the fact that he was bettering the lives of the African people. On his deathbed, Dr. Livingstone made a unique request. He asked his African friends to cut his heart out when he died and bury it in the African soil and then ship his body back to England to be buried with his family. He told him that his heart was now a part of the African people.

The question our dream team needs to ask of us is: Where is your heart? What are your dreams and aspirations and how are you going to keep all of this in balance? Being compassionate and caring includes willingness to take risks—to speak the truth in love and follow your dreams.

Finally, these senior citizens said that they would want to be more involved in causes and relationships that would outlive them. What better way to describe the behavior of a compassionate and caring dream team member as someone who will pour their lives into another's in order to see that person stay in balance in pursuit of his or her dreams? That is what makes up a dynamic dream team.

Wright

Well, Jim, what an interesting conversation this has been. I really appreciate the time you have spent with us today.

Today we have been talking with Jim Cartmill, who is a professional speaker and author. I think this afternoon we have found out why Dr. Denis Waitley calls Jim Cartmill a "rising star" on the national speaking platform. Thank you so much for being with us on *Conversations on Success.*

About The Author

Jim Cartmill is an accomplished speaker and author with a mission to see people bring their lives into focus and balance. He has brought his transformational message of hope, humor and encouragement to over one million people coast-to-coast and around the world. Jim's years of experience as a nationally recognized expert on generational trends, high-performance coach, elected official and successful CEO of Let's Talk Health, a multi-million-dollar nutritional supplement company, give him unique insights into building a mission-driven life focused on balance and relationships.

Acclaimed for both his content and delivery, Jim can capture a crowd, make them laugh, and send them home motivated to create positive change and get the results they want. That is why internationally acclaimed speaker and best-selling author Dr. Denis Waitley calls Jim Cartmill "a rising star on the national speaking platform."

Jim Cartmill

Cartmill Communications

Phone: 619.957.0696

P.O. Box 928

Bonita, CA 91908

www.jimcartmill.com

Chapter 4

DEAN C. DUBOIS, SR. , JD

THE INTERVIEW

David Wright (Wright)

Today we're talking with Dean C. DuBois. You might say that Dean has been laughing with the world since his high school days when he was a yearbook joke editor and perhaps even since he gave his first speech at age ten! He has enjoyed successful careers in public relations, publishing, marketing, and law. His PR background includes service as the Executive Vice President and Director of two local Chambers of Commerce, and affiliations with state trade and business associations and national organizations which provided exposure to local, state, and national audiences. Dean brings a background of humor and lightheartedness that leaves audiences asking for more. He is a native of Gulfport, Mississippi, a graduate of the University of Mississippi with a B.A. in Journalism, a graduate of the Woodrow Wilson College of Law, with a Doctorate of Jurisprudence he has a diploma from the University of North Carolina, Southeastern Institute, in U.S. Chamber of Commerce and Association Management. Dean retired from the military as Brigadier General after forty years of active and reserve service. He served in the Navy aboard a destroyer during the World War II and was recalled to active duty during the Korean conflict. He was then commissioned in the National Guard, and later transferred to the Army Reserve, from which he retired after twenty-six years, and then retired from the South Carolina Guard after an additional six years service.

His awards include the Legion of Merit and the Army Meritorious Service Award. He is a graduate of the Command in General Staff College and War College and the National Defense University. He is a former Vice President of Public Relations and Advertising for Holiday Inn.

Presently, he is President of DuBois and Associates, Public Relations. Dean is the former publisher of *Holiday Inn Magazine, Sports Digest, Fashion Pace*, and editor of the *American Motor Hotel Association Book Directory*. He is the author of *Carolina Decameron, Rx for Rapid Recovery, Is It True What They Say About Dixie? An Unbiased Objective Look at the South From a Southerner's Viewpoint* and *On the Dean's List*. He is presently working on a book of short stories.

Dean's philosophy for living is embedded in the principles of having a serious mind and happy heart, of having a deep and abiding faith, and of maintaining an unfailing sense of humor and a zest for living.

Dean, welcome to *Conversations on Success!*

Dean DuBois (Dubois)

Thank you very much, David. It is a pleasure to be with you.

Wright

Tell me, what is your definition of success?

Dubois

Well, the dictionary is the only place where success comes before work. My definition of success would be that the talent of success is nothing more than doing what you can do well and doing well whatever you can do, without a thought for fame or credit. I like what Herbert Baird Swope, one of the great newspapermen of our time, had as his formula for success. He said, "I cannot give you a formula for success." He reflected for a moment and then added, "But I can give you a sure fire formula for failure—try to please everyone."

Wright

So what do you think it takes to be a successful person?

DuBois

I think for someone to succeed, he should be armed with three or four vital attributes. He must have a great amount of energy to accomplish what he wants to do, and a limitless ambition of purpose. Ambition is critical. He should be possessed of great enthusiasm coupled with a determination to succeed while doing the job with enjoyment and fun. With these ingredients, along with faith, most anyone should arrive at success.

Some people fail because they will not follow or do the things that successful people must do. For instance, the successful scientist must follow a formula just as tourists follow a road map, a builder follows a blue print, and a successful chef follows a recipe. It is not so important to merely want to succeed—one must be willing to do certain things. Follow the rules. This doesn't involve acting like a sheep or anything, for risk-taking comes into play at needed times. Of ambition, Carl Sandburg said, "Before you go to sleep, say to yourself, "I haven't reached my goal yet, whatever it is, and I'm going to be uncomfortable and unhappy until I do it."

Wright

To what do you attribute to your success?

DuBois

The first thing that comes to mind is a positive attitude, and I'm happy to say that I acquired that, I guess, a long time ago. I like the words of Earl Nightingale in *The Strangest Secret*, "We become what we think about." I am influenced by Norman Vincent Peale with his espousal of a positive attitude.

The concept of enthusiasm was always embedded in my brother and sister and me. I think that was a key thing that helped me along.

My parents and my maternal grandparents were very instrumental in my success. During the depression my dad had to work two jobs, but he always found time to be with his children, taking us to a game, for a walk, or down to a neighbor's house to listen to a big championship match on the radio. He was very consistent in that effort and he had a great sense of humor. And my mother was a guiding light. She was an "expression teacher," as they called them in those days. She instilled within me that lightheartedness and sense of enjoying what I do. I got the same treatment and encouragement from my grandparents. I owe my success to them, and others of course.

Wright

So what things do you consider important?

DuBois

I think you can find the basics in the Ten Commandments. I believe you can find them in the twelve Scout Laws. I think I could almost recite them right now for they are very pertinent to a person's success.

Giving back to the community is important. I think a person needs to be a contributor to his community, to give back there, and to his church. I believe in working for the church; I teach an adult Sunday School class. For my community I've been active in civic and social organizations, I have served as president of Easter Seal chapters in Memphis and Atlanta, and I helped organize Jaycee Chapters around Mississippi. I gained a lot of experience in fellowship and tolerance, and learned something from all of those things. But like I said, I think giving back to the community some of what you have gained is essential toward becoming a successful person. It may not be success in gathering wealth, but wealth can also be measured by something more personal—what you've done for your family and how you raised your children. I have four and I hope I have instilled in them these values and commitments.

Wright

As you look back on all of these things you talked about—all of the awards you have received, and the things you have done to achieve your accomplishments, did you set certain goals?

DuBois

Yes, indeed. I learned fairly early—and I wish that I had learned it even earlier—to prioritize my thinking. It was a hard thing for me to do. I would start one thing and then become distracted by something else. I finally learned to wear blinders, you might say, and accomplish one thing at a time.

I would suggest that others do what I did and examine any failures they've experienced so they might gain from them. I failed two or three times with some of my publications and some of my business ventures, but I rolled with the punches, looked for the next goal, and then moved forward.

Wright

You are known as a motivational humorist. Will you define that for our readers?

DuBois

Quite simply, I like to motivate my audience into thinking positively about their lives and their work by showing them a so-called "happy face" while presenting some thoughts for living that can serve some purpose for them.

I use anecdotal humor to make certain points to help them remember that life is short and should be lived each day to the fullest. Start the day off right, with a prayer and look in the mirror as you say, "By George, you did it again! Let's get started!" And rather than saying, "Good Lord, it's Monday!" you could say, "GOOD LORD, IT'S MONDAY!" I like to speak to organizations and show them that these things can be done with a positive attitude and with the attitude of doing something worthwhile, not only for themselves, but for other people as well, for they will then be doing it for themselves.

Wright

Tell me about your two personas in speaking. You speak as the Mayor of Neicaise Crossing, but you're also Dr. DuBois, "M.D.*"

DuBois

As Mayor, I spin stories and tales that make up a lot of down-home humor, sort of like a Lewis Grizzard with a touch of Jerry Clower—although not as bodacious as my late friend Jerry—and I don't wear the white suits with the fringe or anything like that. I'm more like Herb Shriner with down-home stories.

Then there's Dean DuBois, M.D.* There is a big asterisk behind the M.D., so people will notice the footnote under it that reads "Mirth Doctor." I adopted that some years ago, when I heard about "psychosclerosis." When I asked what in the world that was, I found out that you could interpret it as a "hardening of the attitude." I came up with "How to Avoid Psychosclerosis" by Dr. DuBois, M.D.*, and that's where my prescription comes in. That prescription, David, is: "Four L's = A+" which means, "Living on Love and Learning and Laughter, and that equals an A-plus, or Attitude Positive." If you do that, then you should get rid of any negative attitude.

Wright

So that's for all of the mathematicians in the audience.

DuBois

That's right! I have that printed on my card and I have had a lot of fun with it. I have some handouts I distribute, titled "Things to do Today." Number one is to relax, number two is to hug someone, and number three is to laugh out loud. Then I have a couple of other things on my prescription pad, which I give out that say something like, "Rx, just for the health of it: laugh at a minimum of two cartoons a day, tell at least one joke daily, grin out loud and share it, and repeat daily." I also give out feathers and I tell members of the audience to take one out of the bowl as they leave to remind them to keep things light.

Wright

That would be great for everyone in our country who is under more stress than ever before in their lives.

DuBois

Yes, that would be great.

Wright

You served our armed forces for nearly forty years, both on active duty and as a reservist. What did you gain from that besides the satisfaction of serving, and what success did you find in all of that?

DuBois

I happily gained a great deal, and enjoyed my years in service. I learned discipline, even from the first day in boot camp. I am a Navy veteran of World War II having served aboard a destroyer where there was hard work and no goofing off. We were in the North and mid-Atlantic and the Mediterranean leading convoys and watching out for German subs everywhere we went.

In 1952, I was commissioned in the National Guard and I learned a great deal from my experiences there and in the Army Reserve because of the educational program of which I took advantage.

I progressed from the Platoon Leader School, Company Commander School and Command General Staff College, which is like getting an undergraduate degree, to the Air War College which was like graduate school. The other opportunities, such as the

National Security Seminars and serving as Director of the National Security Seminars at Fort Jackson for a couple of years was similar to pursuing a Ph.D.

Through all of that, I learned to become more knowledgeable of my fellow man. Eating and living with men and women from all over the country with various ethnic backgrounds is quite a learning experience. I believe that tolerance best describes what I gained from those experiences—in addition to the educational opportunities I learned tolerance toward my fellow service members.

Wright

Every year near Veterans Day at our church, we play the anthems for each branch of the armed forces, and while each anthem is played, veterans of each branch stand. Most of our congregation would think that you were schizophrenic, for you would have to stand up twice!

DuBois

Well, actually, I would have to stand up three times, David! In high school during the early '40s, I was in the Civil Air Patrol and, of course, it was taken over by the Army Air Corps before the Air Force was formed in 1947. As students and cadets, we learned to fly planes and did reconnaissance over the Gulf of Mexico. I'm happy to report that not once did a Japanese sub enter the Mississippi Sound, thanks to my diligence! Now I stand up for the Army, the Navy, and for the Air Force. Many look around and grin as I explain it.

Wright

As I understand it, you retired as a Brigadier General.

DuBois

Yes, I was very fortunate.

Wright

Who are some of the people who have influenced you through the years?

DuBois

I mentioned my parents and grandparents, but there were others who made contributions. Earl Nightingale's strangest secret, which is that, "We become what we think about," has always stuck with me through the years. Then I became acquainted with Norman Vincent

Peale's positive attitude, which is stated in a different way. James Allen, in his, *As A Man Thinketh*, has a powerful thought, "As you think within your heart, that's what you'll become." So if it appeared that I was heading in the wrong direction, I would come back to these basics.

There were some other folks who are not that famous, but my Sunday school teacher, back in Gulfport, Dr. Ruepert Cook, taught some of the basic fundamentals we are talking about. My other teachers, Ms. Margaret Evans, who taught English and was a delightful lady, and Coach Landrum taught values as well. Coach Landrum was a very likable, down-to-earth, fun guy but very tough.

Lately I've been influenced by Dr. Stephen Covey, and I think I might be getting acquainted with him one of these days in one way or another. I have enjoyed his books. He came to Columbia a few years ago, I believe, when his book, *First Things First*, was released. His lecture was a great experience and I picked up several great ideas from him. I remember a little line that went, "To live, to love, to learn, to leave a legacy," as a kind of line that matches one that I have used for a long time. My take on that has been in my formula, which I mentioned earlier, "Four L's = A+." When *First Things First* came out, it added fuel to my to frequent jumping from one project to another. I took him literally, first things first, and that brings us to what I was saying about learning to put blinders on my eyes and finish a project before I tried something else. That is one of the ways I have benefited. First things first of eight different things, working effectively every day to meet deadlines, eliminating stress, and getting things done, distinguishing between management and leadership, recognizing and eliminating poor work habits, developing high levels of activity to form improved habits, overcoming procrastination, and balancing work and personal life. I have all kinds of things posted on my bulletin board such as, "If you can dream it, you can do it."

Wright

By virtue of the years you have under your belt—all of the things you have done and all of your accomplishments—I'm sure you could give some pretty sound advice to our young people. If you had a platform and could speak to the young people of our nation, what would you say to them?

DuBois

I feel that I could say a lot to them, but I think some of the key things would include that they should not try to fool themselves, they have to work to succeed—they have to study, to think, and believe in themselves. They should have the faith of their own abilities. Self-confidence, without ego building up inside, helps to clear the decks for life's actions, and having faith drives away confusion and uncertainty.

Some other things I would say are: Live life to the fullest, one day at a time. Live simply, expect little and give much. I have that on the back of my business card. Don't be afraid to go out on limb, that's where the fruit is. Don't brag, but remember that it's not the whistle that pulls the train. Learn from the mistakes of others, because you can't possibly live long enough to make them all yourself. Conduct yourself in such a way that your high school would want you to address the graduating class. We all know the Army slogan, "Be all that you can be;" I worked with one general whose motto was "Do it right!"

Wright

That's a good one. Is that your list of do's and don'ts?

DuBois

Yes, and here are a few others: Have an open mind and don't be afraid to change. Learn to disagree without being disagreeable. Have ambition combined with goals and work toward those goals, far down the road perhaps, and set less ambitious goals along the way. Tackle those and achieve them and you will be heading toward the big goal.

Wright

I understand that you discuss the importance of communication and how effective it is to upward mobility.

Dubois

Communication is *everybody's* domain. As soon as you move one step from the bottom of the ladder, I believe your effectiveness depends upon your ability to reach others through the spoken word and the written word. The further your job is from your manual work, the larger the organization, the more important it is for you to know how to communicate effectively. Express your thoughts in writing and in speaking. In very large organizations, whether government or large business or the military, the ability to express oneself is one of the most important skills a person can possess. Effective communication has the power to make things happen, and if it is done well it moves people to react. Communication is another major factor along with motivation and enthusiasm. Be able to communicate and learn how others get their points across. Watch the leaders and observe what they do to communicate well.

Wright

I heard one great speaker say that communication in our country has changed from genuine communication into people taking turns talking.

DuBois

Yes, I'm afraid that's right and it's a dreadful and sorry state of affairs. Sometimes political correctness goes a little too far. It prohibits and intimidates a lot of people and rather than just speaking in a plain and forceful way, they ask themselves, "How am I going to say this and make it sound right and still be politically correct?" Communications is vital in these days, I believe.

Wright

So what other qualities or values have been important to you?

DuBois

I would like to say more about enthusiasm and faith and some of those things. I think that enthusiasm is certainly a value or virtue. I'm working on a book now that goes into a lot of values and virtues and which are which. Enthusiasm is an image of magic and can work magic in all of our lives. I remember my mother saying, every time my younger brother would come in, that, "You look like you're full of enthusiastics." I still use that when I see somebody. I know they think I should say "enthusiasm," but it's a good expression that became a part of me. I believe Dr. Peale once explained enthusiasm to a listener by saying that the word "enthusiasm" comes from two Greek words which mean "in God," or "just full of God," and that's enthusiasm. It can work for you, but if you don't have it, it can work against you!

Another one of my mentors, whom I failed to mention, was Kemmons Wilson, my boss at the Holiday Inns. He was a splendid guy who worked hard but enjoyed relaxing and loved his family; and he treated us as family, too.

Zig Ziglar—that rascal—would reply enthusiastically to, "How do you feel?" by responding, "Fantastic, but getting better!" I use that a lot. In a way, our enthusiasm is what keeps us in touch with the world.

I was impressed by the fact that I have one trait in common with these men—I believe life should be lived with enthusiasm and lived to the fullest. For them life was never for a moment dull. Everything about it was filled with excitement and everything that they did was an adventure. I'm a member of Rotary Club International and I always try to follow their Four-way test: Is it the truth? Is it fair to all concerned? Will it build goodwill and better friendships? Will it be beneficial to all concerned?

I usually end my presentation with "Drinking from a saucer:"

"I've never made a fortune, but its probably too late now.
I don't worry about that much because I'm happy anyhow.
As I go along life's journey, reaping better than I sowed,
I'm drinking from my saucer 'cause my cup has overflowed.
Don't have a lot of riches, sometimes the going is rough,
But I've got folks that love me and that makes me rich enough.
I just thank God for His blessings and the mercy He's bestowed,
I'm drinking from my saucer 'cause my cup has overflowed.
I remember times when things went wrong and my faith got a little thin,
But all at once the dark clouds broke and the sun shone through again.
So Lord, help me not to gripe about the tough rows I have hoed,
I'm drinking from my saucer 'cause my cup has overflowed.
And if God gives me courage when the way gets steep and rough,
I won't ask for other blessings—I've already had enough.
I will never be too busy to help another bear his load,
And I'll keep drinking from my saucer 'cause my cup has overflowed."

—The author is unknown

Wright

I really do appreciate all of this time that you have spent with me today, Dean. It's just been more than a pleasure for me. I have known you for many years and have laughed at your jokes and have read your books and found them so insightful and entertaining. It's really an honor and a pleasure to talk with you.

DuBois

Well, David, I certainly appreciate the opportunity to visit with you and it's been a real pleasure.

About The Author

Dean has had successful careers in public relations, publishing, and marketing and law. His PR background includes service as the Executive Vice President, Director of two local Chambers of Commerce, state trade and business associations, and national organizations. He's also spoken to local state and national audiences. Dean brings a background of humor and light spoken heartedness that leaves audiences asking for more. He is a native of Gulfport, Mississippi, a graduate of the University of Mississippi with a B.A. in Journalism, the Woodrow Wilson College of Law, where he got his Doctorate of Jurisprudence and has a diploma from the University of North Carolina, Southeastern Institute in U.S. Chamber of Commerce and Association Management. Dean retired from the military as Brigadier General after forty years of active and reserve service. He served in the Navy aboard a destroyer during the World War II and was later called up during the Korean War. He then was commissioned in the National Guard, later transferring to the Army Reserve, retiring after twenty-six years, and then retiring from the South Carolina Guard with an additional six years service. His awards include the Legion of Merit and the Army Meritorious Service Award. He is a graduate of the Command in General Staff College and War College and the National Defense University. He is a former Vice President of Public Relations and Advertising for Holiday Inn. Presently, he is President of DuBois and Associates, Public Relations. Dean is the former publisher of *Holiday Inn Magazine, Sports Digest, Fashion Pace*, and Editor of the *American Motor Hotel Association Book Directory*. He is the author of *Carolina Decameron, Rx for Rapid Recovery, Is It True What They Say About Dixie? An Unbiased Objective Look at the South From a Southerner's Viewpoint* and *On the Dean's List*. Currently he is working on a book of short stories. Dean's philosophy for living is embedded in the principles for having a serious mind and happy heart, of having a deep and abiding faith, an unfailing sense of humor, and zest for living.

Dean C. DuBois, Sr., JD

1001 Wildewood Downs Circle, #C-124

Columbia, SC 29223

Phone: 803.419.1169

Email: debc01@bellsouth.net

Chapter 5

ED GASH

THE INTERVIEW

David Wright (Wright)

Today we're talking with Ed Gash. He is a Leadership Development Consultant and owns his own business, Eagle Wings Consulting, "Where leaders learn to soar!" He was president of the national award winning chapter of the Charlotte, North Carolina, area American Society of Training and Development. He worked at First Union Bank for eight years implementing a corporate-wide leadership training program with the Franklin Covey Company and previously managed the training and employment functions at the Federal Reserve Bank.

His versatile career includes being a top salesman in an executive recruiting firm, directing a comprehensive guidance program at an independent school, a decade of coaching winning football and wrestling teams, writing a federal grant that awarded a drug treatment facility, assessment and creation of an overall wellness and fitness program, and working with the Department of Corrections as a probation officer.

He has recently authored a book entitled, *Beyond the Hashmarks,* chronicling his coaching stories as corporate and personal development learning experiences. In the book, Ed's varied background is coupled with coaching experiences and humorous storytelling anecdotes that are an entertaining and enlightening experience for all who read it. He has also been honored at the Franklin Covey Symposium as recipient of the International Facilitator of the Year award.

Ed, welcome to *Conversations on Success.*

Ed Gash (Gash)

Thank you. I'm very honored to be a part of this book which includes such respected leaders!

Wright

Before you established yourself as an award winning facilitator and leadership coach, you were on a different career path. How did your time as football coach contribute to the development of your career concepts of successful leadership?

Gash

Well first of all, I really don't consider it a different career path. I think it was a vocation. I believe all the jobs I've had—probation officer, drug treatment liaison, and all the rest—were not by coincidence; they were part of a grand assignment that I've been given. My time as football coach contributed a lot because it gave me personal development metaphors. My book is about the successful things I did in coaching as well as some of the pretty stupid and unsuccessful things I did in coaching. Hopefully, readers can use those stories to help with their own personal development.

Wright

You use the Eagle Wings performance "PACT" as the framework for your leadership coaching and training, what exactly is this PACT?

Gash

The Eagle Wings performance PACT provides a structure to support performance improvement, leadership development, and teambuilding. It is made up of four levels—Principles, Actions, Courage and Tactics—from which the acronym P-A-C-T is derived. More than just an acronym, the PACT process results in a commitment—a pact—to behave in a way that will move you in a positive direction toward achieving your goals. The framework I use looks like sixteen simple squares; but once you get into it, you realize it is a multilayered approach that can be used for organizational development as well as personal development.

Wright

PACT includes three critical elements: assignment, alignment, and attainment. You refer to these elements as "triple A insurance." What is, in your opinion, assignment, alignment, and attainment?

Gash

I grew up watching ABC News anchor Peter Jennings as a young reporter in the Middle East. I loved watching him broadcast from the Middle East and witnessing the pride with which he would say, "This is Peter Jennings on assignment in the Middle East." He didn't say, Peter Jennings reporting from the Middle East—he was *on assignment*! All of us are here during this time on earth for some kind of assignment, be it personal or professional. The Eagle Wings performance PACT first helps you to identify that assignment. It may be a temporary assignment, such as a project, or a career assignment, or even a life assignment.

Alignment is making sure that what you are doing (procedures), how you are doing it (processes), and what you are doing it with (resources) are aligned with your assignment.

Attainment is simply what you are trying to achieve. Attainment is the final result of the PACT process.

Wright

What do you mean by "guiding values" and what role do they play in the assignment element?

Gash

I grew up in the mountains of western North Carolina and I went to a small junior college in my hometown. Around the south side of the campus was a wall made out of river rocks from the nearby Pisgah National Forest. If you looked very closely at the colorful rocks in this unique wall, you would see they are beautifully smooth. They were shaped and polished by exposure to the rush of cold mountain streams. Their strength and elegance were gained through experience.

Your guiding values are like those big rocks. They are shaped and polished by exposure to life—they become strong through experience. Recognizing your own guiding values is the first step toward identifying your assignment. Do you know what your big rocks are? How sturdy is your wall?

Native Americans teach that if you're feeling pulled toward something, you're probably living your assignment or what they term "vision quest." Guiding values help to pull you towards your assignment.

Mother Teresa was once quoted as saying, "Don't make a big thing out of what I'm doing. I'm only doing what I was called to do."

My guiding values can be summarized with the acronym COACH: Care, Ombudsman, Affirm, Collaborate, Hear.

Wright

In a business environment characterized by change, you say that "organizations get out of alignment," what does this mean and what can individuals do about it?

Gash

One day, after I was finished working out at the gym, there was a chiropractor there offering free assessments. He stood behind me and looked at my ears; then he pointed to different parts of my body and said, "I bet you have pain here and numbness there."

He pointed to the exact places where I had those symptoms and I said, "How did you know that?"

He replied, "Your head is on crooked."

I didn't need him to tell me that—my wife has been telling me that for about twenty years! But I understood for the first time that when my spine is misaligned, it causes pain. So now I visit my chiropractor regularly to maintain proper alignment and take the pain away.

Organizations become misaligned when they are not living out their vision, or missing a strategic plan. Changes in organizational structure resulting from mergers, acquisitions, and reduction in the workforce are also causes of misalignment. When organizations are out of alignment, certain departments are in pain, certain departments are numb, and they certainly are not walking a straight line.

So, how do you align an organization that is undergoing change? Building trust is essential. In order to establish trust, it's important to have personal alignment before achieving organizational alignment. How can we align others if we aren't aligned ourselves?

Since alignment is a process of making a vision a reality, it relates to many factors in the workplace such as: integrity, values/ideas, decision-making, problem-solving, motivation, and empowerment.

Always keep integrity in mind when realigning yourself, members of your team, or organization by remembering the three C's: candor, consistency and congruency. By maintaining candor, you're keeping the lines of communication open by encouraging people to put their thoughts, feelings, and ideas into words. Be consistent by putting words into action and setting an example by practicing what you preach. Establish congruency by creating a team atmosphere and unifying everyone to pursue the same goal.

Wright

How does alignment affect decision-making in solving problems?

Gash

Alignment is the bridge that gets you from assignment to attainment. It's the people process, and purpose, position, and products. Alignment creates a structure for strategic planning and for implementing sound policies that will ultimately yield successful results for both the employees and the company.

No matter what the situation is in a company, there will always be problems to solve, which is another reason why alignment is so essential. It allows for the assessment of limiting factors to get to the root cause of a problem so that you can find solutions and get your team back on track.

Wright

What role does visualizing attainment, living out the vision statement of one's business, work, and life play in success?

Gash

The clearer you can picture the end in mind, the greater the chances of attainment. The most successful athletes visualize crossing the finish line ahead of competitors, or sacking the quarterback, or pitching strikes. If you can visualize success, you can attain it.

Wright

What is the relationship between attainment and needs?

Gash

One way to look at the relationship between attainment and needs is to see attainment as the freedom from being needy. As you move along the continuum towards attainment, you begin to acknowledge your own needs and make a conscious effort to meet those needs. When your needs are met, you are free from them and are able to attain your goals.

People often look at money and think money is a primary factor in attainment. The truth is that most of us want to make a difference, and I call it "getting MAD"—(Make A Difference). We have a need to make a difference. It's the highest need, with almost a spiritual significance; attainment is achieved when we make a difference.

Wright

Sports have played a large part of your leadership development concepts. In addition to your time as coach, you participated in archery competitively as a youth, which eventually lead to your concept of "Target-centered Leadership." Could you tell our readers what Target-centered Leadership is?

Gash

The five principles of archery are: Stance, Draw, Anchor, Aim, and Release. I've created a target center for leadership and living based on those five principles:

Principle Number 1: STANCE—What do you stand for? What do you *not* stand for? This will help set boundaries and guide you in the right direction.

Principle Number 2: DRAW—Draw on the gifts bestowed upon you. Assess your strengths and determine how you can pass them onto others to help them improve and strive toward success.

Principle Number 3: ANCHOR—Anchor to your governing values. Identify any personal values and the values of your company. Evaluate how you will implement those values into improving performance or succeeding personally or professionally.

Principle Number 4: AIM—Aim at a needy starving heart or your "life assignment." Assess the goals of a particular project, foster the skills and talent of the team, and guide how the project will be implemented.

Principle Number 5: RELEASE—Feel the release of joy at having made a difference in others! There's nothing more rewarding than knowing you positively impacted someone's life.

Wright

Thinking about archery (I don't know anything about it but I've watched it a lot), I can understand everything but anchoring in archery. What is anchoring?

Gash

I'm glad you bought that up. When I've not shot in awhile, I have to go back and rediscover my anchor. When you pull back the bow, you always want to anchor in the same exact place. For me, there's a bone in my thumb I always have to place next to a certain place in my jaw to anchor my line of sight. If I'm just a little bit off, it's going to throw everything off. If I've been practicing, I can find my anchor point quickly. We lose our anchors by not practicing. It's a great metaphor for daily living.

Wright

I can almost see that metaphor as a Christian metaphor as well.

Gash

Absolutely. All of this is very Christian based—where do you think I got the name Eagle Wings from?

Wright

Down through the years, you have made the decision of choices in your life, has faith been important to you?

Gash

Oh, absolutely. In my book there's a chapter on "metanoia." I had a spiritual advisor teach me what "metanoia" means. Metanoia means to surrender to a radical change of heart. During my workshops I write metanoia on a writing board. I then write the definition. When I write the definition, I ask, "What words jump out at you?" And they always say "'surrender' and 'radical.'" Well surrender is not necessarily a white flag indicating that you give up— it's about forgiveness, and letting go, and acceptance.

Radical usually makes people think of the sixties, of the hippies and the superlative word "extreme." But the word "radical" is derived from the root word "*radii*," which means to "radiate"—a deeper meaning. This definition changes the context of the entire meaning. We are born perfect, but then we acquire all this crap. I help people unearth the gifts from their past. You've been given many gifts not by coincidence and they're in alignment for a special reason.

Wright

Who are the influential role models and mentors in your life?

Gash

I've been blessed with some wonderful bosses and I've been exposed to some great leaders: Dr. Stephen Covey, Ken Blanchard, Peter Koestenbaum, and I've been blessed with so many scout leaders, friends, and family. To name just one or two wouldn't do justice to all of these, what I call "balcony people," who have helped me with my assignment.

Wright

I've asked many people to define "success" and I get about as many answers as the people I ask. What to you is the definition of success?

Gash

Well, it's pillow talk with yourself. You acknowledge that today you came one step closer to death and you can give yourself a minus one or a plus one. And today, you came one step closer to your assignment, so give yourself a grade. Today you came one step closer to alignment and today you came one step closer to attainment. So if you can ask yourself those questions, sometimes you can fall asleep fairly peacefully. If you don't like the answers, you may have a restless night; but the next day you get up and get ready to do your assignment tomorrow.

Wright

Well, what an interesting conversation, I've learned a lot here. You've got acronyms for so many things—I can't wait till the book comes out so I can see them all.

Gash

I'm the tip of the iceberg when it comes to acronyms. You can't sling a dead cat without hitting an acronym.

Wright

Today we have been talking with Ed Gash who is a leadership development consultant. Ed owns his own business—Eagle Wings

Consulting. As we have found out here, he knows a whole lot about self-development and has some really good sounding methodology that most readers of our books will really be interested in.

Ed, thank you so much for taking this much time with me to answer these questions, it's really been a pleasure.

Gash

Thanks so much.

About The Author

Ed Gash is a leadership development consultant and owns his own business, *Eagle Wings "Where leaders learn to soar!."* He conducts numerous workshops in the areas of Leadership and Personal Development. Ed was president of the national award-winning chapter of the Charlotte Area American Society of Training and Development. He worked at First Union eight years, implementing a corporate-wide leadership training program with Franklin Covey, and previously managed the training and employment functions at the Federal Reserve Bank. His versatile career includes being a top salesman in an executive recruiting firm, directing a comprehensive guidance program at an independent school, a decade of coaching winning football and wrestling teams, writing a federal grant that awarded a drug treatment facility assessment and creation of overall wellness and fitness programs, and working with the Department of Corrections as a probation officer. Ed graduated from North Carolina State University with a BA in Sociology and Criminal Justice. He also holds a Master of Education Degree in Guidance & Counseling from University of North Carolina at Charlotte. He studied at Cambridge University in England and graduated from the North Carolina School of Banking. He is a Master Trainer in Development Dimensions International and Franklin Covey and teaches all of the Franklin Covey Leadership Courses. Ed is certified to teach Situational Leadership for Blanchard Training. Additionally, he has attended the Disney School of Management. Ed is active in his church as a lay minister and leader.

He has recently authored a book entitled, *Beyond the Hashmarks* chronicling his coaching stories into corporate and personal development learning's. Ed's varied background, coupled with coaching experience and humorous storytelling antics, prove to be an entertaining and enlightening event for all. Ed is an avid disciple of Dr. Stephen Covey's "Seven Habits of Highly Effective People." After reading the book in 1989 he immediately discerned a personal mission statement that he lives by today. He has been honored at the Franklin Covey Symposium with "International Facilitator of the Year." Ed attests that this process helped him cope with the toughest challenge to him so far, watching and supporting his wife's recovery from breast cancer.

Ed Gash

4100 Carmel Rd. Suite B-202

Charlotte, NC 28226

Phone: 704.458.9184

www.calleaglewings.com

Chapter 6

STEPHEN M. R. COVEY

THE INTERVIEW

David Wright (Wright)

We're talking today with Dr. Stephen R. Covey, cofounder and vice-chairman of Franklin Covey Company, the largest management company and leadership development organization in the world. Dr. Covey is perhaps best known as the author of *The Seven Habits of Highly Effective People* which is ranked as a number one bestseller by the *New York Times*, having sold more than fourteen million copies in thirty-eight languages throughout the world.

Dr. Covey is an internationally respected leadership authority, family expert, teacher, and organizational consultant. He has made teaching principled centered living and principle centered leadership his life's work.

Dr. Covey is the recipient of the Thomas More College Medallion for Continuing Service to Humanity and has been awarded four honorary doctorate degrees. Other awards given Dr. Covey include the Sikh's 1989 International Man of Peace award, the 1994 International Entrepreneur of the Year award, *Inc.* magazine's Services Entrepreneur of the Year award, and in 1996 the National Entrepreneur of the Year Lifetime Achievement award for Entrepreneurial leadership.

He has also recently been recognized as one of *Time* magazine's twenty-five most influential Americans and one of Sales and Marketing Management's top twenty-five power brokers. Dr. Covey earned his undergraduate degree from the University of Utah, his MBA from Harvard, and completed his doctorate at Brigham Young University. While at Brigham Young he served as assistant to the President and was also a professor of business management and organizational behavior.

Dr. Covey, welcome to *Conversations on Success!*

Dr. Stephen Covey (Covey)
Thank you.

Wright
Dr. Covey, most companies make decisions and filter them down through their organization. You, however, state that no company can succeed until individuals within it succeed. Are the goals of the company the result of the combined goals of the individuals?

Covey
Absolutely. If people aren't on the same page they're going to be pulling in different directions. To teach this concept, I frequently ask large audiences to close their eyes and point north, and then to keep pointing and open their eyes. They find each other pointing all over the place. I say to them, "Tomorrow morning, if you want a similar experience, ask the first ten people you meet in your organization what the purpose of your organization is and you'll find it's a very similar experience. They'll 'point all over the place." When people have a different sense of purpose and values, every decision—*every* decision—that is made from then on is governed by those purposes and values. There's no question this is one of the fundamental causes of misalignment, low trust, interpersonal conflict, interdepartmental rivalry, people operating on personal agendas, and so forth.

Wright
Is that mostly a result of the inability to communicate from the top?

Covey
That's one aspect, but I think the problem is more fundamental. There's an inability—an unwillingness—to involve people. They may

communicate what their mission and their strategy is, but that doesn't mean they achieve emotional connection to that. Mission statements that are rushed and then announced are soon forgotten. They become nothing more than just a bunch of platitudes on the wall that mean essentially nothing and even create a source of cynicism and a sense of hypocrisy inside the culture of an organization.

Wright

How do companies ensure survival and prosperity in these tumultuous times of technological advances, mergers, downsizing, and change?

Covey

I think it takes a lot of high trust in a culture that has something that doesn't change—principles—at its core. There are principles people agree upon that are valued and that gives a sense of stability. Then you have the power to adapt and be flexible when you experience these kinds of disruptive new economic models or technologies that come in and sideswipe you. You don't know how to handle them unless you have something you can depend upon.

If people have not agreed to a common set of principles to guide them and a common purpose, then they get their security from the outside. They tend to freeze the structure, systems, and processes inside and they cease becoming adaptable. They don't change with the changing realities of the new marketplace out there and gradually they become obsolete.

Wright

I was interested in one portion of your book *The Seven Habits of Highly Effective People* where you talk about behaviors. How does an individual go about the process of replacing ineffective behaviors with effective ones?

Covey

For most people I think it usually requires a crisis that humbles them into becoming aware of their ineffective behaviors. If there's not a crisis the tendency is to perpetuate them and not to change. You can create a crisis through artificial ways, well really not artificial, but you don't have to wait until the marketplace creates the crisis for you. You can have everyone accountable on a 360 degree basis to everyone else they interact with, with feedback, either formal or informal, where they are getting data as to what's happening. Then they start to realize that the consequences of their ineffective behavior require them to be humble enough to look at that particular behavior and adopt new, more effective ways of doing things.

Sometimes people can be motivated to do this if you just appeal to their conscience—to their inward sense of what is right and wrong. Many people sometimes know inwardly they're doing wrong, but the culture doesn't necessarily discourage them from continuing that. They either need feedback from people, or they need feedback from the marketplace, or they need feedback from their conscience. Then they can begin to develop a step-by-step process of replacing old habits with new and better habits.

Wright

It's almost like saying, "Let's make all the mistakes in the laboratory before we put this thing in the air."

Covey

Right, and I also think a paradigm shift as analogous to having a correct map, say, of a city or of a country. If people have an inaccurate paradigm of life and of other people and of themselves it really doesn't make much difference what their behavior or habits or attitudes are. What they need is a correct paradigm—a correct map—that describes what's going on.

For instance in the Middle Ages they used to heal people through bloodletting. It wasn't until Samuel Weiss and Pasteur and other empirical scientists discovered the germ theory that they realized for the first time they weren't dealing with the real issue. They realized why is it that women prefer to be delivered by midwives who washed rather than doctors who didn't wash. They gradually got a new paradigm.

Once you've got a new paradigm then your behavior and your attitude flows directly from it. If you have a bad paradigm or a bad map, let's say, of a city, there's no way, no matter what your behavior, or your habits, or attitudes are, or how positive they are, you'll never be able to find the location you're looking for. That's why I believe that to change paradigms is far more fundamental than to work on attitude and behavior.

Wright

One of your seven habits of highly effective people is to begin with the end in mind. If circumstances change and hardships or miscalculation occurs, how does one view the end with clarity?

Covey

Many people think to begin with the end in mind means you have some fixed definition of a goal that's accomplished and if changes come about you're not going to adapt to those. Instead, the end in mind you begin with is that you are going to create a flexible culture of high trust so that no matter what comes along you are going to do whatever it takes to accommodate that new change or that new reality and maintain a culture of high performance and high trust. You're talking more in terms of values and overall purposes which don't change rather than specific strategies or programs that will have to change to accommodate the changing realities in the marketplace.

Wright

In this time of mistrust between people, corporations, and nations for that matter, how do we create high levels of trust?

Covey

That's a great question and it's complicated because there are so many elements that go into the creating of a culture of trust. Obviously the most fundamental one is just to have trustworthy people. But that is not sufficient because what if the organization itself is misaligned? For instance, what if you say you value cooperation but you really reward people for internal competition? Then you have a systemic or a structure problem that creates low trust inside the culture even though the people themselves are trustworthy.

This is one of the insights of Edward Demming and the work he did. That's why he said that most problems are not personal; they're systemic. That's why you have to work on structure, systems, and processes to make sure they institutionalize principle-centered values. Otherwise you could have good people with bad systems and you'll get bad results.

When it comes to developing interpersonal trust between people, this is made up of many, many elements such as taking the time to listen to other people, to understand them, to see what is important to them. What we *think* is important to another may only be important to us, not to another. It takes empathy. You have to make and keep promises to them. You have to treat them with kindness and courtesy. You have to be completely honest and open. You have to live up to your commitments. You can't betray them behind their back. You can't badmouth them behind their back and sweet-talk them to their face—you will send out vibes of hypocrisy and it will be detected. You have to learn to apologize when you make mistakes and to admit mistakes, and to also get feedback going in every direction as much as possible. It doesn't necessarily require formal forums; it requires trust between people who will be open with each other and give each other feedback.

Wright

My mother told me to do a lot of what you're saying now, but it seems that when I got in business I simply forgot.

Covey

Sometimes we forget, but sometimes culture doesn't nurture it. That's why I say that unless you work with the institutionalizing—formalizing into structure, systems, and processes the values—you will not have a nurturing culture. You have to constantly work on that. This is one of the big mistakes organizations make. They think that trust is simply a function of being honest. That's only one small aspect. It's an important aspect, obviously, but there are so many other elements that go into the creation of a high trust culture.

Wright

"Seek first to understand then to be understood" is another of your seven habits. Do you find that people try to communicate without really understanding what other people want?

Covey

Absolutely. The tendency is to project out of our own autobiography—our own life, our own value system—onto other people, thinking we know what they want. So we don't really listen to them. We pretend to listen, but we really don't listen from within their frame of reference. We listen from within *our* own frame of reference and in actuality we're preparing our reply rather than seeking to understand what they are saying.

This is a very common thing. In fact, very few people have had any training in listening seriously. They're trained in how to read, to write and speak, but not to listen. Reading, writing, speaking, and listening are the four modes of communication and they represent about two-thirds to three-fourths of our waking hours. About half of all that time is spent listening, but it's the one skill people have not been trained in. People have had all this training in the other forms of communication. In a large audience of 1,000 people you wouldn't have more than twenty people who have had more than two weeks of training in listening. Listening is more than a skill or a technique so that you're listening within another frame of reference. It takes tremendous courage to listen because you're at risk when you listen. You don't know what's going to happen—you're vulnerable.

Wright

Sales gurus always tell me that the number one skill in selling is listening.

Covey

Yes—listening from within the customer's frame of reference. That is so true. You can see that it takes some security to do that because you don't know what's going to happen.

Wright

We're trying to encourage people in our audience to be better, to live better, and be more fulfilled by listening to the examples given by our guests. Is there anything or anyone in your life who has made a difference for you and helped you to become a better person?

Covey

I think the most influential people in my life have been my parents. I think they modeled the example of not to experience comparisons and jealousies or to seek recognition. They were humble people. I remember one time when we were going up in an elevator and the most prominent person in the state was in the elevator with us. My mother knew him, but she spent her time talking to the elevator operator. I was just a little kid and I was so awed by this person.

I said to my mom, "Why didn't you talk to the important person?"

"I was," she replied, "I had never met him."

They were really humble, modest people who were focused on service and other people rather than themselves. I think they were very inspiring models to me.

Wright

In almost every research paper that anyone I've ever read written about people who influenced their lives, in the top five people listed who most influenced them, about three are teachers. My seventh grade English teacher was the greatest teacher I ever had and influenced me to no end.

Covey

Would it be correct to say that she saw in you probably some qualities of greatness you didn't even see in yourself?

Wright

Absolutely.

Covey

That's been my general experience. The key aspect of a mentor or a teacher is that they see in you potential you don't even see in yourself. They treat you accordingly and eventually you come to see it in yourself. That's my definition of leadership or influence— communicating people's worth and potential so clearly that they are inspired to see it in themselves.

Wright

Most of my teachers treated me as a student, but she treated me with much more respect than that. As a matter of fact, she called me "Mr. Wright" in the seventh grade. I'd never been addressed by anything but a nickname. I stood a little taller; she just made a tremendous difference. Do you think there are other characteristics mentors seem to have in common?

Covey

I think mentors are, first of all, good examples in their own personal lives. Their personal lives and their family lives are not all messed up so they come from a base of good character. They are also usually very confident and take the time to do what your teacher did to you—treat you with this uncommon respect and courtesy. They also, I think, explicitly teach principles rather than practices so that rules don't take the place of human judgment. You gradually come to have faith in your own judgment in making decisions because of the affirmation of such a mentor. They care about you and you can feel the sincerity of their caring. It's like the expression, "I don't care how much you know until I know how much you care."

Wright

Most people are fascinated with the new television shows about being a survivor. What has been the greatest comeback you've made from adversity in your career or your life?

Covey

When I was in grade school I experienced a disease in my legs. It caused me to use crutches for a time. I tried to get off them fast and get back. The disease wasn't corrected yet so I went on for another year. The disease went to the other leg and I went on for *another* year. It essentially took me out of my favorite thing—athletics—and I became more focused on being a student. So that was kind of a life defining experience that at the time seemed very negative, but has proven to be the basis on which I've focused my life—being more of a learner.

Wright

Principle centered learning is basically what you do that's different from anyone I've read or listened to.

Covey

It's like the far-eastern expression, "Give a man a fish you feed him for the day; teach him how to fish, you feed him for a lifetime." When you teach principles that are universal and timeless, they don't belong to just any one person's religion or they don't belong to a particular culture or geography, they seem to be timeless and universal; like the ones we've been talking about here: trustworthiness, honesty, caring, service, growth and development. These are universal principles.

If you focus on these values then little by little people become independent of you and they start to believe in themselves; their own judgment becomes better. You don't need as many rules. You don't need as much bureaucracy and as many controls and you can empower people.

The problem in most business operations today, and not just business but non-business, is that they're using the industrial model in an information age. Arnold Joseph Toynbee, the great historian, said, "You can pretty well summarize all of history in four words: nothing fails like success." The industrial model was based on the asset of the machine. The information model is based on the asset of the person—of the knowledge worker. It's an altogether different model. But the machine model was the main asset of the twentieth century. It enabled the productivity to go up fifty times.

The new asset is intellectual and social capital—the qualities of people and the quality of the relationship they have with each other. Like Toynbee said, "Nothing fails like success." The industrial model does not work in an information age. It requires a focus on the new wealth, not capital and profit.

A good illustration that shows you how much we were into the industrial model, and still are, is where are people on the balance sheet? They're not found there. Machines are found there. Machines have become investments. People are on the profit and loss statement and people are expenses. Think of that, if that isn't bloodletting.

Wright

It sure is. When you consider the choices you've made down through the years, has faith played an important role in your life?

Covey

An extremely important role. I believe deeply that we should put principles at the center of our lives, but I believe God is the source of those principles. I did not invent them. I get credit sometimes for some of the seven habits material and some of the other stuff I've done, but in reality it's all based on principles given by God to all of His children from the beginning of time. You'll find you can teach these same principles from the sacred texts and wisdom literature of almost any tradition. I think the ultimate source of that is God and that is one thing you can absolutely depend upon—in God we trust.

Wright

If you could have a platform and tell our audience something you believe would help them or encourage them, what would you say?

Covey

I think I would say put God at the center of your life and then prioritize your family. No one on their deathbed ever wished they spent more time at the office.

Wright

That's right. We have come down to the end of our program and I know you're a busy person, but I could talk with you all day Dr. Covey.

Covey

It's good to talk with you as well and to be a part of this program. It looks like an excellent one you've got going on here.

Wright

Thank you. We have been talking today with Dr. Stephen R. Covey, co-founder and vice-chairman of Franklin Covey Company. He's also the author of *The Seven Habits of Highly Effective People,* which is ranked a number one bestseller by the *New York Times,* selling more than fourteen million copies in thirty-eight languages.

Dr. Covey, thank you so much for being with us today on *Conversations on Success!*

Covey

Thank you for the honor of participating.

About The Author

Stephen M. R. Covey is the Co-founder and CEO of his own boutique firm—CoveyLink—which is a learning and consulting practice focused on enabling leaders and organizations to increase and leverage trust to achieve superior performance. Recognized as a leading authority on creating high-trust, high-performance organizations, Covey is currently writing a new book titled *The Speed of Trust*, expected to be published in 2006. This book represents more than a decade of research and practice on how creating high trust within organizations propels speed, influence, and results. To accompany his writing, Covey enlightens audiences through engaging presentations.

Stephen M. R. Covey

50 W. Canyon Crest Road

Alpine, Utah 84004

Phone: 801.756.2700

Email: info@coveylink.com

www.coveylink.com

Chapter 7

NITA SCOGGAN

THE INTERVIEW

David Wright (Wright)

Nita Scoggan is a motivational speaker, award-winning author, and trainer. Nita worked at the Pentagon for twenty-five years as a research analyst and illustrator for the U.S. Air Force. Between 1973-1998, Nita ministered during lunchtime meetings for staffers at the Pentagon and the White House. In 1999, she and her husband, Bill, relocated to Bedford, Indiana. Since 2002, Nita has been on the faculty as an Adjunct Professor at Oakland City University, at the Bedford campus. She teaches courses in Business Ethics, Marketing, and Communication, as well as Liberal Arts courses and seminars.

I want to welcome Nita Scoggan to *Conversations on Success.*

Nita Scoggan (Scoggan)

Thank you, David. I'm delighted to be with you today.

Wright

Nita, your career has been very successful and unique in many ways. You're a successful business owner, college professor, author of seventeen books, interviewed on many television programs, been a keynote speaker at many events across the nation, conducted weekly prayer services at the White House, and you have had a thirty-five year career in the federal government. Tell us how you were chosen for ministry at the White House.

Scoggan

David, people often ask me how I was chosen for this important position. Frankly, it came as a complete surprise to me. It wasn't something I had planned to do. I never dreamed I would be invited to the White House. At the time, I had no special credentials, not even a degree. I was a government employee working in the basement of the Pentagon. However, in 1984, Caroline Sundseth, Associate Director of Public Affairs on President Reagan's staff, invited me to start a weekly prayer service and Bible study in her office at the White House. She told me she wanted to have a dynamite Bible class like the one I had been conducting at the Pentagon. She had heard God was answering many prayers and that miracles were happening at our lunchtime meetings.

I was surprised she had heard of our Bible study. She said our ministry was very well known. She also told me she had friends in ministry all over the nation who wanted to move to Washington D.C. in order to conduct these prayer and Bible ministry meetings in her office. In spite of this, she felt strongly that "it was God's class and He would choose the person to lead it." Then she pointed her finger at me and she said," Nita you're the one God has chosen." I was thrilled and I thought that since God has chosen me, He will enable me to do it.

The Bible says that God uses people who are ready and willing. When I accepted the Lord, I studied my Bible three times a day. I got up earlier, gave up my lunch companions, and made a decision that I was going to read my Bible three times a day and I did that every day for six years. I wanted to know exactly what God had to say for my life. As it turned out, this was preparation for the open door for ministry God had for me that I knew nothing about.

I had the honor to lead meetings in Room 180 for almost fifteen years. It was particularly sweet for me, because this room had been the Vice President's office from Herbert Hoover to George Bush. I thought, "What a wonderful place to pray!" It was just a few feet from the Oval Office. As an added benefit, we got to see the Vice Presidents from each administration and other important people during our time there. It was a very humbling experience to think God put me there for such a time as that.

Wright

I also understand you taught daily Bible classes for women during your time at the Pentagon under the auspices of the military chaplaincy program. Tell us about your successes during that time.

Scoggan

I was thrilled to be accepted as part of the military chaplaincy. I never planned it, yet I was recommended by the Pentagon chaplain and was accepted. It was a dream come true for me. My greatest joy was seeing people's lives changed. It is still my greatest joy today. I believed that if I could help to make the life of someone better because I was there to answer a question for them or to pray with them, that was a tremendous success for me.

Wright

Nita, you are quite the author. I understand you have written seventeen books. How did you find the time to do this?

Scoggan

I never planned on writing a book. I was a working wife with two sons still living at home. I was active in our local church, including a position on the church board, in addition to the White House and Pentagon meetings I was involved in. But one morning, I remember getting up early and I had an hour alone in my devotion time before I got ready for work. That morning, I really felt impressed that God was telling me to write a book, about what He was doing at the Pentagon.

I said, "God, I don't have any time to write a book."

And God said," Nita, you've got two hours a day going to and from work in the van pool. You could use that time to write."

I thought, "Well, okay, God," and that's what I did.

After awhile, the van pool members were curious about what I was doing. Some had doubts that I was really writing a book about the Pentagon. Some thought it was a joke. Anybody can write a book, but not many people do, because they won't make a commitment to take the time to do it. But, I was committed to writing everyday.

After many months, I finished the book. Then, I was uncertain about the title. Not long afterwards, I was praying about it and God spoke to my heart and said, "Call it *Pillars of the Pentagon*. I knew it had to be God, because it was quite different from what I had in mind.

I asked God, "What does that mean?"

He said, "The praying women of the Pentagon are like the huge pillars in the building that support and hold up the entire structure."

Most people walking through the building never notice the pillars, and yet they're vital to support the building and the work that's done there. From that day forward, I knew God had chosen the title. The testimonies in that book are very uplifting and give praise to God for His divine intervention in people's lives. That's when my writing career began to blossom. With additional ideas coming from God and my determination to do so, I have written seventeen books to date.

I'm still amazed what God can do, when we are willing and obedient to follow His leading in our lives. God has been so faithful to help me in this effort. I'm glad I've learned to trust Him and allow His power to work through me.

Wright

Do you have a message of encouragement you feel passionate about?

Scoggan

It is so important to have passion for life and to hold on to your dreams. It is equally important to be thankful for all the blessings we have, including our health, job, and the freedoms we take for granted here in America.

God truly is for us and not against us. It is His will to give us good gifts. He can be our best friend and lifelong companion. He wants to help us in all that we do.

This divine relationship though, isn't automatic. We must invite Him into our lives and invest our time and have faith to believe that, "He is the rewarder of those who diligently seek Him."—Hebrews 11:6. He loves us all. He created us all. He wants to restore what we have been robbed of, and He asks so little in return. He's just waiting for us to pray and come into His presence.

Reading the Bible helps us understand what God is like. It gives us something to believe in. Our part is to believe He can and will do for us what the Bible says He will do. Jesus said, "Have faith in God"—Mark 11:22. The Bible says in Colossians 3:23, "And whatsoever ye do, do it heartily, as to the Lord, and not unto men..." He wants to be our best friend and yet if we don't talk to Him, if we don't read His Word, we're never going to draw close to Him and get the blessings He has for us. So I tell people, press into God, read the

Bible, and keep doing your very best work, as if you were working directly for Him. I've seen this method produce some amazing results and many are recorded in the *Pillars of the Pentagon.*

Wright

Would you tell our readers your thoughts on the keys to success?

Scoggan

There are nine essential keys to success. They are:

1. *Do what you say you're going to do.* Personal integrity is priceless. I believe it's the most important key to success. Without integrity, everything else will eventually fall apart. Personal integrity includes speaking well of others in their absence, including your boss, spouse, pastor or priest, etc. It also means doing the best job you can whether someone is watching or not.

2. *Make a positive contribution wherever you are regardless of the situation you find yourself in.* Attitude does determine altitude. As my friends in the Air Force say, "AIM HIGH."

3. *Be thankful and count your blessings every day.* Learn to surround yourself with past successes. Keep their memories close to your heart, especially when times get tough. The level of success in your life depends on you. Give yourself a chance to succeed and apply patient endurance. The Bible says we learn "line upon line and precept upon precept"—Isaiah 28:10. I think that's so important when things are hard for us.

4. *Work daily to improve your knowledge, skills, and abilities.* Make yourself more valuable every day. Learn a new skill or take a course. Develop a new relationship or renew an old one. The more you know, the more valuable you are to others, including your boss and your Creator.
   I have found that bosses, and God, normally use people who are ready. Prepare yourself now for the job opportunity you want in the future, and when the time comes, you'll be ready. Also remember, the most valuable resource in this life is people.

Build relationships—don't burn bridges. You will need other people's help along the way. Sometimes God uses people you may not like to refine your character and help you on your way.

5. *Associate with people who are worthy of your trust.* Ask them for their help. Let them know how you are doing and share your successes from applying what they have imparted to you. You would be surprised how valuable this is to a friend, relative, teacher, boss, pastor, priest, etc. Be careful who you share your thoughts, goals, and dreams with. Keep them close to your heart and among your trusted friends. It is my opinion that this is the most common mistake people make. The Bible says, "Don't cast your pearls before swine"— Matthew 7:6. In other words, be careful whom you share your secret thoughts with or they will be trampled, ruined, and destroyed by the words others speak.

6. *Never, under any circumstances, regardless of the reason or situation, never, never, never, ever, feel sorry for yourself.* Never feel sorry for yourself, regardless of how you feel or how bad circumstances look. God is faithful. "He will never leave you or forsake you"—Hebrews 13:5. You are never alone. There is always hope. Feeling sorry for one's self is the deathblow to focus, motivation, confidence, and any possibility of a successful life. I strongly suggest avoiding people who feel sorry for themselves and who display chronic complaining. Complaining is a sign of an ungrateful spirit and an unrepentant heart. These folk will suck the lifeblood out of anyone who will listen to them. Complaining is also an indication that people have a problem supporting authority. Stay clear of these types of people. Consider them a good example of someone you will never want to emulate.

7. *Stay the course.* The Bible says to, "Set your face like flint"—Isaiah 50:7. Stay on course regardless of what painful circumstances come your way. General Douglas MacArthur said nine words to a

graduating class at West Point in what I believe was one of the most memorable speeches ever delivered anywhere. It was near the close of WW II. The General was familiar with the painful circumstances of war. He stood to his feet and said in a clear loud voice, "Never give up! [he paused for several moments] Never give up! [again he paused for several moments] Never give up!" Then he sat down and I understand he wept openly. Powerful man. Powerful speech. Powerful words.Along that same line, the Bible says, "I can do all things through Christ, who strengthens me"—Philippians 4:13. If we apply these words to our lives and have the courage to take the requisite action, it will give us confidence and stamina to stay the course, to complete the job, endure great trial, and fulfill our destiny here on earth. This is why we were born. This is why we're here.

8. _Find a suitable mentor and be accountable for your progress._ This is a big part of the successful learning process. In days gone by, this was similar to having an apprenticeship. You would work side by side with a tradesman and learn a trade. Usually, it took a couple of years to complete your training. If things worked out, you ended up as a professional tradesman while the "employer" received free work during the training period. Find a teacher you can be committed to—a trusted friend—whose constructive criticism you value. Choose someone with whom you have good chemistry, who is living the life you desire to live. Choose this person very wisely. It is by far the best way to learn any skill. It is the way Jesus taught his disciples. We learn by what we see other people do. Jesus was always there for them. He was teacher and coach. He gave them assignments. The successful ones did what He said.

9. _Teach someone else what you've learned._ This is the best way to give back to society, friends, family, etc. Teaching someone else is how we master what we have learned. If you can teach it, you really

know it. That's the test. In my experience, the best teachers are the ones who also practice what they teach. An added benefit for us is that we remember what we teach and we are remembered by what we teach and do. Stephen Covey, in His renowned book *Seven Habits of Highly Effective People* says, "Leave a legacy." I believe that when we teach someone else what we know through speaking and doing, it will remain after we're gone. It is my strongest intention to teach my grandchildren all I know. It is my intention to teach them what is good and right—things that matter. It is my greatest hope to also teach them how to learn and how to teach others. I cannot improve on Dr. Covey's words. I can only improve on the methods I choose to deliver my message and the effectiveness of its impact.

Wright

You're a member of the National Speaker's Association.

Scoggan

Yes, this is one of the accomplishments I'm most proud of.

Wright

How'd you get started as a professional speaker?

Scoggan

I never planned to be a professional speaker. In fact, I still remember how frightened I was during my first speech in high school. I was petrified and did a terrible job. I just stood frozen and speechless. My speech teacher pointed out every fault and shortcoming I had in front of the whole class. I was so embarrassed. After that, I was determined to succeed in that class and make an A. I made it a point to remember what she said I did wrong. I was determined I was going to improve, and improve I did.

Eventually, as my life progressed, I began to get invitations to speak, mostly to volunteer organizations without monetary compensation. This evolved into speaking at events for pay. My first was at a women's retreat. I received fifty dollars. I was on top of the world! Now I understand that fifty dollars isn't much, but I was doing what I loved and getting paid for it. That is truly one of the great secrets to success. Find what you love and do that.

After my fifty-dollar event, I was so "pumped up" that I decided to actively pursue more speaking opportunities. Many became available through the women who attended the Pentagon Bible classes. They began recommending me as a speaker at retreats or different events at their churches. I stayed with it and I really enjoy speaking. It's a challenge and one I dearly love. I've spoken at universities and organizations all across the nation. I've really grown along the way and I am still amazed at the successful results God has produced through me during this time in my life.

Wright
To what do you attribute your success?

Scoggan
1. *First of all, I attribute my success to faith in God.* I believe God has led me all the way, helping me to know what to do, when to do it and how to do it.
2. *Secondly, I followed the example of my mother's strong work ethic.* She was a great fan and was always in my corner, so to speak. She demonstrated success to me by the way she conducted her daily life. She was a great example to emulate. Many stories about her life are recorded in another book of mine entitled, *The Alaskan Lady*. She was an amazing person. She was also a very determined and focused person. She was a hard worker. I remember her saying, "Don't leave a job half done." She was also the kindest and most generous person I've ever known. She was a very happy person who always liked to "cut up" and have a good time. What a wonderful example God gave me to follow; she was always there for me. I miss her every day.
3. *Thirdly, I believe in the power of answered prayer.* Mother was a praying woman. My grandmother was a praying woman. I am a praying woman. I believed at a young age that God was real and He heard my prayers. I believed answers to those prayers made a big difference in my life. That has encouraged me and helped me all along the way,

because I've had to overcome many obstacles on the road to success. Some people believe that after one gets God involved in their lives, everything is supposed to get easy and there are no obstacles to overcome. I believe the opposite is closer to the informed Biblical understanding of "overcoming." You see, the Bible says, we are over-comers (see 1 John 2:13-14). Therefore, that would imply there must be something to overcome. We start small and work on things over time. Every victory makes us stronger and gives us a better foundation of reliance on God in our faith walk.

We are encouraged by the Bible, because it says, "faith comes by hearing the Word of God"—Romans 10:17. If you believe the Bible is God's Word, it will also work for you, because God is no respecter of persons (Acts 10:34). In other words, it doesn't matter to God if you're poor or rich, young or old, successful or not. He will meet you wherever you are and whoever you are. He is always ready. He never sleeps. He never gets tired. He never gives up on us. He is a respecter of those who have faith and trust in Him. Walking by faith brings the supernatural into the natural realm. As we practice this, we get better and more consistent results all the time.

Our goal is to become like Jesus. He is the Divine Son of God. He is our example. He is our standard of behavior. Most of us, including myself, have a history full of much sorrow. God takes us in, cleans us up and begins the life long process of helping us to become all He has created us to be. My advice is to ask God to help you overcome your obstacles and remember the Bible says not to despise small beginnings (see Psalm 51:17). Build on that, and I believe God will help you become successful, because He is for you, not against you. He wants to become your greatest fan, supporter, and teacher. He is definitely in your corner and wants you to be a successful overcomer.

Wright

Tell us about some major obstacles you overcame on your road to successfully reaching your dreams.

Scoggan

I had some major obstacles to overcome along the way. I can remember when I was six years old a flood came and washed away our house in Texas. We barely got out with our lives. There was no time to take anything with us, not even our shoes. I was cold and wet. It was raining. I know what it feels like to be homeless. It was terrible. It was terrible being poor.

I remember never having enough money. My mother was a single mom much of my childhood. She worked as a waitress, mostly for tips. I remember the depression years. Times were very tough and lean. We did without many things but God was faithful to take care of us. We learned to be dependent on Him for common things such as shoes.

After the flood, we moved to Los Angles, where my stepfather got a job with the railroad. I remember while we were living in "LA" Mother was given twenty dollars by one of her customers at the restaurant near Christmastime. She used it to pay some essential bills and had enough money left to buy my sister, Hazel, and me a new pair of shoes. There wasn't enough left over for bus fare, so we walked a long way to the shoe store. Hazel and I didn't care. We were very happy to have new shoes. It was 1936. Mother was very grateful for the gentleman's generosity.

She always believed God would provide. She reminded us of this story from time to time when we were adults in difficult financial times. She always helped us see the bright side of things. She was a wonderful encourager. She taught us to have faith in God and strive with all our might to overcome obstacles and make better lives for ourselves. Her latter years were better than her former years. She always had more than enough. She had more friends than anyone else I have ever known. Her cup was overflowing.

My stepdad worked for the railroad as a detective. It was hard work and he was gone a lot. In 1938, he went to Alaska because land was free. Mother joined him in 1939. They homesteaded there and built a log cabin south of Anchorage. There was no water, no sewer, and no electric, but it was theirs. It took them about two years to finish the cabin. Hazel and I lived with our grandmother in Texas, during that time.

Mother sent for us in 1942. We traveled on a troop ship. This was during WW II—not the best place for two young girls—but God was faithful to watch over us. Most civilians had to leave Alaska during this time because of the war. The Japanese had bombed the Aleutian Islands. They had also invaded the Aleutians and taken prisoners, which was not something taught in public school or even publicized at that time or even now. We had blackouts and Marshall Law was in effect. It was a scary time. We were allowed to stay though, since

Jack, my stepfather, had been deputized as a territorial Marshall as a part of his railroad work. Mother would not leave him. We didn't have much, but we were very happy to be together.

Jack taught Hazel and me to shoot his firearms and he taught us how to protect ourselves against bears and intruders. We went fishing a lot. The price was right and the fish were great. Jack was an outdoorsman and taught Hazel and me a great love and respect for nature. There was no TV in those days and I spent much of my time reading. I still love to read. I had lots of time to develop my skills in drawing, painting, and sewing.

My dream was to become a professional artist. There wasn't much opportunity in Alaska during that time. After World War II the first university in Alaska was established but my parents couldn't afford to send me to college. That was okay. I knew growing up we didn't have very much money.

I worked during the summer of my sophomore and junior year to buy my school clothes. And you know, that was probably one of the best things to happen to me because when you have to stretch your money, you really learn to be a good shopper. You also learn to really appreciate things. So, I learned to be a wise shopper, stretch money and to be content with what I had.

A love of drawing and art was still in my heart. I went to the school principal in my senior year and asked him if I could enroll in the mechanical drawing class, which was for boys only. This class was the closest thing to art that was offered. Since I was a good student and active in leadership positions in the school, I thought it would be a "piece of cake" to get the principal's permission. I was mistaken. He said no, that the class was just for boys. I said all I wanted was a chance to prove that I could do the work. He said he would ask the teacher and leave the decision up to him. Well, he called me into the office the next day and told me the instructor was willing to give me a two-week trial. He thought a girl in the class would be disruptive to the boys. He told me, "If there are any problems, you won't be able to stay."

I said. "Okay."

I was determined to be a success. I wouldn't even talk to the boys. I was one of the only students who passed the final exam with an A. And you know, it taught me to be very careful to always do my best work.

The first statement on the final exam was to read *all* the instructions before starting. He never said another word. In the instructions, it said, "When you have finished reading this paragraph go to page three to begin." I was one of a few students who read the instructions. Almost everyone else started doing the exercises and other assignments on pages one and two. I made an A in this class because I read the instructions and I did exactly what it said to do. As a result, he gave me a wonderful recommendation. The government hired me as a trainee in the drafting department in the Federal Building in downtown Anchorage and later in Washington, D.C. That's how my government career in art started. It seemed like my dream came true for me. It was creative and challenging work.

Wright

So what are you doing now that you're no longer in Washington D.C.?

Scoggan

We moved to Bedford, Indiana, because my husband's health was failing. He grew up here and wanted to move away from the traffic and the busy life of the city. I asked God to please make me happy in Indiana, because I was leaving all of my friends, some of my family, and our ministry. I didn't want to be a wife who was unhappy. I didn't want to complain about missing all those things I loved. And you know, God really has answered that prayer.

When we came here my husband had to rest a lot and that was good because he regained his health. I decided I would finish my bachelor's degree. I only needed two courses. I finished that and I went on to obtain my Master's Degree in Organizational Management. In 2002, I was offered a position on the faculty at Oakland City University. There again, I never dreamed of teaching at a university. It wasn't in my plan, but what a wonderful, wonderful privilege to have a positive influence on the lives of students.

Of course I'm active in community affairs, and we go back to Washington at least once a year. When we are there, we're invited to the White House to attend the class we started and to have prayer and lunch with friends there. Every year I'm invited to be a speaker at the annual retreat, "The Pentagon Advance for Christian Women." They call it an Advance because military people do not retreat! As a speaker, it's a challenge because the ladies really know the Word of God and have high expectations. So, I seek the Lord's guidance as I fast, pray and prepare. Then, I joyfully share what God has given me to say.

Wright

I always ask our authors if they have a closing thought to share that our readers can immediately put to use and perhaps help change their life. Do you have any such thoughts?

Scoggan

I have some thoughts I would like to share. It is so important for us, when things are hard to never give up. When things seem impossible—financial problems or health problems, difficult work schedules, military separation, and other stressors of life—it is during those times that we need to start praising God.

You know, people don't thank God and praise Him enough. Start thanking God and counting your blessings, knowing that God is with you and is going to help you through your problems.

Something President Calvin Coolidge said played a significant part in encouraging me and helping me to be successful. I want to share that with the readers. He said, "Nothing in the world can take the place of perseverance." We've got to stick to the job! Pray! I prayed a lot and asked God to help me do my best. I asked Him for wisdom on my job and understanding. President Coolidge went on to say, "Nothing in the world can take the place of perseverance. Talent will not. Nothing is more common than unsuccessful men with talent..." I worked with people who had degrees, and I also went on to get a degree myself, but a degree does not insure that someone can do the work. President Coolidge went on to say, "Genius will not. Unrewarded genius is almost a proverb. Education will not. The world is full of educated derelicts. Persistence and determination alone are omnipotent."

Persistence and determination are the most important factors. You can't write a book, you can't be a speaker, or teacher unless you are persistent and determined. *We must keep our focus on our goals and dreams and never give up!*

Wright

Today we have been talking with Nita Scoggan. Nita, thank you so much for this interesting conversation. I've learned a lot today. Thank you so much for being with us on *Conversations on Success.*

Scoggan

Thank you, David. It's been a privilege talking with you and I firmly believe God will use our conversation today to encourage many people to better understand how they can begin to enjoy the results of success in their lives by applying these principles.

About The Author

Nita Scoggan is a national keynote, seminar and international conference speaker. She is the award-winning author of seventeen books, professional member of the National Speakers Association, respected Adjunct Professor and business owner. With enthusiasm and humor she relates success principles learned in her twenty-five-year career as a research analyst and illustrator at the Pentagon. In 2004, Nita was appointed President of the Advisory Board for Oakland City University-Bedford, Indiana. As a member of the OCUB faculty, she teaches Business and Liberal Arts courses. A frequent television guest on national and Canadian programs,

Nita stresses the value of education in order to be more successful. From 1973-1993, Nita gave her lunchtime to God by teaching daily prayer and Bible classes at the Pentagon. Her ministry is credentialed by the Department of Defense Armed Forces Chaplaincy Board. In 1984, Nita was invited to the White House to conduct weekly ministry to the White House staffers. For almost fifteen years, from Presidents Reagan to Clinton, teaching focused on prayer, believing faith and being doers of the Word. Nita Scoggan is a remarkable woman of faith.

Born at her grandmother's home, a two-pound preemie at birth, the doctor declared she had "no chance to live." But live she did! Placed in a shoebox, fed with an eyedropper—without medical aid—her survival was a miracle. She overcame health problems and poverty, giving God the credit for it all. "I believe in miracles! I've seen them, in answer to prayer. I know God can do anything, so I love to pray," says Nita.

Her driving force is to uplift, encourage and empower others to achieve their maximum potential in life. Her motto is "Never give up your dreams-pursue them with patience and persistence."

Nita Scoggan

Maximum Zone Consulting

P.O. Box 2125

Bedford, IN 47421-7125

E-mail: nscoggan@ocub.oak.edu

www.NitaScoggan.com

To Schedule Nita to Speak

Call 1-866-735-2498

Chapter 8

EVA JENKINS, PHR

THE INTERVIEW

David Wright (Wright)

Today we're talking with Eva Jenkins. Eva Jenkins brings more than twenty years of experience to her role as leader of VIP Staffing and VIP Innovations. With a career that had its beginning in business and finance, she has shown companies time and time again how she can pair her knowledge of business with human capital to take organizations to the next level of success.

Mrs. Jenkins has earned a reputation in the Washington, D.C., area and beyond as a change agent who has analyzed and redeveloped the recruiting function for many technology companies to make them more effective and productive.

Ms. Jenkins, welcome to *Conversations on Success*.

Eva Jenkins (Jenkins)

Well, thank you.

Wright

Why did you decide to start your own consulting firm?

Jenkins

I came to a crossroad in my life where I had to choose between having a complete focus on a career position, which took me away from my family very often, or choosing to stay focused on being there for my young son and creating a balance within my professional and personal life. I always had a real desire to build a business of my own, so after more than twenty years of corporate life, I made the decision to start my own consulting firm and try to balance my professional and personal life more effectively.

Wright

So what were some of your biggest obstacles? You came from the corporate world didn't you?

Jenkins

In a nutshell: creating a flexible and viable business plan, defining a business strategy to mirror image the business plan, and obtaining some financing assistance to at least start building the foundations of the business. Since I am analytical in nature, my priority was to focus on creating and defining the business operations policies (accounting), procedures and files, etc., creating marketing collateral, and the start of an e-marketing strategy which was all put together prior to getting out there and selling my services. I just did not want to bring in business I could not totally support! I have seen way too many companies sell generate sales without having the proper solid infrastructure to support and maintain the incoming business.

That is the reason why so many companies fail to achieve excellent customer service and cannot keep their clients. Those companies who understand and appreciate how important it is to gain their clients' trust and provide excellent customer service will somehow sustain themselves even during very slow and turbulent economic times. This was evident during the past few years—all businesses have experienced this to one extent or another!

Wright

So what does it take to succeed in starting your own business?

Jenkins

The absolute and shear determination of wanting to be in your own business, having a real passion for the field you choose, and being tenacious and persistent. I was always told that tenacity was one of my best assets and I am glad I have that characteristic in me. I just love this quote, "Frequently the difference between success and failure is the resolve to stick to your plan long enough to win."— *David Cottrell*

Wright

What were the biggest challenges you faced in the very beginning?

Jenkins

Staying focused—especially the first couple of years. I had gone to so many meetings and listened to so many so-called "experts" that I was thoroughly confused and exhausted. Making sense of all the information and defining a particular niche to market to is absolutely vital. Another challenge was successfully positioning my business, which took some time to define.

Wright

So what are your on-going challenges as your business matures?

Jenkins

Meeting short-term business and financial goals and, of course, continuing to build my organization which will sustain itself for the long run.

Wright

So what types of services does your consulting divisions provide?

Jenkins

I have two business divisions: One is an executive diversity focused staffing firm, called VIP Staffing, LLC, based in Washington, D.C. We primarily focus on identifying excellent "diversity" management candidates. We then follow up by utilizing state-of the-art assessment tools such as the "Profile XT Assessment," which gives feedback on the "Behaviorial, Thinking and Job Interest Fit." This additional and powerful tool helps us present better-qualified candidates and helps the companies and hiring managers with their selection. It also aids in coaching for future and continuous best performance of the placed candidate.

After much deliberation and research, I had opened up an employee training and assessment and organizational consulting practice all centered around delivering the principles of High

Performance. VIP Innovations specializes in helping companies to identify benchmarks and implement the skills, structure and knowledge needed for continued success. If a company can recognize that every employee can positively or negatively influence their organization, then VIP can help them find, train and keep the cream of the crop.

Wright

How does your service help companies?

Jenkins
VIP helps companies refocus their current business strategies and positively re-direct their human capital. We can help companies tap into the intelligence and creativity of their people. With our High Performance Training programs and Profiles Assessment tools, we can help develop caring employees who can collectively focus on the success of their companies. Our process improvement techniques can revamp operations so employees feel like "partners" in the business rather than just "paycheck collectors."

Wright
So, how does a business achieve High Performance?

Jenkins
A High Performance organization achieves superior and sustainable results by clarifying its strategy, streamlining its processes, and creating a culture in which each person is a contributing partner in the business. The standard methodology for achieving High Performance within the workplace has been to break away from the traditional and highly structured model of a business organization to one that is more organic and flexible. Within these organic systems, managers are encouraged to create teams of employees who work together toward a common business goal. The teams are empowered to make decisions and solve problems, they monitor and improve their quality, and each individual employee is seen as a contributing business partner.

Wright

So, what really happens? Why does the theory of High Performance so often get derailed when it is based on sound principles of human behavior and motivation?

Jenkins

The problem is not with the theory, it is in the execution! Our culture is so indentured to the traditional model of organization that, despite our best efforts, it is almost impossible to remove the vestiges of managerial control, division of labor, and the reams and reams of policies and procedures that trap employees into doing things one way and one way only. When well meaning executives, managers, and consultants take hold of the notion of High Performance Management, they often rush to create teams, write new job descriptions, set up feedback systems, and create elaborate reward and recognition programs all in an effort to convince their employees that they are valued and respected and their contributions are meaningful and appreciated and will be rewarded.

Again, these are all sound notions but the problem is that these programs address only surface issues; they do not even begin to attack the traditional notions and customs that continue to prevail. Think of organizational dynamics as an iceberg where only ten percent of the issues are visible on the surface and the bulk remains hidden and potentially menacing underneath. In truly High Performance workplaces managers do not have to "convince" employees they are valued—the employees inherently know they are valued simply by the way the work is organized and performed.

So what's wrong with this picture?

The organization that is *trying* to be High Performance is really no more than a traditional organization in disguise. It has adopted new terminology and is trying out some new human resource management techniques but the organization has *not changed the way it approaches the system of working.* Work is still narrowly defined and departmentalized, and management is still controlling and directing the flow. On the surface it may sound like things have changed but the employees know they are doing exactly what they did before; except now, they are part of a "team" doing it.

Wright

According to your experience, which human capital practices drive financial performance and unlocks the human potential in an organization?

Jenkins

There is no real secret magic formula that can be applied to every single company. VIP has adapted the viewpoint that each company is unique. Our approach varies from organization to organization depending upon each company's organizational needs and position in the marketplace. Some human capital practices can drive financial performance across the board in a company but again, in order for a company to reach its "maximum" Human Capital ROI, each company needs to define their position or market orientation. Then they need to devise their own human capital strategies and align their management practices. However, research indicates that there are three basic findings which yield consistent financial rewards these are: Setting starting salaries; Measuring employee performance and constantly enhancing employee productivity by creating High Performance teams and workflow, and effectively communicating throughout the company.

For example: If you are a company needing to develop new products or create software hardware solutions, or biotechnology firm where you need to be first and you need to have outstanding/best products, then most likely you are considered an "innovative" company whereby you need to attract top performers and pay top starting salaries. This type of company must retain its top talent even in very trying economic times by providing ongoing training pertaining to their field of expertise. This type of company must also place higher emphasis on attracting individual contributors and most of the time these employees understand there will be large disparities among the employees. However, if you take this approach and apply it to an "operationally focused company," this type of practice can and will create very negative consequences.

If a company is "customer service" focused (banks, hotels, retail) then, the crucial Human Capital Management (HCM) practices which will give the highest financial return would be: (1) Focusing on internal equity pay scales for new hires; (2) Performance Measurement systems based on developing new skills; (3) Practicing consistent communications throughout the organization!

Wright

From your viewpoint, what is the correlation between human capital management and having a High Performance organization?

Jenkins

The only way to move toward true High Performance is to adopt a system of HCM that helps measure and execute real changes in the way that human capital (resources) is managed. It starts with the realization and acknowledgement that your human—intangible— capital is as important as your tangible capital and that like the tangible items, human capital needs to measured and accounted for on a consistent basis. Just as you want to keep your equipment in top shape, so should you keep your people in top shape—ready and capable of performing the job they were hired to do. Just as a company seeks investment opportunities for their financial capital to grow, the company also needs to invest in human capital and provide them with opportunities to grow and produce results.

By attending to the needs of your employees, a company allows them to perform to their capacity. This maximum capacity yields high productivity and that is when you truly have a High Performance organization.

Achievement of High Performance requires linking HCM programs, philosophies, and objectives to the following four factors that have the most influence on organizational success:

1. Strategy Development—It is absolutely necessary to create HCM systems where all employees have input into strategy development and have direct responsibility for the achievement of that strategy and associated objectives. This builds the intrinsic self-worth of the employee as he or she understands how his or her actions have a direct impact on organizational success.

2. Team Development—Effective HCM requires the development of autonomous and empowered teams. Encouraging and facilitating employees' freedom to act and think independently produces the positive energy, creativity, and motivation capable of limitless achievement.

3. Leadership and Personal Development—People crave opportunities to improve themselves and showcase their talents and abilities. HCM programs that promote and sponsor individual development spur the desire to

continuously improve. Combined with effective teams, enthusiasm is contagious and everyone wants to be the best they can be, not just for themselves but also for the team and company as a whole.

4. Organizational Assessment—This factor requires commitment to continuous organizational development. In order to remain effective, HCM needs to regularly assess those aspects of human capital that indicate whether High Performance is being achieved. Some factors to consider are loyalty, recruitment, retention, customer care, and intellectual property. By identifying, measuring, and tracking the success within these types of human capital factors, it is possible to modify and improve your overall HCM ensuring persistent High Performance.

High Performance is as critical as it is possible. It is a process that starts with philosophical change and ends with practical solutions that lead to substantial improvement in the way work is accomplished, the way work is perceived, and the amount of work that is achieved. Practicing effective Human Capital Management that encompasses how the entire organization runs and how it evaluates employee success, will create a natural link to High Performance Management that will see businesses emerge as healthy, prosperous, and highly competitive.

Wright

From your perspective and experiences do senior financial executives today realize the importance of human capital management?

Jenkins

Now this is a loaded question.

The term "human capital" is now part of everyday business language. It is a workforce's skills, knowledge, and experience, and is now seen as a critical source of value for a company when managed properly. Managing human capital is now a strategic responsibility increasingly shared by all of the company's leaders. HCM is not a sole responsibility of the company's human resources (HR) office nor is human resource company sole owner of this process.

Tangible assets that determined a company's value used to be what chief financial officers, merger-and-acquisition strategists, bankers, and fund managers were paid to keep track of. Those things were, quite literally, "things" such as: plant and equipment, factories and machinery, buildings, and inventory. They were hard assets that could be measured and used to calculate a return on investment. Those assets were solid and so were the financial decisions based on their value.

But in the world of finance today, things aren't what they used to be. In the new economy, the most valuable assets have gone from solid to soft, from *tangible* to *intangible* assets. Instead of plant and equipment, inventories, and buildings, companies today compete on *ideas* and *relationships*. Assets come in the form of *patents, knowledge*, and *people*. These kinds of intangible assets are soft and squishy, and numbers crunchers and bean counters hate them. How do you assign a dollar value to an engineer's startup experience? How much is a personal network worth? How do you decide whether to finance a new internal project when its only assets are an idea and a team? Hard questions about soft intangible assets are driving finance professionals to develop new measurements, new reporting forms, new tools and techniques for an economy based on intangibles.

Historically, relationships between the finance and human resources functions have too often ranged from adversarial to mutually uncomprehending. But there is a growing awareness that managing human capital requires a strong partnership between these functions, and CEOs and other senior level finance leaders express a desire for even closer collaboration. While HCM is not the exclusive domain of the HR professional, it's an enterprise-wide discipline that must be embraced and driven by line-of-business managers; the HR department is a key influencer. If it chooses to rise to the challenge, HR has the physical and intellectual tools to bring effective people management to the heart of corporate strategy.

Despite all of the awareness, there still remains an undercurrent of discomfort for both functions. Still, today, organizations know little about the return they get for their considerable expenditures on people. And the potential of technology has not yet been recognized sufficiently to help companies manage this intangible asset. So while companies might believe that human capital is perhaps an organization's most critical asset, there is a frustrating inability to manage it in ways supported by good data and measurement.

Consider the following recent figures: companies spend approximately one third of their revenues on human capital expenses, but only sixteen percent of these companies say they have anything more than a moderate understanding of the return on human capital investments

This is a big problem. It means that most companies lack the ability to apply financial discipline to their largest investment. And despite the CFO's emerging role as a "chief resource allocator," human capital remains a vast area of spending where it is perceived that few tools or measurements are in place to help guide meaningful decision-making.

Ever so slowly, this situation is changing. CFOs along with investors and boards are coming to view human capital as a crucial source of value. As a result, finance executives are taking a more active role in the management of human capital, and many are seeking to apply financial discipline to these investments, which means more than slashing headcounts across the board and not giving yearly increases.

Wright

What a great conversation. You tend to make me believe you know what you're talking about. I just wish more people knew more about human capital.

Today we have been talking with Eva Jenkins. So tell me what are some of the ways we can measure human capital when we consider ROI?

Jenkins

Well, once again, there is no one single way of measuring HC ROI. However, here are a few different ways we happen to believe can demonstrate success. Creating a "Human Resource Balanced Scorecard" is one of the easiest ways for busy executives to quickly absorb information.

Another way is to make sure that:

- Organizational goals supported by manpower-driven data,
- People, processes, and technology are aligned around a common goal,
- Anticipate, forecast, and predict future human capital needs and changes, and
- Leverage benchmark data to identify best practices,

The Ideal HCM System should be agile enough to consolidate information and deliver quantifiable results; designed to measure human capital assets and organizational effectiveness, and be able to perform HR-specific analysis and reporting to support organizational goals.

Wright

The whole topic of human capital could be a full book in itself. I really do appreciate all the time you've spent with me this morning Ms. Jenkins. You've been so helpful and so enlightening. There's no question your business will just keep growing and growing because you've got what we need.

Jenkins

Well, let's hope so. I had a conversation with a vice president of human resources several weeks ago and she goes don't even mention that term—she said that she cringes every time human capital management is mentioned to her. There's still a tremendous amount of work ahead. Technology is driving this whole process and once again I think you and I are so aware that with technology, the possibilities are limitless. Unfortunately at this time, within technology, none of the platforms work together to get exactly what we need—not yet, but it is still evolving.

Wright

When I look at my payroll each week, I have about sixteen people working for me in one job or another and when I add up all the paychecks every week that's where I'm spending all my money in human capital. So really this is the largest investment any business owner has.

Jenkins

In today's complex and very unstable economic business climate you have to maximize, I am sure, doing more with less. But then you really have to take a look at your own business philosophy, how you approach your business strategy and set your business goals.

Wright

Today we have been talking to Eva Jenkins. Ms. Jenkins continues to grow and re-shape her own company by applying the very same methodologies and processes her consulting firm is promoting to her clientele.

Thank you so much for being here with us today on *Conversations on Success*.

Jenkins
　　Well, thank you.

About The Author

Eva Jenkins is a visionary entrepreneur whose rich history of accomplishments in business and finance serve as both the foundation of and the fuel for her current success with VIP Staffing and VIP Innovations. Jenkins, a lightening rod for innovative thought and a divining rod for uncovering hidden potential in businesses, is armed with a keen understanding of the dynamics of human capital acquisitions and an astute sense of the best way to leverage that capital. She uses her unique high-performance principles to help companies re-shape their fundamental business beliefs and practices. Her goal is to prepare her clients so that they may respond to, and more importantly anticipate, the precedent-setting HR challenges in today's evolving international global economy.

Eva Jenkins, PHR

VIPInnovations

1717 K Street, NW - #600

Washington, DC 20036

Phone DC: 202.973.0179

Phone: VA: 571.248.8041

www.vipinnovations.com

Chapter 9

JOLI L. ANDRE

THE INTERVIEW

David Wright (Wright)

Today we are speaking with Joli L. Andre. Joli is founder and CEO of Polished Professionals, a company specializing in business etiquette, professional image, and international protocol. Since 1981, she has assisted executives in professional development both in the U.S. and internationally. Fully trained and certified by the Protocol School of Washington D.C., Joli has authored: *Business Etiquette Mastery: The Power Of Executive Leadership* and *Maximizing Your Polished Professional Potential,* an audio program. A former teacher, Joli is a certified image consultant, member of the National Speakers Association, and the International Visitor's Council.

Ms. Andre welcome to *Conversations On Success.*

Joli L. Andre (Andre)

Thank you for the opportunity to be with you today.

Wright

Would you talk to our readers a little bit about your experience and education that qualifies you to teach business etiquette, professional image, and international protocol?

Andre

Yes, I would love too. My earliest training began with professional image, beginning as a model and working in retail clothing throughout college. My college degree included Fine Arts, with emphasis on color and design. I went on to earn the AICI-CIP distinction, which honors the top four percent of image consultants from the Association Of Image Consultants International. My first speaking engagements were actually on image and professional dress. It was through the Association Of Image Consultants International that I heard about The Protocol School Of Washington, D.C. I enrolled and graduated with certification as a business etiquette and international protocol consultant. I earned the ATM-Silver distinction from Toastmasters International and professional level status from the National Speakers Association.

I believe the best experience for my business today to train executives and students, along with developing materials for my fun interactive programs is my background as a kindergarten teacher. After leaving teaching, I became Director Of Education for a pharmaceutical company where I gained experience in: corporate executive training, creating public relations programs, buyer presentations, trade shows, sales, and training internationally.

It was while working within this pharmaceutical organization that I became aware there was no business etiquette training or international protocol classes I could attend to accelerate my business social skills. I truly believe I have been groomed to do what I do, and love the fact that I get to use my love of teaching and corporate experiences to enhance my training and speaking engagements.

Wright

Great! Your first book in 1997 was titled: *Business Etiquette Mastery: The Power Of Executive Leadership.* Can you highlight some of the top tips you gave your readers?

Andre

The book contained the core of what business etiquette is and helped develop readers' knowledge and skills about communication, handshaking, introductions, conversation skill builders, telephone etiquette, e-mail, cellular, correspondence, and business networking manners as well as professional dress, office meeting etiquette, and dining skills.

The best tip to improve your communication skills is to listen. Listen as though there will be a test, and you will listen at a totally different level. A firm, bone-crushing handshake is not appreciated. A good handshake is like a good hug, both palms connecting with two shakes and release.

In an introduction, you mention the client's name first by saying, "June Smith [client] I would like you to meet our company President Joe Walsh."

A conversation skill builder is to not interrupt and to ask questions only for clarity along with being sure your dialogue includes speaking and listening.

For telephone etiquette be sure to return phone calls within a twenty-four-hour period and leave short, concise messages with your phone number said clearly at the end.

For e-mail, watch your grammar and the words you use to create the tone you want the receiver to understand.

Your professional dress is a non-verbal communication and speaks before you say a word. Think about what your image and wardrobe say about you.

For office meetings, honor the participants' time by beginning and ending the meeting at the time you stated.

For dining, pass the community food to the *right*.

Actually, this book evolved into my audio program: *Maximizing Your Polished Professional Potential*. I will be coming out with new products this year to enhance professional social skills for both students and professional people.

Wright

You are an AICI-CIP image consultant; only four percent of image consultants are at your level of expertise. Is it true that many companies are abandoning the business casual look?

Andre

Yes, many companies are abandoning the business casual look and going toward a more executive casual to traditional attire along with revising their dress codes. Employees saw the word "casual" in "business casual" and everyone had their own interpretation. There is a big difference between social clothing and what is appropriate for the workplace. Casual dressing within the work place is one of the biggest challenges faced in professional organizations. When employees come to work in "social" clothing it may affect the work environment as a whole.

Managers say they spend more time being fashion police because of: personal interpretation of the dress code—no detailed or too vague of a dress code policy, employees' non-compliance, inappropriate clothing that causes sexual harassment and flirtation issues, casual attire producing a laid back attitude that resulted in lost business opportunities from a poor first impression, and employees' lack of clothing care and grooming standards. With this said, employers are realizing their dress code policies need adjustment and revisions for the employees who are dressing too casually for work. Pants are too low on hips, tops are too tight, show cleavage, or are too baggy, skirts are too short, attire is too sexy, underwear is exposed with low riding pants, or underwear is seen through clothing, garments are mismatched, stained, or not ironed.

Employee's attire is a reflection of your company. First impressions are made in the first seven seconds; how they are dressed contributes to that first impression.

Wright

Staying with the subject of image a little longer, would you give our readers some tips of looking polished and professional if their company is still allowing business casual?

Andre

First, always look consistently polished and professional whether you are in a business suit or business casual attire of: tops, shirts, and slacks. Have a jacket to cover any spills, extra nylons if you get a run and select fabrics that need no ironing to look fresh all day. Wear your shirts tucked in and have a nice professional look from head to toe with a maintained hairstyle and polished shoes.

Even if you wear a uniform you can have an extra uniform in your locker area. Bring an extra pair of pants or change of shirt to always look clean and pressed. Whether you are in the office, at appointments, attending networking events, corporate parties, or professional development seminars you are a reflection of the company. Understand that your clothes send a non-verbal message. Your clothing and how you present yourself can either sabotage your career advancement, or help it. It tells your customers that since you appear to be able to take care of yourself that you'll also professionally take care of their needs.

Be aware that you work in a mixed gender work place—clothing that shows cleavage, skirts with slits up the side or front, off hip, or slacks that are too tight can be worn socially but are not appropriate for the workplace. Prefer to wear no nylons with pants and not a dress or skirt. Clothing that is too casual can sabotage your career success by sending the wrong message. Always bring items to upgrade yourself such as: an extra coat, tie, heels, earrings, and toiletries to regain a fresh professional look when unexpected clients come to the office.

Wright

You are an international protocol consultant. In this very diverse global market place, what are some of the tips to be culturally and politely correct?

Andre

The international market place is much more formal. People who are in the international market place dine more formally, communicate in a kinder, positive tone, and respect rank and status when addressing others in an introduction. Whether you are going overseas or hosting international clients, you must be briefed on the social protocols and business etiquette of the specific country where you are doing business. This shows respect and will enable building long-term relationships and avoid misunderstandings that may arise from language in conversation, e-mails, gestures, and inappropriate gift-giving.

International companies do their homework to show respect and they would hope that you are equally professional when wanting to do business with them. When employing people from different cultures you should be briefed in each specific country's etiquette to know which staff positions will bring out the best in a particular employee's talent and how people from different cultures may interact with each other. Most importantly, just honor employees' cultural backgrounds throughout the year.

Wright

I bet you could share some great horror stories couldn't you?

Andre

Oh yes! To illustrate that, a U.S. company president was meeting with the president of a Mexican manufacturing company with the purpose of gaining a multi-million dollar contract with this company. The U.S. president planned to attend their meetings and negotiate a multi-million dollar contract, attend banquets in his honor, and build a long- term relationship.

The initial meeting was warm and when the Mexican president asked, "Well, what do you know about me and my country?" the U.S. president just sat back and acted stunned and silent, stumbling to find a few words to say. The Mexican president said, "It is obvious you do not know how to build a relationship with me. I have spent many hours learning about your likes and dislikes and I cannot do business with a person who does not show me equal respect." He just stood up and announced, "Our meeting is over!" This could have been easily remedied by the U.S. executive being culturally briefed on Mexico, along with talking to the Mexican president's executive assistant to ask about his likes and dislikes. This was a very expensive missed opportunity.

Wright

Last year you were selected as a delegate for a U.S. Trade Mission to China and wrote the cultural briefing for the other delegates. What did you learn on your visit?

Andre

It was a lifetime experience and a great honor to be asked to participate. I gave a Chinese cultural business briefing before our meetings began with the government officials, small business owners, and women's groups. We reviewed general Chinese business etiquette, dining protocols, gift-giving and receiving gifts etiquette, presenting of business cards, conversation, and toasting protocols. Even though the Chinese were gracious, you had to be aware of their insistence of rank and status to allow the leaders of China or leader of the U.S. delegation to begin the conversations or offer the first toast.

I was pleasantly surprised to see how modern the Chinese cities looked and how westernized the government officials and executives were in their thinking. What I really loved seeing was how they provided housing for their people at the corporate sites and at the schools. New construction is just everywhere! China is preparing their country to be the number one economy by 2020 and I would love to share my knowledge with U.S. companies desiring to work with China and to brief them on that country's culture.

Wright

Your current business etiquette training includes an audio program, *Maximizing Your Polished Professional Potential.* The program discusses general business etiquette tips and includes a small book *The ABC's Of Small Talk* to help executives talk about anything to anyone. Can you share about how *The ABC's Of Small Talk* works?

Andre

You have to be able to talk about topics other than business. Small talk is the "getting to know you" kind of conversations. The ability to talk on any subject to anyone is really a learned skill. My background is that of a school teacher, so I came up with a simple ABC process where the alphabet is matched up with a word (for example: B equals book) so in this instance you can talk about books you have read, ask the other person what they like to read, and share information in that conversation. It's a simple process of picking an alphabet letter, knowing the matching word, instilling good listening skills, making eye contact, and asking simple questions for clarity to maintain an easy flowing conversation.

Wright

Sounds like that would work in any situation.

Andre

The ABC's of small talk are very easy to learn; during my business etiquette training participants always enjoy the communications segment.

Wright

I'm taking notes here. I have a sixteen-year-old and I need all the help in communication skills that I can get! Now that I know some topics to discuss during a conversation, are there tips to know how to keep the conversation friendly and to build a relationship with a potential client?

Andre

Developing better listening skills is the key. You must like to listen, ignore any distractions, summarize in your mind what you heard, tame any emotional judgments, maintain good eye contact to show you are paying attention, and nod your head or make agreeing sounds to show you are listening. Never constantly interrupt, but do interject questions for clarity, and nurture the relationship by listening and speaking. You want to ask questions—not in an interrupting way—but to clarify what you have said. If they say, "I'm from California or San Diego, my clarifying question would be, "Where exactly in California or San Diego"?

A good conversation contains speaking and listening from both participants. Within fifteen minutes they should know equally about each other enough to begin a relationship. Upon an initial introduction, if the person has an unusual name, ask them if their name means something because there is always an interesting story.

Keep conversations from being one-sided or taking back the conversation to center on you. If they are telling you they just got back from Hawaii, say: "Oh, tell me more about your trip," instead of saying, " Oh, I just got back from Hawaii too and we took a great limo, had VIP this and that, etc." All of a sudden, what they said loses the impact. In order to really build a good conversation, it is critical to be a good listener. There is an old Chinese saying, "A lion does not have to hear itself roar." Give other people an opportunity to talk about themselves by becoming a master of listening. That's what really builds a relationship.

Wright

In your training, you have a section in business networking. Are there "set rules of the road" so we do not sabotage ourselves at corporate social events?

Andre

I can actually share several quick tips that can spare you from sabotaging a first impression. First, it's really important to send an R.S.V.P. response card or telephone call whether you go to the event or not. Arriving at an event where you have not responded can sabotage a first impression because it will put undue stress on the host who is scrambling to accommodate you.

It's also important that you are dressed in professional attire. Being dressed too casually when everyone else is in suits could definitely sabotage a first impression. Eat and drink right away, for it is difficult to talk and shake hands when you are carrying a drink or eating finger foods. Talking too much about your company and how great you are and not sharing the conversation with other people is definitely a good way to sabotage a relationship. Talking with a mouth full of food, interrupting a conversation, and passing out your business cards before building some connection is unpolished.

Some people approach others and say, "here's my business card," giving several to pass around to others without even knowing the individual. Avoid passing out a business card to another until you feel you have a business or personal interest beginning.

It's also difficult to be with people who seem to have nothing to say, who are either negative or passive, and who can't seem to share a conversation. These non-verbal communication behaviors can definitely sabotage your first impression. Having too much alcohol could cause you to say something inappropriate, which could definitely sabotage your company and your level of professionalism at business networking events.

I was just speaking at a conference yesterday where a large insurance company added a new policy that stated no alcoholic drinks with clients are allowed. They didn't want to have to worry about what "appropriate drinking" meant to their agents.

Remember, you are watched and heard more than you realize—especially if you are driving a client. If you were driving a client, show them respect by not drinking alcohol and lessen their concern about safety. You would be mistaken if you believe no one is watching the types and quantity of drinks you are having at a public event.

Another way to sabotage yourself is to use continuous negative talk or tell an inappropriate joke. People think that joke-telling is a way to loosen up a crowd, but you have to be extremely mindful about the kind of joke you express. You just never know how the other person is going to receive it; maybe they are of a certain ethnic or cultural background that would find your comments offensive.

Remember to put your cell phone on vibrate—answering your cell phone and talking to your caller while talking to others is rude. If you are in conversation and your cell phone vibrates, apologize, recognize who called, then turn the phone off without answering. If you begin a conversation on the cell phone you are sending a message that the person on the phone is more important than the person you were having a conversation with. If you need to place a call or if you have an emergency, excuse yourself and walk to a quieter area.

Wright

At networking events I can never remember names. Are there some tips you can give that will help our readers remember people's names so we can look polished and professional?

Andre

Yes, I have a few quick tips to share since most people, including myself, will admit that they sometimes don't remember names. Forgetting an acquaintance or a client's name as they approach you, especially when they remember your name, is embarrassing. I never imply I have forgotten a name. I keep upbeat and friendly maintaining full listening mode. If an introduction must be made, I say, "Do you know each other?" If not, they usually introduce themselves and I hear the person's name. Usually, through the conversation, I hope to get enough information to remember. If not, I ask for their business card again.

You must change your mindset by saying, "I'm going to remember people's names today," and never fill your mind with a self-fulfilling negative prophecy by announcing, "I never remember names." Try to engrain yourself with techniques and make it a game that you are going to be remembering names today. The first tip would be to hear the person's name really distinctly—listen and concentrate on getting the name right, have them repeat his or her name for clarity and repeat it back immediately saying: "Robert, it is nice to meet you." If you mispronounce it or if you didn't hear the name correctly, write the name down phonetically so you can visually see it and say it. If you have been introduced incorrectly, always say something.

When I introduce myself as Joli Andre and they hear "Julie," it's very important that I say it's Joli—"J-O-L-I." Thinking I am being polite by not saying anything only causes confusion and being introduced as "Julie."

When you first hear a person's name, use it right away in the conversation. Make a name association. For example, if her name is Barbara you might say, " Oh, my mother's name is Barbara." Make an association with a person and place, or rhyme the name with an object or something. You *must* have a visual or word connection with names to remember them. Remembering names of people whom you just met or do business with is an impressive way to build relationships. You can always request his or her business card or ask if someone knows the person you just spoke with. Upon leaving a group or conversation use the person's name again and shake his or her hand when you say good-bye. You can request a business card during the beginning of a conversation when you hear an obvious mutual connection or at the end of the meeting. If you have no connection, then say it was a pleasure meeting him or her.

Wright

Part of your business etiquette training includes a live dining tutorial during lunch. Are there some quick tips you can share with our readers so they can feel more comfortable at meals with clients?

Andre

Yes, actually a dining experience can tell a lot about an individual and is one of the most fun segments in my business etiquette training. A few tips include the following:

- The community food such as salt and pepper, salad dressing, rolls, and butter are always passed to the *right* and your V.I.P. would always be seated to the *right* side of the host.
- Your drinking glassware is on your right and your bread will be on your left.
- When you are toasting you would raise your glass but don't drink to yourself.
- A napkin left on your chair will let your waiter know you will be right back, and when finished with your meal put the napkin back on the left side of your place at the table.
- You begin to eat when the host either begins to eat, tells everyone to begin, or when everyone at your individual table is served.
- If a cold meal such as a salad or sandwich is served, then you can wait until everyone at a large rectangle table is served.
- When having a meal with a client and his or her food is not appropriate (maybe it had cheese on it and they asked for it not to have cheese), be sure to send your food back and kept warm until your client's meal is ready to be served.

Wright

This is such a hectic business world of e-mail, phones, and cellular, would you share with our readers some tips for this area of doing business?

Andre

Our new technology has made it so much easier to keep in touch with each other. E-mail is still a written correspondence where writing protocols should be maintained. Use good sentence structure, grammar, proper spelling, and greetings when speaking with clients. Internal e-mails can be more casual and use cellular text messaging where appropriate.

Watch your tone in your e-mails—the words you select or the phrases you use create a "tone" and can easily be misunderstood, especially dealing with international clients.

To honor people's time, keep telephone business conversations brief, and professional. When calling always ask, "Do you have a moment?" When leaving a telephone message, say the phone numbers slowly and separately without combining numbers like 95-60 say "9-5-6-0." Not knowing how much time a voicemail box will give you, state your name, reason for calling, and your phone number right away. As you are finishing the message, leave your name, company, and the last thing you say is your phone number, slowly and clearly.

This new technology really keeps us connected and there's no excuse for not returning a phone call or an e-mail within a twenty-four-hour period. When using your cellular in close quarters, either keep your voice low or wait until you are in an area where you can be alone. Your politeness and consideration will be appreciated. Hopefully these few tips will be helpful.

Wright

You believe that business etiquette is something you become; will you finalize the interview here with thoughts on etiquette and whether we need to get back to the basics?

Andre

The truth be known, business etiquette skills are really "life skills." You use them at work, socially, and at home. Once you have the polished professional techniques and realize how confident they make you feel, they become "second nature." With employees putting in extra long days, there is a serious need for helpful guidelines and more politeness in the workplace. Business etiquette skills will help you feel confident in any situation while putting others at ease. This is why I'm so passionate about teaching business etiquette, professional image, and international protocol. I know these skills are foundational in relationship building, which is so vital to financial success.

The way you dress, communicate, and the social skills you demonstrate create an image package that commands respect, inspires trust, projects professionalism, and heightens the perception level of your company. Business etiquette used with valued clients or in managing a diverse work force involves the social skills of doing business with people of various generations, genders, and cultural backgrounds. Remember, it will be the small things you do that will make the biggest difference in how polished and gracious you appear, how your behavior influences your customers, and ultimately how your level of excellence is raised.

Wright

I really appreciate this conversation, it has been very informative and some things you've said here I'm going to start using before this book comes out.

Today we have been talking to Joli L. Andre of Polished Professionals, a company specializing in business etiquette, professional image and international protocol. Joli is trained and certified by the Protocol School Of Washington, D.C. as a Business Etiquette and International Protocol consultant, a certified image consultant, a member of the National Speakers Association and the International Visitors Council. Thank you so much Joli for being with us today on *Conversations on Success*.

Andre

Thank you for the privilege of sharing my thoughts with those reading *Conversations On Success*.

About The Author

Joli Andre is the founder of Polished Professionals®, a company specializing in Business Etiquette Training, Leadership Programs, Professional Image, Communication Skills and Cultural Etiquette in the Workplace to "polish" professionals, students, and management. Since 1981, Joli has assisted executives in professional development both here and internationally. She has been an entrepreneur and small business owner since 1987 and is fully trained and certified as a Business Etiquette Consultant by the Protocol School of Washington D.C. She is the author of *Business Etiquette Mastery: The Power Of Executive Leadership* and *Maximizing Your Polished Professional Potential (CD-ROM)*. Joli holds a K-8 school teaching credential, is an awarded Toastmasters ATM-Silver speaker, a member of The National Speakers Association, and listed in *Who's Who In Professional Speaking*.

Joli L. Andre

Polished Professionals®

Phone: 858.759.9560

Email: joliandre@polishedprofessionals.com

www.polishedprofessionals.com

Chapter 10

STU NEEDEL

THE INTERVIEW

David Wright (Wright)

Today we're talking to Stu Needel, The Technology Teddy Bear™ and President of Stu Needel Communications, LLC based in Baltimore, Maryland. He is an internationally known speaker, trainer, consultant, author, actor, musician, drummer, percussionist, and drum circle facilitator who has devoted his life to Making The World A Small Village™ through his passionate dedication to studying, analyzing, practicing, and teaching communications of many types. Stu is an experienced speaker, as comfortable on a general session stage in front of and interacting with thousands of people as he is in a management briefing or small training room for days on end with a small sales or customer care department. Stu has been a musician nearly his entire life, playing and sharing music as a drummer, percussionist, singer and keyboard player. He also shares his love of drumming and music as a drum circle facilitator, creating group drumming experiences that are at minimum foot-tapping and very often life-transforming. As a technologist, Stu has managed IT departments of many sizes, consulted for many organizations and individuals on technology strategy, and developed and led many different courses, workshops and retreats on many technology topics, particularly those focused on effectively and powerfully applying technology to human issues. Above all else, Stu is a tireless humanitarian and philanthropist teaching vital personal subjects such as interpersonal communications, public speaking and business presentation, customer care and training. He is involved with numerous non-profit organizations that he cares deeply about. Carrying out all of the above talents and services, Stu happily and gratefully travels a great deal each year, having discovered his love of travel at the age of 2 when he made his first flight from Baltimore to Los Angeles, so much so that he's added Travel Consultant to his repertoire and recently launched his own travel seminar for business professionals—*Enjoy the Journey: From Road Worrier to Road Warrior*—at the 2005 National Speakers Association Annual Convention. He's definitely a man with a mission. Stu Needel, welcome to *Conversations on Success!*

Stu Needel (Needel)

Thanks David. What a pleasure to be finally having this conversation. I've been looking forward to it. Thanks for inviting me to be a part of the interview series and the book.

Wright

You emphasize your mission of making the world a small village in most of your publications and promotional material and yet your reputation and expertise is in technology, music, and communications. What do these seemingly unrelated topics have to do with each other and how are they relevant to our book's theme? What does this have to do with success?

Needel

Ha! In the words of Shakespeare, "That IS the question," the great question that occupied, entertained, and truthfully disturbed me for hours and even years of never-ending exploration, debate and discussion in my own mind and with selected advisors, whose perspectives I sought and whose opinions I trusted. I have, obviously, as you so completely described, a very diverse background and have struggled to define, if someone asks me "what do you do?," a way to describe it without spending an hour with them just to completely describe what I do. Not just to save time and make the task easier, but much more importantly, to provide a context—I really love context – to contain and integrate all of my passions, expertise, and answer my own question of what it really is that I'm all about. It turns out I had the answer all along, given to me by Sarah Victory, an extraordinary consultant and coach I'd worked with years ago. Just as so many amazing inventions take place, she seemed to come up with the marketing phrase *"He makes the whole world a small village!"* in a moment, but at the time I thought it was just cute and clever, but nothing like the all-encompassing mantra that describes everything I'm about today.

"Making the world a small village," the final version of Sarah's original gem I eventually and thankfully discovered as the ideal "box" for everything I'm about, succinctly described the whole theme of creating a sense of intimacy, bringing people together, facilitating relationships, and facilitating communication, all of which is the common theme that runs through all of the work that I do. Whether relating it to drumming, technology, applying technology, teaching technology, and all the music work that I do, the theme and joy for me is that each brings people together in some way or another and in addition, almost organically provides a discovery of true human potential by showing us and others what's really possible. Relating this theme to travel, we don't have to question and struggle to see how it brings people together physically, but I really see travel as an exercise in testing the human spirit, meeting people and getting out there that's not necessarily done by someone just traveling, so it seems as if there are threads through all of this after all.

After about 30 years of doing this, from my days in high school when I first played music professionally and also started research on exotic uses of technology to bring people together, there were threads of relationship in all the areas of expertise that called me. I've always known I want to make a profound difference in the world, but this process made it obvious that my unique way of fulfilling that is by inspiring and educating people, and bringing them together, literally, virtually, and metaphorically, in many different ways. I wanted to say that in a profound and succinct way and suddenly I could hear Sarah's brilliant phrase reverberating in my mind. I finally crafted it into "making the world a small village." In fact, my Technology Teddy-Bear moniker that you so cleverly mentioned was the first phase of this process, when I wanted people to understand that while I work with and love technology and have a great deal of expertise, I ultimately use it to bring people together, having them discover capabilities they had that they never knew, which is where the teddy-bear came in—being the ultimate huggable, touchable entity. That brand has made a large impact in effectively communicating everything that I do. Now the new mantra explains the meaning and relationship that runs through all of it.

Wright

So that's where your alias came from.

Needel

That's right. Some people actually thought I was only referring to my own appearance and personality, since I certainly do have "teddy-bear qualities" (especially when it comes to hugging!), but I was mostly conjuring the connotation of teddy-bear as a concept.

Wright

I do see the theme that connects all your work and philosophy but how did you manage to transition from music to technology to communications?

Needel

The music started very early. As you said, I've been playing music a long time. It was my family's hobby, how we entertained, and essentially our signature—I'm blessed to come from a very musical family. My mom played organ and my dad was a singer and a cantor, actually a lay cantor in many Jewish congregations and synagogues. I was surrounded by music in my family, my immediate family and my extended family from the very beginning. As a matter of fact, my mother proudly bragged her entire life that she "gave" me my sense of rhythm by inundating me for the nine months she carried me with perpetual drumming on her stomach. She was a very musical woman. How it evolved from there to technology was one of those failure-becomes-the-success stories.

I was actually in the midst of embarking on a professional music career and at some point in my teens scared myself into thinking that as a drummer, especially on tour, I would be around too many drug dealers and drug addiction and that's not what I do, not to mention I don't want to be a starving musician. I basically talked myself, initially, out of this music career that I was definitely on the track to achieve with all the effort and time I invested and the successes I had at that point. Still in high school, I was being offered some amazing opportunities, but I apparently was too scared of the initial success. Oh if I only knew then what I know now.

My next calling was to immerse myself into technology and it started in audio. I clearly recall my earliest inspiration being my Cousin Fred's mock radio station in his basement. He had to lift me up to put me on the stool to sit at the console, but even at 5 years old, I knew what it was and what it meant. I could communicate, entertain, and connect to everyone. I worked heavily in recording engineering and sound design for theatre because it was the closest thing to music and performance without actually being a musician, which for whatever reason I was obviously shying away from. That was the link from music to technology. Then the communications came as a result of realizing that I was committed to and fascinated by more than just "the stuff." I believe in people, love working with people, and my commitment is not just to the technical side of that equation, but more to the heart of the matter; the meat. I know that I profoundly love everybody on this planet, as fellow human beings and as members of my extended family. I also believe in teaching people how to have similar experiences and for them to develop the abilities to see and work with technology as I do.

A large part of my work is training in many forms and that's where I went as you said, from music to technology to communications and where this whole thought process began: realizing the relationships and the connections with all of the passions and talents that I have and have had. Actually in the last five years I've been integrating all of it together, including my music background, my audio expertise and experience, and my music performance experience which until 5 years ago, despite having 30 years in technology, never involved any kind of drum synthesizers. Now I play and love both electronic and acoustic drums. I've integrated all of my talents, backgrounds and expertise into the collective of what I do. What a wonderful way to work. I now get to use all of my resources, which are also my passions, and they now have become major elements of my business and practice. It's an exciting unification process, if you will. I recommend this to anyone who has a similar "diversity" of background(s).

Wright

I saw the Blue Man Group in New York a few weeks ago. Oh my goodness!

Needel

I agree. I met their casting people and seriously considered auditioning for them a few years back. I just didn't want to commit myself to one project and one process only, but I love their work and their contribution. They're an amazing group. In fact, Blue Man Group is really many groups and productions. They are in many cities and I've seen several of the shows. Cirque de Soleil, whose work I also love, also have many different productions running simultaneously and I've seen several of theirs as well. Both of these organizations provide some of the most incredible live theatrical and performance art experiences available today. I send or take friends, family, and clients to their shows regularly and highly recommend them to anyone else.

Wright

You speak in many articles and in your seminars about the George Bernard Shaw quote whose essence is I want to be thoroughly used up when I die. Can you share that quote with us and its meaning in your life?

Needel

Oh David, I'm so glad you asked about that. Shaw said these words almost 100 years ago now. It was in 1906, and he was interviewed for an article on life purposes and I venture to say they were examining success as well. He was actually referring to Shakespeare's Macbeth and some of the classic dialog from Macbeth specifically. Here's the entire response to the question of what it meant to him to have a meaningful life purpose:

> *This is the true joy in life, being used for a purpose recognized by yourself as a mighty one. Being a force of nature instead of a feverish, selfish little clod of ailments and grievances complaining that the world will not devote itself to making you happy. I am of the opinion that my life belongs to the whole community and as I live it is my privilege - my privilege to do for it whatever I can. I want to be thoroughly used up when I die, for the harder I work the more I love. I rejoice in life for its own sake. Life is no brief candle to me; it is a sort of splendid torch which I've got a hold of for the moment and I want to make it burn*

as brightly as possible before handing it on to future generations.[1]

It's an amazing, empowering message that I heard, originally quoted by Werner Erhard, Founder of the Est Training, now 25 years ago and have used it as a guiding light ever since because it so completely explains what I'm really about. I am constantly exhausting myself in physical, emotional and mental ways and I love doing so. I don't mind working hard because that effort "expresses" my enthusiasm and passion for the people in my life, my work and projects, and even the areas I play in. I work hard and play equally hard. I know why I'm doing it and what I'm working for. In fact, in some ways I thrive on the intensity and I believe it's a model for most people to live their life. Instead of holding back, reserving myself and waiting for Goudeau, I'd rather give it all that I have in every moment that I have to give it. Obviously, this concept is significant in my life.

And for those interested, I rest and recuperate as intensely as I work, so there's a great deal of equilibrium. I truly believe in balance and harmony.

Wright

If you had to summarize your strategy for success in only one or two points or phrases what would they be?

Needel

That's a great question given what I said earlier about what I went through to represent what I do. I actually had this challenge given to me several years ago when I was asked to speak, on the spur of the moment, to a chapter of The National Speakers Association and asked to summarize in one word, what it means to be successful. I ended up coming up with two of those one-word mantras. Loving acronyms like I do, I felt compelled to create an acronym rather than just a word. Maybe that's cheating but I just happen to have a passion and a love for acronyms. Why say one word in one word when you can communicate so much more AND make it memorable and clever?

The first one was simple, literally. For the acronym to work, I spelled it creatively as: s-y-m-p-l-e. It represents: sharing your most precious life examples or experiences or expertise or education. The

---

[1] Source: *The Quotations Page* http://www.quotationspage.com

"e" can represent, obviously, many apropos things, but we'll use experience. As I said before, whatever you do, whether it's in terms of choosing a career, a new job, passion, avocation, or hobby, whatever it is that you're deciding on, do whatever it is FULLY and share your joy and experiences with other people. Just remember to do whatever you're most passionate about.

I offer both impromptu and on-demand career and job consulting for friends, clients and colleagues. My biggest concern for them is that they do what they love to be doing, not just pick a job or a position based on the benefit packages or the compensation. That's not a reason nor is it a formula for long-term success and happiness. People should really do what's appropriate for them based on where their passion and joy is. The same applies to my fellow speakers, particularly professionals. We should all be speaking on what we're experts in and most passionate about. I realize passion isn't the only selection criteria, but I know tangibly from experience how valuable following your passions is and how costly not doing so is!

The other one was the showstopper because it just appeared to me out of nowhere, amazingly similar to the Technology Teddy-Bear and the original version of Making the World a Small Village. Perhaps "in the moment" is where all of the best creativity happens. We all talk about tenacity and perseverance, but rather than a single word, a phrase resounded for me and that was: don't ever give up. Of course, the acronym for that empowering statement is "DEGU," d-e-g-u. A Degu, as it turns out, is actually a small animal, I believe a rodent, that is ironically notorious for being this very tenacious, gregarious, never-stopping little creature that can do almost anything it sets its mind to. It does the kind of work that a beaver does but yet it's smaller, more versatile, can swim, travel on land, and it's just an amazing animal. Degu, the word and the creature, then symbolizes DEGU, the mantra: don't ever give up! No matter how hard the job is, no matter how hard the project is, the work you're doing, the financial dilemma you're in, the relationship you're struggling with, the acting career you so badly want to develop, no matter how resistant that prospect is being to your repeated attempts to close the deal...whatever it is you dream of, don't ever give up! If that's not a motive for success, what else could possibly inspire you? There are so many stories told by countless business gurus about well known business leaders who endured a long line of business failures before the one huge success. Why them and not so many others who attempt to make a business a success? They believed in Degu! Don't ever give up, ever!

I believe in this concept, particularly conveying it to others, so strongly that it's now even on my business cards!

Wright

Stu, How have you actually applied these principles in your life and how do you convey them to your clients and audiences?

Needel

In terms of the DEGU principle, I think my life is definitely, both accidentally and sometimes intentionally, a demonstration of that. We'll start with my music career first. As I said earlier, I started in music. What began as a hobby was becoming a career and even with a hiatus where I intentionally interrupted and redirected where I was focusing myself in technology and audio and eventually into IT, it was always there in the background. In retrospect, I never gave up the dream of playing music, playing drums, performing and eventually the dream became so much louder than the current reality and the demand to do it was unavoidable where I had to bring it back into the foreground the way I have.

The same goes for my work that I've done in technology. Whether with implementing and working with new technology or working with people, I am well known for not giving up in many different ways. When it comes to teaching, I've been teaching technical topics now for more than 20 years, and I particularly love teaching stuff that most people would despise teaching because of its technical nature, ambiguity, difficulty in conveying the concepts, and just plain abstractness. I probably love more than anything being able to come up with effective ways for communicating those kinds of concepts, issues and abstractions to people in whatever way I have to. Whether it's physical movement and animation or analogy or humor or games, that's one of the reasons I love training so much. It allows me much more diversity in communication than just doing a keynote speech from the front of a room with 10,000 people. I get very involved, very interactive, so it's another way that I don't give up. I think that the DEGU concept is so powerful in so many different ways. The more you commit yourself, the more incredible the results you can produce, sometimes even outside of the realm of which you had originally planned to do. That is how I apply the amazing DEGU principle.

As for the "SYMPLE" principle, if I haven't used variations on the word "passion" a hundred times already during this interview, we need a new accountant. I can't NOT do, speak about, support, write about, and return to what I'm most passionate about. I lack both the understanding of why and empathy for people who knowingly get involved in jobs, projects, and relationships that they really don't care about, don't love, and don't see a purpose in. I'm certainly sympathetic, but even if it was them settling for what they thought was the best they could get, that kind of thinking is debilitating and even deadly. Whether they know it or not, they could be doing much better.

Wright

Stu, if you wanted to, you could create a resume and flaunt the career you've amassed, just in your work with associations and non-profits. What's compelled you to do that much work in non-revenue generating activity and how does that contribute to your and others success?

Needel

As I said before, once again further endorsing Shaw's incredible declarations, I don't think I could do everything that I do professionally and personally without having a sense that I'm making a contribution in the world, in my industry, certainly in my family and in the community. I just have a very tangible need to contribute, to give back, and most importantly, to support causes and organizations I consider vital and that's what I end up doing. That fact didn't really dawn on me until 10 years ago, when I realized how strong that need was and how much joy and satisfaction I derive from this kind of work, and ultimately how much of a difference this work really makes. I think the first significant amount of non-profit work I did was with the Independent Computer Consultant's Association -- this goes back now about 13 or 14 years. I became very involved with ICCA, which, at the time, represented my industry and my trade. I found the biggest trade association I could find of the kind (it really was the ONLY one) and jumped right in at the chapter level. I attended national conferences and I eventually became president of the chapter and just loved supporting the industry, especially since I had been doing it for about 10 years by then and wanted to more formally support people just entering the business and wanted to have some impact in the shaping of the industry. I went on to other organizations as well and now am proud of and cherish my intense involvement with The National Speakers Association and with multiple chapters within. It is just a really profound sense of joy and satisfaction that I get, both in terms of the contributions that I can make to my friends, colleagues, fellow members and the community and from the spiritual "return" on all of the investment.

People seem to think that volunteer work and community service is done selflessly, for the sheer joy of giving, with little or no dividends in return. While I have no expectations in that way and DO volunteer solely intending to contribute, there are significant dividends. They're obviously not in cash, but the results in terms of relationships, quality of one's work, personal network, inspiration, leadership development, and education are endless and extraordinary. In fact, there is business to acquire. That's just not my intention going in. It's more of an evolution and ultimate result that happens just naturally and very organically. I build my business based on referrals and word of mouth and that happens as a result of ALL of the work that I do, paid and volunteer.

By far the bigger benefit for me is the satisfaction of the contributions that I make on so many different levels. I wouldn't trade that for the world. If I was deprived of being able to work with non-profits and do community service, it would be as horrible and depriving as having limbs removed—it's a very significant part of my life that I take very seriously with a very personal investment.

Wright

If success is truly based on communications and if this makes possible that small village that you talk about so enthusiastically, how will that small village enhance our lives and facilitate a new level of success?

Needel

Great question and a very simple answer. Communications, coupled with trust and relationship issues are at the heart of so many supposedly more complicated issues in organizations and populations, whether involving companies, industries, communities, countries and even our entire world at large. One of my unique abilities is being able to trace threads and commonalities in otherwise unrelated and often seemingly complicated issues. By doing this "threading" when teaching technical and abstract concepts, I'm able to relate and connect concepts and entities with the strength and reliability of a double-stitched seam. See, I'm doing it now, even in jest! The same applies to understanding underlying issues and conversely, the unlimited success of any organization.

Here those 3 threads are the staples of any small village. Constant, clear, and meaningful communications, trust among the members, and ultimately, continuously evolving and nurturing relationships. The threads that bind the small village can provide seamless integration of the largest populations as well. By developing the human infrastructure of a small village, ANY organization can build the foundation that nurtures morale, creates harmony and loyalty, and creates long-term success regardless of the size and type of organization and community. All communities are comprised of people and people thrive on communications, trust, and relationships.

Regardless of the group or organization size, where you typically find issues of tension, the common element that brings those organizations together is when they discover their commonalities, their elements in common, and their relatedness. Taken one step further, we would be addressing intimacy, high morale, team spirit, esprit de corps., and my favorite phrase applied to organizations—joi de vivre, the beautiful French phrase for "joy of life." There are many words and phrases for it, but all of it just refers to people feeling like they belong, that they're connected, loving what they're doing, and ideally that they make a difference. If you apply that to making the world a small village, a small village being an environment where an individual is most visible and relationships are nurtured and not destroyed, it's as simple as that. Within my work in this very general area, there are two areas that I focus on, because they mean the most to me and I'm convinced they are the two most critical elements: People and technology.

There's the human element, which I do increasingly more work in—which is all about facilitating ways to have people feel they're a part of whatever population I'm working with at the time; making them feel that their contribution is necessary, vital, appreciated and in demand and making them feel that they want to be a part of it. I can convince you that you are, but the question is: are you motivated to be and both of those have to really be a part of that equation.

At the other end of the spectrum, some would say, is technology. That is, the technology that the organization uses, the ability of its people to understand and use it and the perception the organization and its public has of that technology. Are the organization and its people seen through the technology or does the technology itself "show up" more loudly than those it is supposed to support?

I use technology to prove that it doesn't matter where you are and where I am, that if we're working together, if we're collaborating, or even if we're a family wanting some private time together even when we're not, we can accomplish this using some very accessible technology. The only limit is in your ability to accept the power of these tools.

I am frequently in situations where I'm out of town and an important event is taking place somewhere and I want to be part of it. There are numerous technologies that let us, as best as we can, circumvent all of the barriers to being there in person and in the flesh, yet still "be there." Those include web and video conferencing, instant messaging, and other collaborative technologies. I'm not there in the flesh, yet I'm able to see, hear, and interact as much as technology does allow today, which is pretty intensively. In a very unique and different way, that therefore gives me the ability to make the world seem, in another way, like a small village.

You talked about my extensive traveling and all the work I've done with making travel enjoyable and embraceable, and at least tolerable for some people. That's how I came up with "From Road Worrier to Road Warrior." I call myself "The Road Scholar." Too many people hate travel, and I've worked out some very amazing ways, very simply, with just ordinary stuff that's out there, ordinary knowledge, resources, products, other things that make travel, I'm hoping, not just tolerable, but actually exciting, challenging, and invigorating. Especially if your job requires a lot of travel, I have suddenly made it possible for you to feel like you can get anywhere in the world very easily without much of the trauma, especially today, since September 11th, without the supposed heartache and agony of traveling and everything that goes with it. Therefore, the end result in that case is almost literally making the world a small village, since you can get up and go to any place in the world today as easily as walking through the village used to be. My goal is making people feel like they're connected and related, no matter where they are and no matter who they are.

Wright

In that connection, a great deal of your work is in areas that most people would prefer not to spend their time doing such as public speaking, traveling, and technology. Why do you think you gravitated to so many areas that others avoid?

Needel

There are two aspects to it. One is that they just happened to be, for some reason for whatever reason, the things that have attracted me the most. I go back to my mantra on simplicity or "SYMPLE." My most precious life experiences, expertise, etc., those are the things that drew me for whatever reason. Many people talk about speaking as being a calling. Not something you pick as a career, but rather something that picks you as a vehicle. I love that concept and agree with it wholeheartedly. That's pretty much the way it's been for me and the same is true in other areas as well.

I could not tell you what ultimately attracted me to technology. I believe, initially, it was that first "session" in Fred's studio, but I also think it was more than even that, as profound as that experience was. My father was not very mechanical. He didn't even have a workshop—I was the one that built the workshop in the house, did the handy work around the house, and was just fascinated by the way things worked and how things happened. I was the kid that took stuff apart and put it back together. Technology has always embodied many elements of fascination for me. It's simultaneously science, art, and the humanity that needs and uses it. I'm convinced that it involves being able to communicate on a large scale and being able to support humanity. That in itself may be what appeals most to me.

Turn it around though and once I have this expertise is, I want to make it available. It's impossible for me to learn something or know something and not want to turn around and publicize, evangelize, and promote it because that's just my nature. I'm a teacher, I'm an educator, and I'm an informer. The inbound part of it, they found me—the teaching, the speaking, playing music, and especially playing drums.

Finally, once I receive or learn something, I want to give it away, which goes back to my involvement with the non-profits and community service. I'm compelled by my own nature to give away what I have. There's the full circle where I receive this, let's say the blessing I consider it to be of loving to speak in public, so much so that I did it as a very young child. Seeing the trauma that speaking creates for so many people, I can immediately contribute to that need for knowledge and confidence, and as you probably know David, as the executive of something of a speaking education empire, public speaking is one of the number one fears of adults, worldwide. It's not something people look forward to, people that don't normally do it. If I can make some difference in that realm of people having a major fear of something that is such a big part of life these days that's a contribution that I get to make in the world. If I can contribute to one person being less uncomfortable and more effective at speaking in public and making presentations, even in a small company, I've had a success. Some people there's no difference for, whether they're speaking in front of five people or five thousand. They've made a difference in the world and certainly made a difference to individual people. That's certainly the way I feel about it.

All these things that have found me, I automatically want to find an ability and an opening with people that normally would not want to be hearing about such horrible activities. It is possible to travel, still have a family, and still be loved and remembered by your kids. You CAN speak in public, be impressive, be effective, and be living when it's all over. You CAN master and use technology in amazing ways despite not thinking you have the aptitude or personality for such "techie" topics.

All these things that otherwise, before Stu Needel came along, may have seemed insurmountable, I show can be done. If Stu can do it, YOU can do it! That's one of the biggest joys in life that I have.

Wright

Hey Stu, while we're on the topic of facilitating people doing activities they never thought possible, please explain to me the significance of group drumming, drum circles, and how something seemingly so primitive relates to making the world a small village and to creating success?

Needel

How did I not dwell on that topic until now, especially with the strong emphasis I've placed on that work in recent years? Thanks for the reminder David.

Drum circles and the other group drumming experiences I create and facilitate are just another chapter in showing people what they're capable of, not to mention seeking out opportunities to make music with people. While music has been such a powerful part of my life from the very start, I'm amazed at the number of people who music is not that important to and perhaps more tragically, how many people don't realize and never explore their own musical abilities. Music is such an incredible way to express ourselves, it's a shame when people don't realize that, so...I formally began creating opportunities for people to explore their musical, particularly rhythm, abilities in what are typically known as "drum circles" as well as participatory experiences when people get to play along with me and by themselves, when I'm performing as a drummer and percussionist.

Drum circles, particularly facilitated drum circles, are group experiences where people come together to make in-the-moment improvisational music together, facilitated by a conductor of sorts, otherwise known as a drum circle facilitator. The phenomenon has been spreading across America and other countries for nearly 40 years now and can ultimately be attributed to the efforts and dedicated life of one extraordinary man, Arthur Hull, President of Village Music Circles, of Santa Cruz, CA. I've known Arthur for 5 years now, have studied with him extensively in Hawaii and Maryland, and consider him both a beloved mentor and friend.

Drum circles, as Arthur has developed them, allow people on the surface to experience the joy of discovering their own innate and natural sense of rhythm, while playing with others around them. At a deeper level, the benefits of group drumming typically include and can be directed towards team building, stress reduction, relaxation, listening skills, negotiation, and pure unadulterated human potential. While unfacilitated drum circles have been around for thousands of years as integral parts of culturally specific ceremonies, rituals, and traditions, facilitated circles are a twist on this rich history, designed to give anyone a non-religious non-culturally-specific experience of hand drumming and the incredible results and benefits are widely known. I'm a proud member of the Drum Circle Facilitators' Guild, whose members include people like me who have made a portion of or their entire professional lives about sharing the joy of drumming with the world.

As much as I love performing as a drummer and percussionist, having the opportunity to play with and facilitate people playing as a "percussion ensemble," some for the first time in their lives, is one of my most cherished experiences. You can't believe the profound benefits that drumming has for so many people. I see it on a regular basis. What better way to facilitate making the world a small village than by doing what used to be how all villages communicated to their members and how many villages in third world countries still do? By the end of any group drumming experience, that small village ambience is definitely palpable! People who were strangers moments ago are now close friends!

Wright

How would you define success for yourself, in general terms that could apply to anyone?

Needel

It's kind of a synopsis of everything I've said. It is really several things: picking what you love to be doing or having it pick you. Finding the things that you most love, most care about, most are interested in—there has to be passion there. Passion is such an important criteria for me. Once you have the things that you love and as you so eloquently described, I do a lot of things that I love. I'm not a mono-interested kind of guy; I obviously have quite a diversity. Once you have that palette of things that occupy your time, your fascination, and your dreams, the next step is to take them out into the world and as Shaw said, be thoroughly used up by them.

In my early days in information technology, I was known for working 18-20 hour days. Not because my job required it, but because my job, as I defined it, was to learn as much as I could about the industry that I was in, the company that I was working for and then of course, my actual job as well so I would work long and hard past the end of the regular day, whatever that means anymore. I would just work long hours to learn and experiment and play long after people left the building. Luckily I had access to the building as a network manager. I had the privilege not everybody has, but I did and I exploited it. Then I would continue after I went home—I would read, study, think, and write and that's continued to this very day—it's just my nature.

That is the critical element of success: it's finding what you love to do and doing it with all the gusto that you can find, muster and that obviously involves sacrifices. That involves a really serious set of life-balance principles that you can continue to meet the needs of your family, friends, and colleagues who think you may be a work-a-holic. I certainly have been accused of being just that. In the long term when you really manage a life, not just a business, for me I know I find that I'm much more happy than if I just go through the motions and do the minimum required, that's never exhilarating for me. I want to do more, I want to get more, and I certainly want to give more. I think for me the essence of success is to give it all you've got in ways that are most pleasing for you. That's where absolute balance is.

There are a lot of people who work very hard out there. There's not a shortage of that. Sometimes the people that are working very hard are not working hard at what they love and that's just a tragedy. Work hard, but work at what you love doing and then, of course, the work is no longer work, it's play. That's not a fantasy. It's the ultimate formula for success. I live it and I see it being proven by the most successful people on the planet.

Wright

Well what a great conversation! I really appreciate you spending all this time with me today to answer these, what I consider to be important, questions. I'm sure that our readers are going to learn a lot from all that you have experienced and have talked about today.

Needel

It's my pleasure to be a part of this book David and equally a pleasure to be talking to you today. Thanks for this opportunity.

Wright

Today we've been talking to Stu Needel, the Technology Teddy-Bear, who is an internationally known speaker, trainer, consultant, author, performer, and musician. He has devoted his life to making the world, in his view, a small village through his passionate dedication to human potential by studying, practicing and teaching communications of many types. Stu, thank you so much for being with us today on *Conversations on Success*.

Needel

My pleasure. Thank you, David.

About The Author

Stu Needel, a.k.a. The Technology Teddy-Bear™ is President of Stu Needel Communications, LLC of Baltimore, MD. Stu personally and through his company is committed to "Making the World a Small Village" ™ by promoting human potential through communications, technology, and music. Stu is a professional musician (drums, percussion, vocals, and keyboards) and a drum circle facilitator, specializing in creating powerful musical experiences for novice and experienced drummers alike.

Stu Needel Communications, LLC

7 Slade Avenue, #204

Baltimore, MD 21208

(866) 688-8788 Find and Fax Me - Anywhere!

(443) 845-1715 Cell(PDA) – SMS Messages

Email: stu@stuartneedel.com

www.stuartneedel.com

Chapter 11

L. E. "LEE" MCLEMORE, PH.D.

THE INTERVIEW

David Wright (Wright)

Today we are talking with L. E. "Lee" McLemore. He is a nationally televised speaker, trainer, author, and one of the most sought after performance coaches today. His clients range from multi-Grammy© award-winning artists to corporate executives and entrepreneurs who follow their hearts and are living their dreams.

Dr. Lee's unique talents allow him to "peel back the onion" to expose and resolve the key challenges that are blocking you on your journey. He assists his clients to remove, take away, or dissolve what always held them back, what has created anxiety, and what has stopped them from being and performing at the level of awesome excellence they have dreamed about or glimpsed in their reveries.

Dr. Lee, welcome to *Conversations on Success*.

Dr. L. E. "Lee" McLemore (McLemore)

Thank you so much for having me.

Wright

Right in the beginning, would you define success for our readers—what does success mean to you?

McLemore

Absolutely. The definition of success—to obtain an outcome or to achieve a goal—is the definition I think society has come to know. I look at success in a little different way, and my objective today is to hopefully shift the paradigm we currently have on success.

There are three presuppositions about the way I like to think of success. The first is that success is an emotion—it's a feeling or a state of being. Secondly, success is the journey, not the destination. The emotions we have or the feelings we hold will determine our destination. Let me explain. In my opinion, I feel that our culture has conditioned us to view success as something that we have to obtain, to look forward to—the End Results—if you will.

More significantly I feel that we have been conditioned to rely on external sources for our feedback—our bosses, our society, and the social norms that have been projected onto us. We could say that success is basically a subjective status and how we determine it is based on the criteria of others. Everyone tends to have their own criteria to measure success, which could include: a six-figure salary job, the Lexus (or whatever car you're driving based on the status car of the year), or we may even base success on the zip code in which we reside. These are some external indicators of success that society has placed on us whether we choose to accept them or not.

I like to think of success as an emotion—it's that state of mind—that "well being" we feel when we have accomplished those external milestones. Now let me be clear that in my world, success is not defined by the object that is acquired or the task that is completed, but by the emotional component those things yield or the, "Yes I've made it!" or the, "Yes it's done!" Ultimately, in the work I do, I've discovered the success that people are looking for is that feeling, not the tangible.

Some people though, are not even aware of what this feeling is, and they keep driving and acquiring things, yet they still do not have that mechanism in place to say, "Yes I've made it!" or, "Yes I have it!"

So, how do we measure success? First let me say that I do not want to paint a picture portraying that material things are bad, or that if we are working toward obtaining material things, then we are shallow. That's not my point at all. In fact, I think we all deserve and should have the multi-million dollar home with the eight-car garage; we live in an abundant world. What I want to suggest here is that we need to develop a mechanism to know when we have achieved it (i.e., what will we see, hear, and feel when we have success.)

Some of us have found success with raising wonderful children and/or finding a loving relationship that is successful. It's not the title or the reward for the completion that makes a person successful. Take for example, a successful businessman or a successful speaker. Success is what that person is feeling at the moment and time they have reached or achieved their outcome; it's what makes them successful. The questions I like to ask for clarity is, "How will you know?" I believe that, again, success is a journey and not the end of the road. The definition, as I said earlier, is the achievement of something desired, planned, or obtained—something that you have— the status perhaps.

The interesting observation I have found in the work I do is that the success tends to be determined by the measurement by others (i.e., the boss's approval), it's the criteria we are looking at.

I would like to take us back to the emotional aspect of this, so let me talk a little bit about the work of David Hawkins, M.D., Ph.D., in his book, *Power vs. Force*. In this book he talks about how emotions have energy; we know that from science all things have energy and that is also my belief. This coupled with the "Law of Attraction," which has been taught by people like Deepak Chopra and Wayne Dyer, suggest that if we resonate with the vibration of success then we are going to attract those things to us that resonate at that successful vibration.

Now, here's where I want to begin to shift our paradigm before we move on to the next question. The old paradigm is that if we work hard and accomplish much then we will be successful. The new paradigm I want people to embrace is, "If we feel successful, then we will accomplish many things."

So how do you find that feeling, you ask? The feeling is found in the joy of doing what you like to do and in feeling the passion for doing what you want to do. Remember that feeling comes from finding the joy and passion, and the joy determines the emotion of your success.

Wright

Why are some successful while others are not?

McLemore

Excellent question! That one question started my journey and my career. It began back when I was working in the medical field more than twenty years ago. I began to observe that some patients heal and other patients do not. Given the same injury, given the same healing opportunities and same resources, one patient would make progress in a different way, different speed than others. I began to observe very quickly that this difference was the six inches between their ears! I'm not talking about intelligence and I'm not talking about an individual's "smarts," but about his or her belief system—"what" a person believes. Those who believed they were going to get better, got better. Those who believed their recovery was going to be difficult, found it was difficult. Those who thought they would not get better, you guessed it—they did not get better.

Because I talk about abundance and I teach how to manifest and how to create abundance, I am constantly asked, "What about people like Donald Trump, Oprah Winfrey, or even people who may have a less than ethical way of doing business?"(Which we're not mentioning those names here.) Some people seem to get ahead by being ruthless and underhanded, yet they become successful. What about karma? Well to that I say, "We must not be so quick to judge someone else's success by our criteria." We don't know "the truth" about their life—we only see one perspective.

When you look at people like Donald Trump, Oprah Winfrey, Tom Cruise, John Travolta—very successful people by anyone's standard—they enjoy and love what they do. Donald Trump loves the art of the deal, the art of negotiating and when he is in that vibration of enjoyment and success, he is going to attract those deals and business opportunities to him that are even going to make him that much more successful. Oprah Winfrey loves talking on her talk show and creating an environment where people can communicate pearls of wisdom as well as empower people to grow. If you have ever heard John Travolta on any one of his interviews he will talk about how much he loves what he does. People who have worked with him have even commented that it was a joy to work with someone like him because he is always in this vibration of joy and love. That's what brings abundance into our lives and that's what brings success into our experience.

What I'm talking about here is taking the "Performance Enjoyment Theory" to the next level. The Performance Enjoyment Theory simply states that the more someone enjoys doing their job, the better they will be at that job and the more productive they will become. I take it one step further and say that the more people not only enjoy what they do but truly find their passion and are able to hold the vibration of success, the more ability they have to accomplish greater success and to excel beyond their wildest imaginations.

My work has continued to evolve, as we would all hope to, and now the studies I have been working with, the techniques that I have been using, follow some great visionaries from the field of energetic DNA. On my television show I've had the opportunity to interview Margaret Ruby who is the founder of Possibilities DNA and Gregory Braden who is the author of many books and one of the most recently published, the *God Code*. Both have spoken of "genetic emotional lineage." Not only can we say the color of our eyes, and the color of our hair is linked together but also the emotional traits as well. There have been studies in Europe that have pinpointed the phobia genes— DPU-2. What has been discovered is that mental illness and phobias are genetically linked.

It's my belief that our genetic make-up also holds the information that is related to success.

Wright

Are you suggesting that we are predisposed to success?

McLemore

Absolutely! But let me explain that before you say, "Well okay, if I'm predisposed, I'm not even going to try; it's all in the genes." Yes, it is in the genes, but we can transcend that. We acknowledge the fact that some children are born into wealth or successful families and some people have the "luck of the draw." We also hear statements like, "We are trying to break out of the projects," or "break out of the chains of poverty." You see, these are in the mind-set or attitude within our genetic code. Each gene holds more than 80,000 stories throughout our lineage passed down from our mother's father's mother's father's mother's father and so on. As we come into this lifetime—are born—we are emotional beings. When we begin to feel rejection, or failure, or lack of success, then that emotion triggers all the other stories in our lineage with that same vibration. So when we first begin to feel that vibration of rejection, failure, or lack of success, we then create other experiences in our life to *prove* that failure or that lack of success. Remember the Law of Attraction?

This is how a belief is formed. You have the cause plus the evidence, which equals the belief. That's the structure of a belief:

Cause + Evidence = Belief

Understanding this structure allows us to go in and remove, reframe, and alter these stories. These stories are blocking you from achieving your greatness, and by removing them we are able to create your heart's desires.

Now there are equal amounts of stories of success and I don't want to paint a doom and gloom picture, but these stories and genes may be lying dormant until those stories are triggered as well. We want to increase the evidence of successes within your life, create and strengthen that vibration and then, using the Law of Attraction, bringing back to you those people, places, and synchronicities that are going to create abundance and success in your life.

Wright

How does one transcend or change their destination or destiny?

McLemore

I think it's very easy. This first step is to begin to challenge and change those beliefs that make you feel diminished, or not worthy, or lacking. Then, day by day make the conscious choice to live in that vibration of success or whatever it is that you want. People may read this and think I'm crazy and that's okay, it's been done before, but changing our destination is really that simple.

As one of my all-time favorite motivational speakers, Jim Rohn, says, "You can't change your destination overnight but you can change direction and direction determines destination." It's those day-to-day conscious steps we take that will determine our future.

I work in three areas of helping people transcend or change their situation. It's my belief that we deserve and are entitled to anything and everything we want. There is enough abundance in this world for us to have an abundant life.

When I begin working with someone or a group, I tell them I'm a very simple person, I'm not going to make this hard because life is intended to be lived with grace and ease. I want to keep things extremely simple for them, so I ask them three simple questions: "Who are you, what do you want, and do you have a strategy to get it?" Now, each one of these could be an entire chapter and may eventually be one day, but I will try to shorten it for our purpose here.

"Who are you?" Is one of the most important questions and people will give it only a glance; they think they know but are missing the boat. This is pretty consistent among those with whom I have worked.

In my experience I've noticed people tend to misinterpret their job role, job title, job functions, life functions, church functions, and society functions as their identity—who they are. If you ask someone, "Who are you? He or she may reply, "I'm a lawyer," or, "I'm a doctor," or, "I'm a deacon at a church." People tend to define themselves as what they do. To that I say, "No, you're not." That is a behavior or a role you have. But it is not who you are.

You are the "Essence of God's light," you are the essence of perfection that chooses from time to time to be the deacon or chooses from time to time to be the lawyer or chooses from time to time to be whatever, for a certain time period each day. But your title is not who you are because with those titles come the mind-set or a set of predisposed rules and preconceived regulations of how they should operate. Those "rules" are limiting. You see, if we can separate the behaviors or roles from the true self ("Essence of Perfection") then we will be able to access more resources that can be used to create what we truly want.

The best example I can think of is the one about people who have taken on the identity of an alcoholic. Ask them who they are and they might say, "I am an alcoholic." They are even encouraged to admit this in Alcoholics Anonymous (AA). When a person introduces himself or herself during the AA meeting, the introduction is stated, "Hello, my name is John, and I'm a alcoholic." I have nothing against AA or any other twelve-step program—everything has its place and serves a purpose. My hat is off to any program that helps anyone on his or her path. But what I say immediately when I hear someone in my presence say, "I'm alcoholic," I must say, "No, you're not, you're a person who has or may have a behavior (i.e., drinking) that does not serve you in your life."

Who are you? The best response is, "I am the essence of God's light, I am love, and I am the innocence of perfection who has at times engaged in a behavior that has not served me." Now once we separate behavior from the essence of the person we are much more empowered to see and access resources within ourselves to change our behavior.

It's amazing—just by using this simple philosophy you can see someone's light click on and they say, "Oh, well, I'm not that bad person, I just engaged in a bad behavior." You see, with the role or title of an alcoholic come certain expected behaviors or burdens. Thoughts such as, "I will always have to watch myself around alcohol. I will always be an alcoholic. Every day may be a struggle, if only I can make it one day at a time," show how much energy is spent in the behaviors or thought process of NOT drinking. With a title such as an alcoholic, we then assume a role or stigma that carries with it a disease process and expected behaviors that can be disempowering. Once we can separate the power from the person by finding out whom they are, what their values, strengths, and weaknesses are, then we can decide what they want.

Now, "What do you want?" is another area where people say they know what they want. The first time I ask people what they want I'm amazed to hear that the first thing they say is what they *don't* want. Someone may reply, "I don't want to file bankruptcy," or, "I don't want to end up in the gutter." It's no wonder we don't accomplish anything when we keep focusing on what we *don't* want!

I wonder what would happen if we were to focus on what we wanted? Starting with what you don't want is one way to begin nonetheless, because maybe if we can find out what you don't want then we can jump off to the next point, and decide what you *do* want. Sometimes it takes us a while to get around to what we want. I think it's because most people have not been given permission to dream. They have been told not to dream, or not to use their imagination, or they can't have it, so don't build their hopes up. I think this is an abundant human race and I think we can have everything, so what we have to do is establish who we are and move toward reclaiming our abundance.

Once you have those two components then the strategy comes very easily, because now you have a lot more resources to access and you can just plug away. Other people probably have achieved what you want to achieve, or have acquired what you want to acquire, because they've already laid out the roadmap. The strategy is pretty easy: We can model behavior from someone else, if we have that clear understanding of who we are and what we want to have or where we want to go.

Wright

You seem to pull from many different theories or philosophies. How did you arrive at this point in your life?

McLemore

I've been very fortunate to have some phenomenal and gifted teachers in my life such as Peggy Dean, to whom I want to give acknowledgement. She has helped me lay down a great foundation of human behavior with the study of "Neuro-Linguistic Programming." Margaret Ruby, whom I mentioned earlier, has taught me about the energetic world of DNA. I read a lot, as one must in order to be a student of life. I have this hunger and thirst to continue to read and to grow.

I really feel I'm here to help other people grow and to help them remove what blocks them from achieving their outcomes. I can only help people get to where I am, so I have to continue to evolve and move to new levels so I can help people get to their new levels. I never take anything for granted when clients come in to my practice. When they come in they can give me some really quirky beliefs. My curiosity kicks in and I want to know what makes them that way or how do they know that to be their true.

I also want to step back and say that everything I have said here—the techniques and the theories—well, none of these are original with me. I gather what I have to offer from "collective consciousness"—others' books and life experiences. I'm not creating and I haven't created any new technique, nor I do have any secrets that aren't out there already. I'm a very simple man learning processes and principles from very different people, and from diverse philosophies and putting them together in such a way that I have found works well for other people. It's not my job to say I have this technique and I can help you. That is emphatically not the case. My job is to unpack your belief systems and to help *you* hold a mirror in front of you to enable you to see how you are blocking *yourself*. Then you have the choice to step over the hurdle or not. It's up to me to help YOU create abundance.

I think that the most successful coaches or facilitators are the ones who have the most tools in their toolbox. The "Law of Requisite Variety" states that the part of the system with the most requisite variety is the part of the system that is in control, and here requisite variety simply means choices—we create choices. I'm blessed to have several tools in my toolbox that can help individuals create these choices so they can ultimately reach their destination or their success whatever that may be—whatever will generate that sensory based information within themselves.

Wright

Do these techniques you teach work both within a corporate setting as well as with individuals?

re

itely! I have clients across the board, from corporate CEOs,
® Award-winning artists to individuals who are simply
to take their life situation to the next level. Because I believe
osophies are so simple, I'm not teaching a system, I'm really
in and working with that individual, within his or her own
ystem.

n map this over individually and I have mapped it over various
nies across various types of industries. We will address the
questions, "Who are you, what do you want, and do you have a
:gy to get it?"

ie difference between the corporate client and the personal client
d be how the, "Who you are," and, "What do you want,"
rporates into the company as a whole. Then the individuals who
:e up the executive team or the leadership create another
:son"—the company—and we have to make sure that their
ividual missions and visions dovetail with the mission and vision
:he company. So the added component in working with a company
giving or breathing life into this additional entity called the
mpany and making that a human person as well.

I like to call what I do as "the investment in human capital." It's
ie one thing I think organizations tend to let go by the wayside
/hen their budgets get tight. They'll upgrade their computers or they
/ill buy systems that cost perhaps thousands of dollars to put in
place. How much time, or money, or whatever, do they actually invest
in the critical aspect of their business called "human capital"? We are
only as strong as our weakest link, so give me your weakest link and
then we can strengthen the company's chain of success.

Wright

You mentioned several times three questions, "Who are you, what
do you want, and do you have the strategy to get it?" Does the success
of your client rely on the strategy you help them develop?

McLemore

Actually no. It plays a big part actually, but it's not the main
determining factor. The strategy to me is the easiest part. The major
block is generally found in the first two questions. You see, people
have a false sense of self as I mentioned earlier. The fact that you've
taken on the identity of your job, role, function, or the identity of the
church we mentioned, or your life's role, or whatever it may be as who

you are. My work helps separate that behavior in order to be able to access the resources to move forward.

After you have the two steps of who are you and what you want in place, then the strategy is the game plan. It can change—we can alter the game plan any way at any time necessary—but it's very easy to stay with because you have a greater sense of self and of accomplishment. Keep in mind that within the first few minutes we're going to find out what success feels like. It's that vibration in which we are going to resonate and it is that vibration which will bring people, places, and synchronicities to you because of the Law of Attraction.

Our old paradigm suggests that we have to stay with our strategy and work hard to achieve our outcomes. So one might say, "Yes, the strategy is the most difficult part." Let's shift the paradigm—keep that vibration of success, whatever it may be for you, with grace and ease. Remember the Law of Attraction: When you hold the vibration of success or whatever it is that you are wanting, then you will attract those situations to you that hold that vibration.

People might say, "Oh that sounds too simple." It is—stop making it difficult! Life is not a struggle. Our ancestors and our parents struggled; the struggle has already been done, let's not repeat that. Let's step into our greatness and create the life and abundance we deserve and are entitled to.

Wright

When I consider evolution and growth, are you saying that the question "who are you" must be asked all the time?

McLemore

Yes, it can be asked all the time until you get to a point of understanding that you're are an Aspect of God's light, you are Love, you are Unconditional Love; that's when you have those synchronicities and you find those moments in time where you find bliss. What you're tapping into is the inner source of love, and that's how you know you're on the right track—when you are working or implementing a strategy and you're in that moment where you're joyful and living the passion.

Whether you come in personally or I talk with you on the phone (I do a lot of my sessions on the phone), and I hear you drop that passion in your voice, I know we've lost that vibration. Then we have to find it (i.e., what happened this past week, that caused this loss of vibration?). Your answer might be, "My boss came in and did something," or, "My boss did this to me," or "I have a situation at home, I have a teenage daughter and this crisis arose," When that crisis arose, you were no longer enjoying the moment of that experience—you went into a lower vibration. We can tackle all crises with joy, love, and passion; when we do, we are going to find those crises are much easier to deal with because we are able to access our resources.

Have you ever been in a situation and then five minutes later just think, "Why didn't I think of that?" This happens because when you get in those lower vibrations you're not able to access the resources you know. You have the answers, you have the wisdom; you're just not able to access them because you're resonating out of a lower vibration or lower energy level.

My job as a coach is to keep you primed and to keep you in that passion and in that glory. I'm not going to say you should walk around living all the time in this euphoric field. Come on, that's not reality, but when we go into a lower vibration we have to learn what the lesson is there. We live our lives in perfection every moment of every day. When we have a crisis and get a sense of the lower vibration, one of the first things we need to do is to say, "Great! What can I learn from this?" Then you will see the situation without judgment; you will see it as neither negative nor positive—it just is. Only after you place meaning on it does it become positive or negative. Do you follow me on this? If you have an encounter, you can either see the negative side or the positive side, but you can't see both. The moment we reframe the situation to understand the positive aspects, and we learn that lesson, then that encounter is no longer negative, it's simply another lesson. Then we can take that lesson and build on it and return to the vibration and it is going to bring to us those things that are synchronistic in life.

Wright

To summarize this, what would be your key bullet or thought for someone, perhaps one of our readers, who is looking for success in his or her life?

McLemore

Stop looking at success as what you want, and make success what you are—find that vibration. Whether you believe it or not, there has been a lot of research done on near death experiences and what I have heard and believe to be true is at the time we transcend (the Bible calls it the judgment day), also called the "Life Review," we're asked three questions: What did you do with the life I gave you? What did you choose to learn? What/whom did you choose to love?

Now I don't know about you, but when I stand before God on that glorious day, I want to say that I lived my life to the fullest, I loved everything I possibly could every moment, and I learned everything I possibly could. You have to live each moment with passion. It's the little things pulling you down that you need to get rid of, and you need to find out for yourself what makes you feel successful today. Then you need to keep that vibration, and just watch the abundance begin to trickle in and grow.

Wright

Today we've been talking with L. E. "Lee" McLemore. He is a nationally televised speaker, trainer, and author. He helps his clients take away or resolve what has always held them back and/or what has created anxiety for them and stopped them from operating at the level where they are intended by God to operate. I think we have found out today he really knows what he is talking about; at least I'm going to think about the things I have learned here today which might be the key to success.

Thank you so much Dr. McLemore for being with us today on *Conversations on Success.*

McLemore

I thank you for inviting me here.

About The Author

L. E. "Lee" McLemore, Ph.D., a national televised trainer/speaker/author, is the president of Peak Performance Consultants, Inc., and founder of the Institute of Alternative Modalities. His clients range from multi-Grammy® Award winning artists, CEO's, VP's to single entrepreneurs. Dr. Lee's unique talents allow him to "peel back the onion" to expose and resolve the key challenges that are blocking you on your journey. He assists his clients to remove, take away or dissolve what has always held them back, what has created anxiety, what has stopped them from being and doing at the level of awesome excellence that they have dreamed about or glimpsed in their reveries.

"As we hold the space for change, behavior patterns shift, empowering beliefs emerge, passionate energy flows through, and focus is on the choices that bring them to success and peace in their life in spite of naysayers around them. Everyone has the potential, however, some need assistance to access it." Dr. Lee believes that many can coach, but few can truly find the leverage it takes to create massive behavioral changes. His sessions are interactive and provide the arena for live problem resolution. Not only do his clients learn new strategies, but also they are able to experience real-life applications.

L. E. "Lee" McLemore, Ph.D.

Institute of Alternative Modalities

Phone: 404.876.5140

Fax: 404.420.2228

www.iofam.com

Chapter 12

MARJORIE BLANCHARD

THE INTERVIEW

David Wright (Wright)

Today we're talking with Marjorie Blanchard. Ms. Blanchard has earned a reputation worldwide as a compelling motivational speaker, accomplished management consultant and trainer, best-selling author, and entrepreneur. In 1983 she was chosen Speaker of the Year by *New Women* magazine and American Express. She was co-recipient, along with her husband Dr. Kenneth Blanchard, of the *1991 Entrepreneur of the Year Award*, from Cornell University.

She is co-author of *The One Minute Manager Gets Fit* and *Working Well: Managing for Health and High Performance.* Marjorie is well versed in a variety of topics and often speaks on leadership and empowerment, team building, customer service, managing change, and life planning.

As president and cofounder of Blanchard Training and Development, she works diligently with her husband to develop the company into one of the premier management and consulting and training companies in North America.

It's my pleasure to welcome Marjorie to *Conversations on Success.* Thank you for being with us.

Marjorie Blanchard (Blanchard)
I'm delighted to be here.

Wright
Before we dig into some real specifics relating to success in business and life, I know our readers would appreciate a little background information about you. I'm always curious about the life journey of our special guests and their early influences, experiences, mentors, and such. Will you tell us a little about your background?

Blanchard
Well, even though we live in California and have for about twenty-five years now, I was raised on the East Coast. I was born in Rochester, New York, the oldest in a family of five—four girls and one boy. My brother is eighteen years younger and actually, he's replaced me as president of our company. I'm right now the head of the "Office of the Future," which is a wonderful job for me. Tom and I are the bookends of this family.

My mom and dad met at Cornell, where I also went to school and where I met my husband. I'd say that the biggest early influence, besides being the oldest person in the family and having young sisters and a brother to feel responsible for, was we moved quite a bit. My dad worked in the meat packing business and in order to progress and work his way up, we moved about every three years. That was quite a remarkable experience as I look back on it. I didn't necessarily like it when it was happening, but what it did was make me feel very close to my family—my major reference group.

Another big influence, I would say, was when I was about six. My parents bought a piece of property on one of the Finger Lakes. Throughout my whole growing-up years we would spend the summer camping out there. I think that made me pretty close to my family. We had some marvelous times enjoying everything from camping out to evenings without television, a lot of good reading time, time alone, and just a lot of family time. Ken and I committed to that when we got married.

I married right out of college and had a wonderful experience at Cornell. We spent about ten years in the academic world and then Ken was eligible for a sabbatical. We came to California, discovered this amazing climate and decided to stay here. Two or three years later we started our company—Blanchard Training and Development—now the Ken Blanchard Company. We just celebrated our twenty-fifth anniversary in the company. Ken and I have been married forty-two years.

Wright

Oh my! That's odd in this culture.

Blanchard

I keep thinking someone is going to come and interview me about that. We have two children, both in their thirties and two grandchildren. Our daughter and son both work in our company. In fact, we're transitioning the leadership of the company to them. We have about 300 people in the company right now and they're spread across the country and the world.

Wright

That would be a great book title—*How to Stay Married*.

Blanchard

It would be, wouldn't it?

Wright

You couldn't say anything about one minute in it, that would be for sure.

Blanchard

Somebody did do a study of married people. In order to get a population that was big enough, he had to get down to people who sort of liked each other and decided to stay married.

Wright

I've got to hear more about this. I've never heard of a "company of the future." What in the world is that all about? It sounds like I want to go to work for you.

Blanchard

It's a wonderful thing.

Wright

What do you do in the Company of the Future?

Blanchard

Well, what happened was in 1997, I was very much up to my ears with being president and getting very frustrated because there was so much happening in our industry regarding the technology, e-learning, the whole boom in the dot com business, and the Internet. I just had this growing stack of articles to read and conferences I wanted to go to and things we needed to do research on, because we could see them on the horizon. We had a wonderful year that year and I petitioned our family to create this "office of the future," which would consist of five people in a little think-tank. Our goal was to get smart on some of these issues we didn't know very much about, and study the trends and the literature, and to prepare our company for some big changes.

We started some experiments with distance learning within the company. We also protected a relationship we had with the company that was putting some of our core intellectual property from our books onto very, very interesting interactive programs.

Then when 9/11 came along and our clients couldn't or wouldn't travel, we were ready. We actually had alternatives to classroom training. What we're now doing is more of a blended approach where people learn a lot more before they get to class so that when they're in class they get to practice and really apply what they're learning to their very own situation. It was a godsend, honestly, because we had previously done a lot of talking but not a lot of doing in that area.

We did a big international study—a lot of our international business is growing—and we were able to spend about four months studying about twenty-eight countries, to look at what some of the opportunities were. We're doing a lot of pushing in the company still, to get them to use existing technology and much less future technology. We continue to work on these study topics, trend watches, and scenario planning, and all the things the smallest companies are too busy to do. Most businesses are so busy with the present they ignore the future and then get surprised.

Wright

As you work with organizations across America, are there one or two issues that seem to stand out above the rest—areas of concern for corporate leaders? For example, are leadership problems occupying most of your attention, or perhaps change managing and cultural issues?

Blanchard

Well, I think all of those are huge issues. Our core technology is in the leadership area, both on a platform for volunteer organizations and in corporate America. I have recently been looking very carefully at this retention issue. There are some very clear signs we could have a big labor shortage in the United States, certainly by the year 2010, that will make what we experience in the late '90s look minor. So what I'm encouraging people and our clients to do is, first of all, take that issue seriously. Start looking at your own retention figures and where you might be losing people you want to keep and that kind of thing.

One of the reasons people leave an organization is because they don't like the way they see people being treated, or they don't feel they are developing in their career. It almost always boils down to the fact that they don't have a very good relationship with their manager or leader. They don't feel they're being coached, or nurtured, or given enough attention. What I'm warning and encouraging people through white papers and other methods is to make sure people feel like they're in a culture where it's a great place to work, where they would recommend their friends to come and work. You can't start doing that when the chips are down—you've got to do it all along the way.

Almost all of Ken's writings have to do with honoring people, paying attention to them one by one—not as a group necessarily—and understanding that your people are your main competitive advantage; you really do get back what you give to people in terms of loyalty, etc.

Wright

Don't you wish more corporate presidents would talk like you do?

Blanchard

You know, some do but what they don't know is how to go from where they are now to a culture they want to have. Sometimes they start by reading the books we've written and they get excited and inspired. Maybe they have one of our speakers come in, or Ken will come in and hold a workshop, or one of our speakers will speak during a meeting to get them excited about how things can be different. Then it becomes a series of things they put in place to act on their good intentions. Most of the companies we work with are great companies already; they just want to get better.

165

Wright

I was in intrigued by the titles of your books. Both of them focus on health and wellness in the workplace—*The One Minute Manager Gets Fit* and, *Working Well: Managing for Health and High Performance*. First, how did you find yourself writing on the topic of health in the work place?

Blanchard

I was a little ahead of myself. Those books actually came out in the 1980s, around 1986 or 1987. I got very interested in this whole idea of whether a manager can make someone sick. What we found was, we would talk with somebody one time and they'd be fine and when we talked with them two or three months later, they would be ill or missing work or hating their life or whatever. What we'd find is they'd gotten a new manager.

In the book *Working Well*, Dr. Mark Tager—a physician with a very holistic approach—and I went around asking questions like, "What do managers do that makes people sick?" and, "How can you create a culture where that's not happening?" It was that area we really started focusing in on. We wanted to know just how important managers are to the people who report to them and to those who depend on them. We wanted to know what to do to convince them they can do a lot in this area and they are very, very important. That was the beginning of that whole thing.

Negative relationships between managers and employees really do show up in absenteeism. You can keep your job pretty much with twenty percent of your energy. You can also give a 100 percent of your energy. We continue to look at that gap between twenty percent and 100 percent, saying that's really where a company's competitive advantage is.

You go into Starbucks and you know those people are turned on, they really like what they're doing, and they're giving good service. It's because they know they're treated well and they're growing, etc.

Wright

I'd love to dig a little deeper if you don't mind. Were there some specifics you discussed with people in these managing jobs? Did you give them any advice about what they could do to not make people sick?

Blanchard

I think the biggest piece of advice I would give to managers, and probably to parents and spouses also, is that you need to spend one-on-one time with the people whom you depend upon and who report to you. Now, what I encourage managers to do is to set aside fifteen to thirty minutes once a week or, at a minimum, once every two weeks to have a one-on-one meeting individually with the people who report to them. The unique thing about this meeting is it's not another little mini-performance status check. It's really a meeting to talk about what's on the mind of the people who report to you.

The meeting will start out with the manager asking, "What's on your mind?" So it's a responsibility to the manager to have the meeting and commit to it, make sure that it's a top priority, and that it happens consistently. It's really the responsibility of the direct report to bring the issues.

I've been doing this now for a number of years and you'd be amazed at what's on people's minds that have to do with their own career, or they may be concerned about an aging parent problem, or maybe they've heard something through the company grapevine that needs some kind of clarification. Just the fact that somebody will take the time and honor that time to provide the communication infrastructure so many organizations want and don't have is important to employees. It gets rid of any feelings of alienation and isolation very prevalent in a lot of organizations—you need a touch-point in an organization.

I think it works just the same at home—having one-on-one time with each one of your children, even if it's once every other week for a half hour. What I've found with my own people is that they save up things. They come in and I ask, "What's on your mind?" They've got this little list of things they want to talk about, because they know that, that time is protected. It's not an interruption and it actually saves me time because they aren't interrupting me while I'm doing something else. They know they're going to have that focused and concentrated time. This is just one of the things we try to keep in place.

When we do leadership training we state that this training will only come alive if you make sure you create a place for people to have this connection—that's so meaningful. That information is being proven in so many of the retention studies—people don't leave companies; they leave managers. People don't leave marriages; they leave spouses. There is a need we have to connect. If there's one thing people could do it would be to rely less on group meetings and to make sure you have these one-on-one meetings.

Wright

In your experience do you think the employee knows it is a confidential time as well?

Blanchard

Well, it usually is, and you certainly set up the rules for that. You can decide how you want to make that work. What people appreciate more than anything is your time. Now, I would say initially, it can be a little awkward if you've not done that before. We give people questions like, "What's going on in your job that I might not know about?" We get things going at first but after awhile, even the shyest will take the opportunity and feel comfortable talking to their managers.

I got this idea from a fellow who was running a D'weinersnitzel restaurant. He had three restaurants that had a remarkable low turnover, both in the management staff and in the frontline staff. When I talked with him, he said the only thing he was doing differently was requiring the store manager to meet individually with these teenagers who were working for them, fifteen minutes once a week. It took these managers three and a half hours once a week to meet with these employees. Why anyone would go down the street for fifty cents more an hour if somebody's taking an interest in them, particularly at that age where it may be their first job? They appreciate somebody on a consistent level making time for them.

Wright

Marjorie, you and your husband, Ken, were awarded "Entrepreneur of the Year" back in 1991. Many of our readers are either thinking about striking out on their own or they're in the middle of a turbulent entrepreneurial adventure. First, what are your feelings about entrepreneurs in general? And secondly, can you address one or two big picture issues that most entrepreneurs face and struggle with?

Blanchard

I think entrepreneurship is a mixed blessing frankly, having been an entrepreneur. I remember reading a book called the

Entrepreneurial Women by Sandra Winston, years ago. It was refreshing to see in print some of the things I had experienced.

One of the things she said was that very often entrepreneurs become entrepreneurs because of some disruptive event. I call them "cosmic boosts"—something that shakes them out of their comfort zone like getting fired or having some kind of tragedy happen at home where they need to make more money or something that gives them energy. Cosmic boosts are important because you need energy if you're going to be an entrepreneur. You'll need a lot of independent energy and you'll have to keep that energy going on your own. You generally don't have somebody coaching you, so you'll need to have a boost into this new world.

Sometimes a cosmic boost is as simple as feeling like you aren't going to make progress in this bigger organization and now's the time. You obviously need to have the resources and you need to know what the business is. Sometimes I suggest to people, for example, if they are going to think about starting their own travel agency, maybe they ought to work for somebody who has experience in that area of expertise for a while—get to know the ropes before going into a brand new venture without really knowing about it.

Entrepreneurs have to be pretty independent. I think you need to be able to pat yourself on the back and take responsibility for what's good and bad and not rely on other people.

I think there are some characteristics of successful entrepreneurs. Often people who are successful entrepreneurs had parents who where entrepreneurs, or grandparents, or uncles who were, so they were able to see what it was like to be in an independent situation like that.

In many ways there's a lot of freedom but then there's also a lot of responsibility that comes with it. I don't think entrepreneurship is the only way to be successful in life. I think you can be successful within a larger organization if you are clear about how you're going to save the money you make, etc.

There are periods of time in a person's life when being an entrepreneur may not be the best choice if there are mouths to feed and heavy monetary responsibilities.

You can also see some tremendous successes. I started as an entrepreneur with a partner and one of the things I learned was that having a partner was a bit like getting married—I had to figure out how we were going to work together. There are also a lot of wonderful joys that come with it. You're pretty much responsible for yourselves and if you hit on a good idea and can figure it out you could always get a good group of advisors. You can do some wonderful things. I heard someone say only about seven percent of businesses make it to twenty-five years; we recently celebrated our twenty-fifth company anniversary. It's not a walk in the park, but it can be successful.

Wright

Regarding the "cosmic boost" you were talking about, I was fairly successful in business one time, I went to $40 million in about five years which would be about $150 million today and everybody says, "Boy that's great! You must have planned." If they only knew. I started working for this company and I thought the owner of the company was an idiot. So I thought I would change companies. I changed to another one—a bigger and better one—I thought would be bigger and better and that owner turned out to be an even bigger idiot, so I started looking around. I loved the industry; but people who were mistreating their employees headed all the companies. So I just opened my own business.

Blanchard

That's a good cosmic boost, but at least you knew the business and knew what it took, that's important. I do believe you do need to know the business. In our own company, we were out of business a few times and didn't even know it. So there are stages when you're growing that can get you in trouble—you get over-extended, or you're *too* successful. We put out a four-color catalogue one time and we almost drowned in the response because we really didn't know what was going to happen. I look back at several points in the history of our company when God was definitely watching over us—we were very blessed to survive.

Wright

Many of our clients are pursuing success at many levels in their careers, in relationships, and concerning their health. I know you do quite a bit of personal development consulting and life planning. Will you share with our readers some advice that may address some of the more bedrock fundamental principles we all deal with in our pursuit of success?

Blanchard

I think my biggest advice probably goes back to moderation. I have known many people who've worked very hard to be successful. They've finally reached the pinnacle of success only to find they've probably lost their most significant relationships and lost their health as well. I think young people see that more clearly than even our generation. They are already asking questions about balance. It is necessary to continue to consider how you can keep nurturing the things that are truly the most important—your health and your relationships—while you're on your journey to success. You can maybe work really hard for a few months but if you just keep the burner turned up all the time, something's going to give.

In the case of our relationship, Ken and I made some decisions about things we would and wouldn't do. For example, we decided we would make every effort in the world to be together on weekends even though Ken does a lot of traveling and I was traveling for a while. That sometimes meant flying home on Friday night and leaving Sunday afternoon, but it was a commitment we made. We have a summer cottage at Skaneateles that was used by my family during our get-togethers. Ken and I made time for each other to go there in the summer.

It's amazing, if you put your own goals out there, other people's lives will fit around them. If you don't have goals about setting aside time for your family, then you get ticked off by all those other folks who interfere with that. You need to be stubborn. We have some rituals and some times that we really protect; when we don't protect them we feel pretty badly about it. It took us a while to see where those real stresses were; but I think you need to put that little bit of structure in.

I love the idea of "date night." We didn't have this when Ken and I were first married. I just think that's the coolest idea. What it indicates is that a couple is going to put their relationship, at least for one night a week, ahead of everything else. They're going to get a babysitter and they're going to spend some time talking together, or going to a movie, or doing whatever. What it shows is they're committed to that primary relationship ahead of a lot of the other things taking their time.

This refers back to redefining balance for yourself, not so much as structuring a strict nine to five, but in regards to establishing those priority areas and making your schedule reflect those things you say are important.

It's the same with health. I've walked now for years out on the golf course with two other women. Just knowing they're waiting for me even if I get back at night gets me up and going at six in the morning. They give me support and some structure for my good intentions. I think that's kept me balanced over a long, long period of time. You'd think by now I'd be totally self-sufficient but I'll tell you, if those ladies weren't involved, I might not be getting up. I went this morning even though I was out late last night. First of all it is fun, we complain about how we feel, we solve the problems of the world, and we talk about how great we're going to look when we're seventy-five. It might be hard to get my clothes on and get out there but my persistence shows I'm acting on my good intentions.

Wright

Sounds to me like you don't make a whole lot of short-term plans. Regarding the cottage you and Ken go to, did you go there as a child?

Blanchard

I did. It was our touchstone. Eventually Ken and I bought a cottage near my parents' cottage. We're now fortunate to be able to spend nine weeks there because we've transferred a lot of our leadership responsibilities here. Our children love to come too and they want to bring their children. So it's one of those things that has been a nice balance for our busy schedule.

Wright

I have a warm feeling just thinking about all the memories that must be running around that cottage after all these years, going all the way back to your childhood.

Blanchard

The biggest thing we decided was not to have television there.

Wright

Is that right?

Blanchard

We have never had television up there. I'll tell you, when our children were teenagers they would complain saying things like, oh, the Olympics this, and what about the soap opera? I would tell them they could walk over to their grandmother's and watch it; but we've never had television there. Now the children come up and it's the first thing they tell their friends. They puff up a little and say, "Well, we've never had television here." It causes us to have more time together to play games, have campfires, and pay attention to each other on a different level than we do at home.

Wright

That is a wonderful thought. Before we wrap up today, do you have any final thoughts for our readers? Can you share with us any information about up-coming books or incentives you're working on?

Blanchard

I think that one of the most interesting trends I'm following now is this idea of "spirit at work and spirit at home." I really believe people want to lead at a higher level. They really want to believe their lives are making a difference. They really do want to work for an organization that they sense either lives by its values, or is committed to some portion of the common good, or perhaps even has some kind of religious connection. I believe that when we hear people—especially young people—talking about "meaningful work," they're expressing a desire to be part of something bigger—to have something that gives extra energy. I believe that that takes thinking.

One of Ken's books is called *Gung Ho*. The first secret of *Gung Ho* is meaningful work—how is what your doing connected to what's beneficial to the organization, good for society, and helpful for the common good. I think that's also something families should spend time talking about.

We need to be asking questions like what is it that's bigger than we are? What are the volunteer things we're going to do or how are we going to make the world a better place? That kind of energy I think will sustain us though what I believe is a tremendous barrage of bad news in the media. We really have to work on keeping our spirits up. We have to be with other spirit-minded people, and I also think we have to realize that the only reason the media does well is they report bad news. You have to be careful as a manager, or as a parent, not to let yourself to begin to think that the world is changing and people just aren't as good as they used to be.

As a manager I remember that bad news rises and personal victories stay hidden. You've got to go looking for those personal victories and focus on what's good. You have to keep yourself inspired.

If I had any advice it would be to encourage people to understand that they need to focus on the bigger picture in their life. They need to know where they're headed and what's important; then they need to spend some time each day remembering that. Some people accomplish this with prayer, some with meditation. Whatever method you use, I think you have to recalibrate every day, because there's so much out there threatening to drag you down.

Leadership, I think, is about going somewhere and it's about creating an exciting look at where we're going; then people want to follow you. That happens at home and, I think, also in the office. It can happen in your own department, it doesn't always have to come from the top.

Wright

What a wonderful conversation. You sound like one of the most thoughtful and levelheaded woman I've ever talked with.

Blanchard

That comes from being sixty-four, right?

Wright

Well, I've got you by two years—in March I'll be sixty-six.

We've been speaking today with Marjorie Blanchard, best-selling author, speaker, management consultant, and entrepreneur.

Marjorie, thanks you so much for being with us as a guest on *Conversations on Success*.

Blanchard

Well, it was a pleasure.

About The Author

Dr. Marjorie Blanchard has earned a reputation worldwide as a compelling motivational speaker, an accomplished management consultant and trainer, a best-selling author, and an entrepreneur. Recently, she was chosen as Speaker of the Year by *New Woman* magazine and American Express. She was also co-recipient—with her husband, Ken Blanchard—of the 1991 Entrepreneur of the Year award from Cornell University.

Co-author of *The One Minute Manager Gets Fit* and *Working Well: Managing for Health and High Performance*, Margorie is well-versed on a variety of topics. She often speaks on leadership, balance, managing change, aging parents, and life planning.

As co-founder of Blanchard Training and Development Inc., she has worked diligently with her husband in developing the company into one of the premier management consulting and training companies in the world. She served as president of the company from 1987 to 1997, leading its rapid growth and success. She now heads the firm's unique Office of the Future—a think tank charged with shaping the future of both the training industry and the company.

Marjorie received both her bachelor's and master's degrees from Cornell University and her doctorate from the University of Massachusetts, Amherst.

Chapter 13

PAT MAYFIELD

THE INTERVIEW

David Wright (Wright)

Today, we welcome Pat Mayfield, president of Pat Mayfield Consulting, LLC. Pat's expertise is based on two decades as a national award-winning sales executive in multi-million dollar businesses. Today Pat is a successful business consultant, professional trainer, and accomplished speaker. Audiences love her practical advice based on real-life examples that she presents with humor and enthusiasm. Pat's most requested programs are "Top of the Tree Leadership," "The Negotiating Tool Box," "The Competitive Edge," and "Please Don't Drink from the Finger Bowl!" She holds MA and MBA degrees, has authored four books, and is a contributing author to *Leadership Defined*.

Pat, welcome to *Conversations on Success*.

Pat, in your Competitive Edge program, how do you outline the ability to succeed?

Pat Mayfield (Mayfield)

The first step is to be the best you can be in your chosen field. Knowledge or expertise is the most valuable factor in gaining the competitive edge. Those with the greatest knowledge, expertise, or skill set will have almost guaranteed success.

The second step is to use your knowledge and your talent. No matter how much knowledge or skill, *using* the knowledge and *implementing* the skill is what creates the success. How much potential success never turns into real success? Too often, the greatest ideas, thoughts, and talents are not publicly shared.

The third step is to have the desire to succeed. Success simply cannot occur without the desire or the motivation to succeed. David, this begs the question, "Is motivation more important than expertise?" We have all known individuals who had a medium amount of talent but a high level of motivation to be the best—and they were. The simple formula is that the individual with expertise *and motivation* will have greater success.

The fourth step in the Competitive Edge program is the ability to portray success. The perception of confidence, power, and success plays an essential part in the world of competition. The key is to feel successful from the inside out, not the outside in. The more confident one appears, the more confident one is perceived. A fundamental part of success is looking and acting like a winner.

The fifth step is to be prepared for success. Being prepared is more than just being knowledgeable, planned, and practiced; it also means mentally positioning the body and brain to embrace and accept success.

Scientists claim the brain cannot distinguish the difference between fantasy and reality. If this is true, then we must prepare our brain and body for success before it happens. We must plant the seed of success so the brain accepts it as reality. The brain will then relay that success image to the rest of the body. When it comes time to compete, the body will have a full expectation of success and will respond as such.

The sixth step is to know who you are and to be true to yourself. The person who has clearly defined beliefs and values will understand who he or she is. A deep sense of character will keep a person strong in the face of adversity. How others perceive us will be reflected through their verbal and non-verbal reactions. If our competitors view us as less competent, our psyche may accept their opinions as reality. The strong individual will be impervious to the negative opinions of others.

The seventh step is to be better, not bitter. The perfect life is rare indeed. Along life's path, we may find challenges and challengers, disappointments, and discrimination, and rejection and loss. What is significant in success is not what happens in our journey but how we react to it. Reactions require responsibility.

Whether and how we overcome difficult circumstances makes the difference between failure and success. To spend time being bitter, resentful, or having a heart filled with vengeance undermines one's ultimate goal of success. Learn to let go of the hurts, the pain, and the disappointments. Focus on being better, keeping your energy clear and positive.

The eighth step is to be thankful, humble, and generous with gratitude. Success happens because of others. Doors are opened, agreements are made, talents are utilized, and support is given to the successful. Be humble in the face of success. Success is a blessing; humility, a treasure. The wise winner shares the credit lovingly, gratefully, and generously.

Wright

Pat, in the corporate world, you were responsible for several successful multi-million dollar businesses. How did you build your success strategy?

Mayfield

David, here is a case of having a strategy and a plan, sticking with it, and watching it work. This was one of the most fun strategies I ever experienced.

My first management assignment in the corporate world was being the sales manager for the Western region. The Eastern region had dominated the Region of the Year award for many years, and eight years had past since the West had won the title.

My goal was to win the title the first year I took the job, but it took the first year to restructure and reorganize the region. The region was inefficient in people, territory, and account assignment and had to be fixed before we could work effectively.

The good news was that the sales force was willing to work as a team and had tremendous selling skills. Several were new to the company and highly motivated to succeed. A vital factor was that everyone on the sales team wanted to win the Region of the Year title.

Since we didn't have it together by the first fiscal year, the goal was to hit the ground running the first quarter of the second fiscal year. The theory was that if we took the lead in the first quarter, the East would not have enough time to catch up. Since the East had just won again, they were still enjoying the end-of-the-year numbers and were in no hurry to get started on the new year. We went to work selling hard on day one of the new year. We hit the ground running, writing orders.

Our team agreed that we should keep quiet about our strategy. Not even my boss was told about our plan. So when we were in the lead in both the first and second quarters, the other regions and upper management paid little attention to us, because most thought we were just gaining on low numbers from the year before. Actually, our numbers were good for the year before, just not enough to beat the East.

My boss began to realize what was happening in the third quarter but fortunately did not share it with the other regions. Amazingly enough, it was not until the beginning of the fourth quarter that the Eastern region realized we had a serious chance to win, and then they pulled out all the stops.

The company is an East Coast-based company with a high percentage of major accounts in that region. We knew that it was possible for the Eastern region to gain additional advertising or returns dollars to support their sales. They gained tremendously on us the last quarter, but it was not enough for them to beat us.

We finished that year with a twenty-two percent increase on a double-digit, multi-million dollar base. No special deals, no additional funding—just strong motivation to win with lots of focus on the basic business and strong customer service. I credit the sales force for creating the strategy as a team, working as a team, and taking the honors with our theme, "The West is the Best!"

Wright

I understand you created and developed a successful national sales force for a division of a large corporation. What did you learn from that experience?

Mayfield

That assignment was one of those unexpected and unplanned gifts of a career. Literally, I was starting a sales force from scratch. I knew no one in that industry, and yet, my assignment was to build a national sales force and develop this business into a multi-million dollar one.

Since this sales force was composed of manufacturer's representatives rather than employees, I knew it would have different needs and wants than my former employee-based sales force.

Because I had a strong sales background, I knew I could train salespeople on a lot of topics. But I was also aware of the characteristics of a great salesperson that are not trainable skills. So I developed my "Three-E Theory of Energy, Enthusiasm and Empathy." These characteristics are valuable in sales but almost impossible to teach. I began to look for these characteristics in everyone I interviewed. It takes a lot of energy to be successful in sales; enthusiasm has to be genuine, and empathy is needed for both the company and the customer.

During the interviewing process, I became aware of the "great interviewer" syndrome. Not all great interviewees will make great workers, and some of the worst interviewees will make great workers. I was careful to check and double-check the references, which helped to reinforce my first and second impressions of the candidate. Also, awareness and understanding of body language became critical in selecting the best sales people.

In addition to learning to read body language, some of the most valuable lessons I learned were: 1) To support, not supervise, 2) To make sure their needs from the company were met, 3) To respect and honor each individual, 4) To celebrate individual success, 5) To celebrate team success, and 6) To train by example, not lecture.

This team delivered a profit nine years out of the ten. When I left that position at the end of ten years, seventy-five percent of the sales force were original hires. The people on this special team remain professional colleagues and much-cherished personal friends today.

Wright

As a consultant, you've helped a lot of individuals and organizations reach their goals. How important is the celebration and the sharing of success?

Mayfield

Celebration of success is extremely important. Although motivation varies from person to person, I saw firsthand the value of celebrating, paying tribute, and rewarding the successful. Let's face it—we're not always successful year after year, but when we are, it's nice to pause and pay tribute. We're always thankful for accomplishments.

Every year I hosted an annual awards dinner for the national sales force. Most of the sales force would tell me that while they enjoyed getting together at the trade show for a nice dinner, they didn't need a plaque or award. They knew when they had done a good job and when they had not; they did not need a trophy to remind them.

Yet each year I awarded at least three prizes, and every year I watched the sparkle and the gleam in the eyes of the winners when they received their awards. If not but for a moment, they knew deep inside they were proud of what they had done, and so were we.

In addition to the big celebrations, I think one of the greatest opportunities for managers is to celebrate and reward the small successes throughout the year.

Many managers will celebrate the big successes but fail to understand that those who are struggling or having difficulty need frequent encouragement and support as well as the small celebrations of triumph. Even those who continually produce need an occasional positive stroke or two.

Little things mean a lot—a kind word of public support, a hand-written note, a congratulatory e-mail with copies sent to upper-management, a lunch or dinner, a gift certificate, a book or a music CD. Verbal hugs can make the difference in pushing harder for success. The phrases "a job well done" or, "you can do it" can never be overused or worn out.

Wright

Pat, could you tell us more about that concept of external and internal success?

Mayfield

Success comes in many different configurations and is relative to many circumstances. Success may be individual and have no relationship to others. The successful individual understands that not all success is built on competition.

External success—often the strongest motivator for competition— is how others receive and perceive another person's success. External success includes fame, media attention, publicity, trophies, plaques, titles and financial rewards. Some may find greater satisfaction through the adoration and respect of others than through their own perception of themselves.

Internal success is how satisfied or fulfilled an individual feels about his or her own accomplishments. Self-improvement may be so fulfilling to the individual that external success has little or no value to them. Self-improvement and internal success is what is valued.

The irony of success is that some who reach the top and experience external success may not feel internal success. Yet others who never reach the top and experience external success may feel tremendous internal success.

David, I'd like to share a great example of internal success with you. Before entering the business world, I worked with the Expanded Foods and Nutrition program in Oklahoma City. Fifteen people were hired as training aides in this federally-funded program. The aide's job was to enroll low-income homemakers and teach them home-management skills. Many of the fifteen aides hired were also low-income.

Each aide was to enroll thirty-five homemakers in this free program. The aide visited each homemaker weekly to teach her information the aide had received from the training. My job was to manage the program and conduct the aide training each Wednesday morning.

What was exciting was that we could actually quantify the results—we could measure growth and success. One measurable success was when the homemaker had food in the pantry at the end of the month.

Another great success was when several of the homemakers decided to return to school to get their diploma. These homemakers discovered they were capable of learning new ideas and skills; they had gained the needed confidence through this program. These small step-by-step successes didn't hit the front page but were significant internal successes for all of us.

Wright

In addition to having written a book on negotiating, you conduct numerous negotiating seminars. How important to one's success is the ability to negotiate?

Mayfield

David, it's a topic that is close to my heart and one I continue continue to see as a major ability needed to achieve success.

We don't work or live in a vacuum. To be "self-made" is almost impossible. We need others to set the example, teach us the skills and the theory. We also need others to critique us, to provide advice, and encourage us along the way. How one negotiates this support and advice is critical to reaching the desired result.

Success requires excellent negotiating skills, even if and when you have to negotiate with yourself. I experienced this recently when I needed to decide whether to continue working on an annual project. The decision was not clear-cut. The emotional rewards had outweighed the disadvantages in the past.

To help understand all the pros and cons of the decision, I went back to the basics of making a list and writing it down. Even seeing that the disadvantages outweighed the advantages, I still had to negotiate with myself. My value system of each pro and con helped me to understand that leaving this project was the right decision. A bit of prayer also helped to finalize this decision and, most of all, accept it.

Long-term success requires negotiating skills that yield mutual benefits. The zero-sum game of winner-take-all will ultimately diminish strong long-term relationships. The wise negotiator will learn and understand the value of being a fair player. Being tough but fair can be an asset that benefits everyone involved.

Wright

Pat, you've shared with me that a lot of the success in your new company is because of networking. Will you please share with our readers these networking skills?

Mayfield

Relationships are not only important in negotiating, they are critical in building a support system. Networking has become so valuable in business that many organizations frequently sponsor networking events. The purpose of these events is for participants to get acquainted and further build professional relationships.

As much as I'd like to share that my networking was a planned strategy that yielded success, I have to admit that most of my early networking success was simply random. The first networking event I attended was sponsored by the Tri-Valley Convention and Visitors Bureau. I had recently moved from my work on the East Coast 3,000 miles away to be closer to family and to start this new consulting business. Even though it was my first networking event in this community, I learned the power of networking that first night. That one evening of networking yielded two important introductions.

The first introduction was with Carol Sofranac, who was then the sales director of the PG&E Conference Center. Carol contacted me three days later to ask if I could conduct a manners program for one of her clients. The program on manners resulted in the publishing of the successful book *Manners for Success*™ and multiple local and national training programs on protocol and global protocol in numerous industries.

That chance meeting helped to form the offerings of my company today. If it weren't for that chance three-minute meeting with Carol Sofranac, I wonder if I would have ever added a manners program. But at that moment, I was new, I needed the work, and it was a topic I knew. And as for that first client, I continue to conduct training programs on several topics for them throughout the country today.

The second introduction was with Gail Gilpin, the Pleasanton Director of Economic Development, who asked me a few days later to conduct a project with the city. It was an honor to be asked to fulfill a contract for the city, especially since I was so new. Today, I frequently work in the public sector.

Although I may never be able to repay those who were so instrumental in helping my company get established, I will be eternally grateful. The key now is for me to help others get established or to grow their business.

The purpose of the networking process is to create and build mutually beneficial relationships. The success in networking is to build connections and relationships—not to just shake hands and exchange business cards. Shaking hands properly and business cards are only tools in the process.

Here are my suggestions for networking from my *Building Professional Connections* program:

1. Build a model of professional connections that will be mutually beneficial.
2. Have an introduction that is brief, does not sound like a commercial and is informative and pleasant. If you're new, say so.
3. Get out of yourself. Focus on others. Ask questions about the other person and their company.
4. Listen carefully with focus.
5. Exchange business cards with respect. Read their card rather than just stick it in your pocket.

6. Avoid the hard sell, but let the person know quickly and professionally what you do and what your company offers.
7. Shake hands—palm to palm, web to web, firm but not hurtful; and just two to three shakes. Make sure your hands are warm, clean and dry.
8. Work the crowd. Do not stay with anyone for more than a few minutes. You can get together with them later to build the contact. Be gracious when you move on.
9. Know why you're there. Have a strategy before your arrive.
10. Understand that the food is not the focus. When you're eating, you are not networking. Once you sit down, you take yourself out of the networking process.

Wright

Do you believe it's true that success produces more success?

Mayfield

Yes. I believe that most of the time that's true. Some will experience success that is once in a lifetime, but many experience continual success.

A lot of successful people are really quite modest. When I'm consulting with modest individuals, I encourage them to share their success with their clientele. Clients and customers like to see the plaques, certificates, or trophies for work and for community service exhibited by those they employ or hire.

In business, these icons of success can illustrate successful experiences, longevity, and know-how. People are drawn to the successful, because past behavior is used as a predictor of future behavior. Clients and customers want the person they hire to be successful.

The Oscar® icon is so important to the external and internal success of those in the movie industry that it is not unusual for the icon alone to be the most important part of the success. Winning the Oscar® may be ultimately more important than what they actually did to win it. Just winning an Oscar® is sufficient enough to establish credibility and future success. The same is true about the Tony Award® for theatre, the Clio Award in advertising,

Wright

Do you believe it is important or even possible to envision one's success before it happens?

Mayfield

The first time I heard about *seeing one's success before it happens* was on a Carol Burnett interview. She smiled that wonderful big smile of hers and told the interviewer that she truly believed, "If you can see it, you can reach it." Before that interview, I had utilized the power of positive thinking but never considered consciously envisioning a desired success.

Envisioning is more than dreaming—envisioning takes the dream from the general to the specific. Envisioning takes the "I want to" to "I will." Envisioning, coupled with telling yourself you will be successful in a *specific situation*, can be a powerful suggestion of success.

How does one envision future success? Take every element of that success level and implant it in your thoughts: the space, the people, your appearance, and your actions. How will you feel before, during, and after? Be thorough in envisioning every element possible. The more you see, the greater the possibility you will have to reach it.

Envisioning is helpful in many ways. Today, I make it a practice to envision every presentation ahead of time to instill the aura of success. To increase the reality, I always try to see the room in advance. When possible, I stand on the stage to have a better feel for the room and audience. Seeing the room, combined with feeling the energy of the room, is a tremendous help in positioning the brain and body for a successful program.

Not only is envisioning about ourselves, we often can envision the success of others. When I first began my selling, one of my first major meetings was with Terry Lundgren, who was a buyer at Bullocks Department Stores. Terry was not only respectful, he told me "no" more nicely than anyone in my entire selling career. Although he did not want to purchase what I was selling, he treated the product like it was gold.

As a new salesperson, that meeting meant a lot to me. I knew then that Terry was special and would become very successful. Years later, I worked with Terry when I was with another company and we were both rising through the ranks. Today, Terry is the CEO and Chairman of Federated Department Stores, a mulit-billion dollar operation.

Another individual I've recently met, whom I also envision being highly successful, is Anwar Robinson. I first met Anwar when he was a member of the Jubilee Singers at Westminster Choir College in Princeton, New Jersey. When I saw Anwar perform a solo at the New Jersey Performing Arts Center in Newark, I knew he had something very special. He was one with the stage that night; his performance transcended to a level that I cannot describe with words. He was totally immersed in that song. It was an incredible performance.

In 2005, Anwar was a top contender in television's "American Idol" competition. Now millions of viewers have seen this talented young man perform from his heart and from his soul. Not only is Anwar extremely gifted, he's one of the nicest young men I've met. He is as generous with his gratitude as he is with his gift.

Envisioning takes "It's beyond my imagination" to "I can see it happening." Envisioning requires mental stretching to take us to a higher and greater level of accomplishment.

Wright

Do you think that most success is planned or that luck plays a major role?

Mayfield

Early in my career, I strongly believed that success meant having a five-year plan. Always. However, I discovered that the good Lord had other ideas for me along the way, so many of the five-year plans didn't work out. Even though for the bulk of my career I have actually had long-term goals, I have learned to appreciate and honor the unexpected and to explore and listen when the detours occurred.

As I look back on my total career, many of the jobs and opportunities came through random meetings. More often than not, these were the individuals who were willing to give me a chance. Because I've moved so many times—nineteen times, if you can believe it—all over this country, my career has taken many twists and turns. Moving nineteen times was definitely not a plan.

Based on what I've learned and what others have shared, it's wise to have a plan but wiser to be open to the unexpected that can enhance your plan. Some of the detours not only changed my plan, they changed my life.

Be cautious in veering too often and too far from your plan. Jumping from idea to idea can create and result in a sideways strategy. When one jumps around too much, he or she may never reach the destination.

As I look back over my journey, many of the most fun and rewarding experiences came from chance meetings. The job in Oklahoma City with the Expanded Foods and Nutrition program came about because of someone I met in Kansas City. My business career began because I met someone on an airplane who offered me my first job in sales. My work in protocol came through a chance meeting at a networking mixer.

Plan or no plan, success is about the people you meet and learn to know along the way and the ability to listen to them and to cherish the relationship. Luck is relative and is actually a wonderful blessing.

Wright

What is your take on the statement, "Most success is simply just showing up?"

Mayfield

I see this in a couple of ways. The first way is that if you don't show up, you'll miss the possible luck and serendipity that can happen. So just showing up really is a part of the formula of exchanging energy that creates opportunity.

If this premise is true, then why do so many not show up? Maybe they're new to town or new to business; the feeling of being new is often difficult for some to overcome. Also, as home-based businesses and small businesses of fewer than five employees continue to grow, it is essential that smaller companies avoid isolation and show up at the networking events to build those significant, mutually beneficial, professional connections.

Another factor that may prevent people from showing up is shyness. According to Dr. Bernardo J. Carducci, Director of the Shyness Research Institute at Indiana University Southeast, approximately forty percent of our country considers themselves to be shy; a rate that has remained stable for over twenty-five years.

However, being shy is not a detriment to being successful. In fact, many of the leaders of the great companies analyzed in Jim Collins' book *Good to Great* considered themselves to be shy and reserved. Yet these great leaders understand the importance of showing up.

Sometimes, the hard-working folks are just too tired. One of the true-false questions on my networking quiz is, "If you're really tired, you should not attend a networking event." I'm always amazed at how many incorrectly answer "true." Take a five- to fifteen-minute break and get out there. Learn to push yourself. The most successful always do.

My second take on just showing up is about having the knowledge and expertise we talked about earlier that gives one the competitive edge. To be successful on a consistent basis for the long term, showing up simply is not enough. Eventually, one has to deliver the goods.

Wright

Success is not always easy. In fact, many successful people have experienced failures along the way. How do you believe most persevere on their road to success?

Mayfield

Knowing who you are before you're successful and staying grounded is how most persevere. Over the course of my career, these are some of the comments I have heard the most successful say: "Be true to yourself," "Keep balanced," "Focus on the reality, not the fame," "Keep your ego in check," "Don't forget to keep and maintain your reputation" and, "Adapt the best you can to the loss of privacy, intense scrutiny, and criticism." The challenge is that often we don't know who we really are before external success hits.

Understand that the more externally successful one becomes, the more requests, demands, and responsibilities will be placed on them. My favorite advice for all the challenges we face, whether in success *or* failure, is to simply, "Keep the Faith."

Wright

What an interesting conversation. I certainly thank you for taking this time with me today. Your thoughts and stories on success for our book *Conversations on Success* are greatly appreciated.

Mayfield

David, thank you so much. I'm grateful for the opportunity and have truly enjoyed working with you.

About The Author

Pat Mayfield, the president of Pat Mayfield Consulting, LLC, is an accomplished speaker, professional trainer, and successful business consultant. Pat's first-hand expertise is based on two decades as a national award-winning sales manager. Audiences give high marks to her practical, use-right-now ideas delivered with humor and enthusiasm. "Top of the Tree Leadership," "Negotiating Tool Box," and "Please Don't Drink from the Finger Bowl" are three of her most popular presentation topics. Pat also offers organization leadership facilitating. She holds MA and MBA degrees and has authored four books.

Pat Mayfield

Pat Mayfield Consulting, LLC

P. O. Box 10095

Pleasanton, California 94588

Phone: 925.600.0584

Email: pat@patmayfield.com

www.patmayfield.com

Chapter 14

SUSAN LANGLITZ, PH.D.

THE INTERVIEW

David Wright (Wright)

Today we are speaking with Susan Langlitz, Ph.D., a professional speaker and author of *Have Confidence Will Travel* and *EUREKA! Build Communication Confidence and Enhance Work Relationships: Simple Steps and Proven Solutions*. Dr Langlitz is a keynote speaker and the founder of SL Associates, a training and consulting company specializing in interpersonal communication and confidence building.

Susan has been published in the *Los Angeles Times, Chicago Tribune, Seattle Times, Newsday, Philadelphia Inquirer, Miami Herald, Detroit Press, Baltimore Sun* and has been quoted in the *Journal of Training and Development*. Dr. Langlitz has made several television and radio appearances. Her clients represent a multitude of industries and organizations in the private and public sectors.

Susan, welcome to *Conversations on Success*!

Susan Langlitz (Langlitz)

Thank you David, for the opportunity to share some thoughts on confidence.

Wright

You have written a book on confidence. Why confidence?

Langlitz

In my twenty years of experience, one question I've been asked most often is, "How do I become more confident?" Specifically, people want to exude confidence in a particular area of their lives, such as public speaking, social events, conducting business meetings, and garnering interpersonal respect. After hearing the inquiry dozens of times, I thought that I'd explore confidence further.

Wright

Are self-respect, self-image, and confidence the same thing?

Langlitz

Self-image and self-respect are certainly akin to confidence. If I have self-confidence, I would tend to possess a healthy self-image and would convey self-respect. However, let me offer a definition of confidence: Confidence is two-fold. First, it involves a skill or capability in a particular area such as playing the piano well, or giving a presentation with ease. Secondly, confidence is an internal, positive feeling people experience when they are demonstrating or performing a skill in which they are confident.

For example, people describe emotions like pride, joy, elation, or fulfillment while they are playing the piano effortlessly, giving a presentation with aplomb, hitting a soaring golf ball, writing exquisitely, etc.

Wright

Dr. Langlitz, how did you prepare for your book or conduct your research?

Langlitz

I conducted research in two ways. First, I studied what the academic experts discovered about confidence. Those professionals included university professors who spent an inordinate amount of time examining the topic of confidence.

Second, I interviewed ten people who are extremely confident in their respective professional fields of work including: business, politics, music, sports, religion, and social acumen. In particular, I was interested in how they became confident, what steps they took, and if there were any common denominators.

Wright

I bet that was fun just researching it.

Langlitz

Yes, and interestingly, between the research and the ten interviews, I found very consistent information.

Wright

So would you draw for us some universal principles?

Langlitz

Sure. In fact, the feeling of confidence transcends all venues— politics, business, sports, music, etc. Two aspects are most striking. First, each person I interviewed had a keen desire and motivation to become more confident in their chosen area. Second, sometimes against all odds they would persevere to gain the outcome of confidence.

Wright

Could you say more about perseverance and how people got their confidence?

Langlitz

To illustrate the collective voices of experience, I'd like to quote President Calvin Coolidge who said, "Nothing in the world can take the place of persistence. Talent will not; nothing is more common than unsuccessful men with great talent. Genius will not; unrewarded genius is almost a proverb. Education will not; the world is full of educated derelicts. Persistence and determination alone are omnipotent."

The point is that only over a period of time can one's persistence and determination in experiencing trial and error, toil and tears, and results, produce a powerful sense of confidence—there are no short cuts.

Wright

You just lost all the people who can't postpone instant gratification.

Langlitz

And therein lies the paradox. We live in a world of instant consumerism—fast food, ATM machines, digital cameras, on-the-spot stardom, and the like. Unlike those commodities however, confidence cannot be immediately obtained.

Many people want the confidence without doing the work, or they want confidence after a few weeks. The truth is, however, it is the protracted *process* of gaining confidence rather than the end result itself, which is significant. Confidence is something you earn.

Probably the best example of that statement was from an Olympic swimmer I interviewed who won gold and silver medals. I asked him how he felt when he won the gold medal. Was he beyond overjoyed?

He said, "I would have been disappointed if I hadn't won." Then he offered an explanation. "It is like the guy who is running down the football field and makes a diving catch and wins the game. Everyone is surprised except for the player because he has run that pattern over and over and over and over again." Such was the way of the Olympic swimmer, and this is the way one gains confidence.

Wright

Does confidence pertain to one area?

Langlitz

That's a good question. Academicians speak of "confidence within a context," meaning that a person can be confident in one role but unsure in another. For example, I might be confident both socially and meeting new people, but panic with the thought of giving a presentation. Or I can be stellar in geometry but not understand algebra. Similarly, I can be a brilliant and confident lawyer but not an effective parent.

Wright

Is it fair to say that people are confident about those things they are good at or that they enjoy, and not confident about things they are not very good at and do not enjoy?

Langlitz

Yes. Interest and confidence are compatible because you need the desire to continue building confidence.

Wright

Is confidence genetic—either you have it or you don't?

Langlitz

Experts would argue that there is a genetic proclivity, interest, and leaning toward a particular area in which one develops confidence such as sports or music, however even more so is the desire to work to develop one's confidence. The ten people I interviewed said that the ratio between their genetic ability and the actual application—the hard work—is more like twenty/eighty. A couple of people said forty/sixty, but overwhelmingly it is the application of skills over a considerable period of time.

Wright

How long did it take on the average for those people to feel confident?

Langlitz

Five to ten years for that feeling of mastery. I'd like to add that there are degrees of confidence. For example, feeling as though I could play a solo at Carnegie Hall is different than performing a recital at a local community gathering. Even so, the feeling of confidence would still fall in the five- to ten-year range.

Wright

This may seem like an odd question, but how will I know when I am confident?

Langlitz

It's a great question and to answer I'd like to quote a highly confident, successful CEO of a fifty billion dollar company. When I asked him to define confidence, he said, "It's an inward feeling or conviction that you are fully qualified and able to perform a series of tasks at an exceptional level, as well as anyone and better than most."

Wright

Dr. Langlitz, what is the bottom line for how people become confident and then will you offer practical suggestions for those of us who would like to be more confident in our chosen field?

Langlitz

The bottom line is, people who are confident have achieved that confidence through:

1) hard work and repetition,
2) discipline,
3) focus,
4) guidance from others, and
5) feedback from others.

Another characteristic of confident people, while not required, is their exposure to a confident role model during their formative years.

Wright

What do you mean "exposed" to a confident role model in their formative years?

Langlitz

A child can observe a parent or significant person who is confident at a particular skill, and can learn vicariously through that observation. For example, let's say a child goes with her parent each time the parent purchases a new car, about every three years. Or the child watches the parent regularly resolve conflict in a proactive manner with a neighbor or family member. The child can learn negotiating skills while watching those interactions. Of course ultimately, the child needs to apply the skills himself or herself.

Wright

And again, what are the practical skills I can begin to apply to build my confidence?

Langlitz

There are seven steps:

1. Identify a specific area of your life and possess the desire to build confidence in that area. Others can inspire you, but you have to be willing to do the work, design the plan, and be persistent. There must be a commitment, an investment, and a sacrifice. This applies to all chosen areas whether it is in relationships, a sport, politics, music, business, or religion. Keep in mind, the key is to focus on one skill. It would be very difficult to build more than one area of confidence at once. In time you can move to a second area of desired confidence but be razor-focused with one area of confidence. Several people said you have to love your desired area of confidence in order to master it.

2. *Study and become a scholar or "expert" on your desired area of confidence.* Specifically, surround yourself with role models; talk with people whom you deem confident, form networks with other people who have more experience in your area of confidence. Read books on the subject. Look for patterns, trends, and similar ideas in what they suggest or in what you read about confidence. You will see the overlap. Notice the practical steps they take to achieve that confidence.

3. *Write down your goal and be specific.* For example, you may want to become so confident in giving presentations that you can move away from the podium and engage the audience and have fun. Or perhaps you want to field every ground ball that comes to you and throw the person out at first base. You may want to cook meals for dinner parties where the guests are satisfied to the extent of asking for your help at their dinner parties and requesting recipes.

4. *Visualize yourself as confident.* When you are in quiet moments such as in the shower or when you can concentrate, see yourself confident in your chosen area. Visualize yourself composed, relaxed, and exuding a high level of confidence. As simple as this seems, there are powerful consequences to practicing visualization.

5. *Write down a plan to gain confidence.* Segment your plan into achievable, incremental steps. For example, before I give a presentation, I write down an outline of what I'm going to speak about. Second, I hone my major point and secondary points. Next, I research content areas for my presentation along with pertinent examples to support my points. I rewrite the outline several times before it looks right. Last, I practice and practice and practice until I feel that I "own it."

6. *Find a mentor or coach.* Identify someone who can give you feedback on your chosen area of confidence. Plan to have him/her observe you and give you feedback. Make certain you are very clear on your expectations. A colleague of mine wanted to ensure she was getting her point across clearly during meetings. She asked a peer, whom she considered an excellent communicator, to watch her during

particular meetings and provide feedback. She asked the person to observe her tone of voice, her gestures and to note if her points were illustrated with excellent examples. After six months, her colleagues inquired what she was doing differently, because it was obvious she had improved her communication abilities.

Another friend of mine wanted to build his confidence in his demeanor through the way he walked, specifically his posture and his dress. He researched business fashion and the way business schools taught etiquette. He asked for feedback from a business consultant who helped him achieve his goal of building self-confidence. People began noticing him at his company. Within a year, he was promoted and now teaches basic confidence skills.

7. Practice and consistently apply your skills. This is where the eighty percent comes in. There are no shortcuts—no instantaneous results. Practice, trial-and-error, re-adjusting your course, and persistence will give you the confidence you are seeking. The payoff is tremendous.

Wright

Dr. Langlitz, that sounds doable and motivating. I'm curious though, even when I'm confident can I lose it?

Langlitz

Interesting question. The Olympic gold medal winner I interviewed told me an enlightening story about himself. He said that while he was training for the Olympics, the coach brought in a younger, less seasoned high school team so that they could practice. During an informal competition, one of the high school swimmers beat the Olympian at his best stroke. The Olympic gold medal winner told me that the experience really shook him. It knocked him off balance for a period of time. However, in his current wisdom, he calls losing your confidence, "temporary negative evidence." Isn't that an encouraging attitude!

The solution is to go back to the fundamentals of how you initially gained confidence. For the Olympian, he went back to his basic skills and practiced with more focus.

I do think we can be tipped off-balance for a number of reasons, such as the occurrence of a family illness, getting criticism from someone, or being preoccupied. The remedy is to go back to the basics and refocus.

Wright

What are the tangible rewards of confidence that people reading this book can gain? How would they feel, change, or be different?

Langlitz

Most people who are confident in their chosen fields express a strong sense of purpose or sense that they are making a difference in society and in their families. People also say they believe they're expressing a life goal or mission when they exude confidence in a chosen area. Some people feel happier when they are noticed and rewarded through accolades or positive feedback from others; some enjoy a tremendous sense of wisdom and mastery of a skill or field. Yet others have a quiet sense of intrinsic motivation or self-satisfaction.

Wright

Dr. Langlitz, thank you for an interesting conversation. Do you have any final thoughts for our readers?

Langlitz

I truly believe that you can strengthen and build your confidence regardless of upbringing, background, or past. Today is a great time to begin! Have faith in yourself, extend yourself, persevere, and practice and, over time, your confidence will increase. And that is a tremendously gratifying feeling; no one can ever take it away from you.

Wright

Thank you again, Dr. Langlitz. Today we have been speaking with Dr. Susan Langlitz, who specializes in interpersonal communication and confidence building. You can read more about practical ideas and strategies on how to build confidence in her book, *Have Confidence, Will Travel.*

About The Author

Susan Langlitz, Ph.D., is President of SL Associates, Inc., a professional speaking and training firm specializing in workplace communication. She has worked with hundreds of companies representing a multitude of industries including: finance, technology, communications, insurance, healthcare, hospitality, travel, government, associations, and academia. Dr. Langlitz conveys wisdom, knowledge, practical ideas, and humor while incorporating audience interaction into all her presentations.

Prior to starting her business in 1997, Dr. Langlitz held management and director positions in both profit and non-profit organizations. Susan is a former CareerTrack trainer, corporate manager, association director, and professor. She taught at Ithaca College in New York and at the University of Maryland. Her practical business experience and strong academic background make for a rare, desirable blend in today's complex business world.

Dr. Langlitz has been published in the *L.A. Times, Chicago Tribune, Seattle Times, Newsday, Philadelphia Inquirer, Miami Herald, Detroit Press* and the *Baltimore Sun,* and has been quoted in the *Journal of Training and Development.* She has made several media appearances including radio and television.

Susan holds a Ph.D. in Human Development from the University of Maryland, an M.A. in Communication Studies from Emerson College and a B.S. in Health Science. She is the author of *EUREKA! Build Communication Confidence and Enhance Work Relationships: Simple Steps and Proven Solutions* and *Have Confidence, Will Travel!*

Susan Langlitz, Ph.D.

P.O. Box 19926

Alexandria, VA 22314

Phone: 703.299.9060

Email: info@slassociatesinc.com

Chapter 15

SANDY K. ALLGEIER, SPHR

THE INTERVIEW

David Wright (Wright)

Today we are talking with Sandy Allgeier. Sandy is a consultant, trainer, and coach whose focus is on assisting organizations to maximize their human assets. She began her consulting practice in early 2000. Previously, with twenty-five years experience as a human resource professional, she directed human resource (HR) functions in a variety of Fortune 500 business settings.

Today she is a faculty member for the Society for Human Resources Management, and instructs HR professionals across North America. Sandy specializes in assisting organizations become better places to work with a focus on building those critical people skills so needed by leaders at all levels. With a practical down-to-earth approach, Sandy openly shares her knowledge, ideas, and personal experiences to benefit her clients.

Sandy, welcome to *Conversations on Success.*

Sandy Allgeier (Allgeier)

Thank you David!

Wright

As a Human Resource Specialist with more than thirty years experience, you have observed all kinds of organizational situations. Can you describe what success looks like when it is clearly there?

Allgeier

Let me start by saying that from my experience, the typical business model, or traditional way of looking at things, is that when you have profits, you have success. What I have learned though, is that organizations with leaders who focus on supporting and equipping their employees to achieve the results will achieve *lasting* success. So, I think that it is a little bit misleading to only look at the absolute bottom line. If you dig a little deeper, sustainable success comes from truly focusing on those people in the organization—the employees—who are going to create the success. The employees are the ones who impact the customer and the customer drives the organization's success.

The best example I can provide is with one of my current clients. Elmcroft Assisted Living is a business that provides homes, care, and services to senior adults who need help with daily living functions, but who are not in need of skilled nursing care. Elmcroft is a privately held organization and exemplifies what I mean about focusing first on the employees, who will then deliver the type of service the customer needs. The leaders of this organization have made a decision to focus first on their employees, whom they call associates.

They clearly believe that they will be the best in their industry by creating the best possible work environment for their associates, who will then in turn create the best living environment for their assisted living residents.

The Elmcroft leadership team puts its money where its mouth is too. They not only measure sales and profits, they closely monitor and measure employee engagement and employee retention. Managers are rewarded on employee-centered issues and concerns as a **first** measure of success, not just some generalized afterthought.

At Elmcroft, leadership discussions center on the values of patience, kindness, humility, respectfulness, selflessness, forgiveness, honesty, and commitment, which results in service and sacrifice. Managers and front line employees are invited to stay with the organization when they deliver results based on those values. They are also invited to leave if they cannot. Now, don't misunderstand—

the leaders of this organization are not totally philanthropic in their approach. They expect to make a profit and they are delivering on that expectation. The difference is in the way they approach it.

I believe their approach ensures long-term success. And, what is very interesting to me is this: in their business, the relationship between the employees and the senior adults they care for is the greatest determinant for customer satisfaction. In that industry, facilities are very similar from competitor to competitor. The services and food options are very similar from one provider to another. The pricing is nearly identical. What makes the difference? The difference is how the customer feels about the quality of care they receive on a daily basis!

Wright

You specialize in helping organizations maximize their human assets. What is the most important lesson you have learned about organizations and employee effectiveness?

Allgeier

We've all heard this about buying a piece of property—"location, location, location." From my experience working in organizations, I think it is really basically as simple as, "leadership, leadership, leadership." Let me explain a little bit more about what I mean about that. There are those who are leaders as a result of the position they are in—positions of authority. And then there are those who are leaders as a result of the impact they have, regardless of position.

It has really been a wonderful treat for me to observe leaders through the years. Those who stand out are leaders who clearly have a vision—a big dream about what the organization's future can be. Their impact seems to come as a result of talking frequently and openly about that dream, as well as engaging employees who can see themselves as a part of that vision or dream. These leaders who share their dreams are better equipped for success and effectiveness.

Secondly, when you combine that with leaders who are truly honest, who have unquestionable integrity—including being willing to share good news as well as bad news—employees learn to trust those leaders. Leaders who are big dreamers yet honest, able to maintain a sense of humor, able to laugh at themselves and have fun, find themselves more often able to gain the commitment of the employees of the organization. And, when it is time to say, "Let's go take that hill," they have employees willing to do whatever it takes to get it done.

Several years ago, for example, I had an opportunity to work in a large financial services organization that was being acquired by an even larger Dutch firm. I was working as a leader in Human Resources, supporting the business unit president. The acquiring organization was analyzing the business to determine how it would consolidate divisions. Basically, several thousand employees in this business unit didn't know whether jobs would remain in Louisville, Kentucky, under current leadership, or if the acquiring company would choose to base the business out of Baltimore, Maryland, where it already had its divisional offices. This was, as you can imagine, a time of high anxiety for employees, with insecurity creeping into the minds of everyone.

Bob, our leader at the time, told me that he believed one thing, "People need to know whatever we can tell them, even if it isn't good news." He clearly believed that we needed to keep our employees totally informed and make sure they had confidence that leadership was being 100 percent honest during this difficult time. He told me, "We must be extremely proactive in communications, and even if we don't have anything to tell them, we need to tell them that." He was the head of one business unit in an organization of several large and diversified financial services business units.

There was no real news on the status of the acquisition and transition plans coming from the corporate offices of our entire company, so Bob began having conversations in the lobby of our divisional headquarters building, calling them "lobby talks." Basically, once every seven days or so, he would go down to the lobby level of this large atrium-style building. He would turn the lavalière microphone on and update the employee population on what was going on with the acquisition transition process.

Many people would crowd into the lobby, some would hang out on the staircases—anywhere people could squeeze in—just to hear a word about what was happening. He would tell them good and bad, such as, "Here are the things that are going in our favor," and, "Here are the areas where I do not know whether or not we will achieve our goal in having this business located here," and, "I am just very, very committed to keeping you updated."

This was so interesting because nowhere else in that large organization did any other leader or Business Unit president take that type of role in communicating to the employee population—only Bob.

These lobby talks over time became known as "Bobby in the Lobby." Eventually, employees from other business divisions in the company would attend those lobby talks—even though they needed to travel to our location—just to hear an update about the acquisition. Ultimately, the decision was made to run the business from Baltimore and not Louisville. Naturally, that was a huge disappointment for all of us at the Louisville location because we knew that most jobs would be eliminated. And, since there was already a business unit president in Baltimore, Bob was advised that his services were no longer needed in the organization.

Here is the fascinating end of the story. As is typical when finalizing the merger or acquisition process of a publicly traded company, a final shareholders' meeting was held to formalize the final process. Word started circulating within the organization that all of our business unit employees were planning on attending the meeting. Now, as shareholders, of course they were invited. However, it was highly unusual for employees to attend.

At the published time of this meeting, about eight hundred employees from our business unit headquarters building walked across the street, crowded into the ballroom of a large hotel, to be in attendance at this meeting. As was also the standard process, each business unit president of the company being acquired was formally introduced to the shareholders attending. When Bob was introduced, the entire employee population in attendance gave him a standing ovation that lasted about ten minutes. That was an amazing testimony to honesty and integrity—and how it impacts people in the most amazing way. Even in the most challenging and difficult circumstances, leaders can gain the commitment of employees by being honest and open. And, by the way, our business results during this time of intense difficulty actually improved—we did not experience the typical employee turnover you expect to see in these uncertain times.

Wright

You also do quite a bit of work with the Society for Human Resources Management as a faculty member and instructor. What is your approach to helping HR professionals become successful?

Allgeier

Unfortunately, human resources management is not always considered to be the most highly valued function within an organization. There are some very well intentioned HR professionals who alienate themselves by becoming the "HR police force." In all reality I believe that the HR function has the potential of having more impact on organizational results than any other functional area. Why? Because again, it is through effective employee engagement and the resulting performance that long-term organizational success is achieved. And, the HR function can have the greatest impact on employee engagement *when* it is performing effectively.

While I have had the opportunity to teach HR functional knowledge and skills, I think my greater impact has been on helping HR professionals build stronger interpersonal influence and to increase effectiveness as a result. HR professionals can often get hung up on "the rules" or the "the policies" and that is sometimes legitimate. However, HR professionals who are able to become trusted internal advisors—not the HR police force—clearly have greater impact in their organizations. So, through "Interpersonal Influence Workshops" and one-on-one coaching, I've had the chance to help many HR professionals make a powerful difference in their organizations.

I also teach HR professionals how to be strong business partners. Basically that means it is important to get to know the critical issues of the organization—really understand what makes that business or organization tick—and then be able to make the connection between the business strategies and HR strategies.

Wright

You know, most of us who have been in the business world for a while have had experiences with HR professionals and it is not always viewed as being successful or even pleasant. As an HR professional yourself, what do you believe equates to success for the human resource profession?

Allgeier

It is definitely *not* the HR police force! I do think that success for HR professionals means you must possess personal credibility. To do that, you must be a respected expert in your field—you must know the business of HR management—so that you can provide value-added knowledge and services to both management and non-management within the organization. You must also establish personal credibility in this way.

You also must be willing to get your hands dirty. The best HR professionals are willing to leave their "safe" environment and get out and work with the people of the organization. So, for example if your business is insurance sales, you are working occasionally with the insurance sales person in order to understand how insurance sales works and its challenges. If you are in the restaurant business, you are putting on a uniform and working in that restaurant in order to understand what that is really like.

When I worked in the Assistant Living business, I was the senior vice president of Human Resources. I needed to understand what an employee goes through, for example, during the process of trying to bathe an elderly and frail adult, especially someone with Alzheimer's disease. That was not particularly an easy thing for me to experience, but very necessary in order to be effective and credible in that organization.

Additionally, HR professionals must be perceived as beyond reproach professionally, morally, and ethically. This can be tough—to be viewed as very approachable and yet at the same time totally objective and somewhat "separated" from their organizational peers so that there is no risk of being seen as overly aligned with management or non-management. Ultimately, this can lead to HR professionals leading a bit of a lonely existence. HR professionals really need to be involved in professional HR organizations like the Society for Human Resource Management (SHRM) so they can have friends and healthy working relationships without having to worry about being beyond reproach.

HR professionals also must have a very strong passion for understanding and supporting the organization's cause. Whatever it is that the organization does, HR professionals must be able to clearly connect with the employees' impact on the results of that business and then get passionate about supporting the employee process for impacting results.

Last, but definitely not least, HR professionals must be able to quantify the financial impact on any HR initiative for the business. It took me quite some time to develop that understanding and skill. For example, if you are complaining to line management that turnover in the organization is a problem, you must be able to show your organizational leaders—especially the financial leadership—the devastating financial impact of turnover on the bottom line. I think

HR people traditionally struggle in that area because some of these areas are very difficult to quantify. But there are some excellent books and materials available to assist HR professionals speak in dollars and cents terms to gain their leadership's support for employee related initiatives.

Wright

You often work with leaders at all levels of organizations to help them become more successful. What have you found are the most common challenges or problems this group has in creating personal success?

Allgeier

I have had the opportunity to coach several executives and leaders. I have found that their problems are rarely (if ever) in the technical or functional capacity of performing their jobs. Most leaders or managers are highly functionally competent. If I am dealing with marketing people, they know marketing, if they are finance people, they know finance, and so on. It is most common that their challenges are in dealing effectively with the "other players in the game." Some struggle with peers, and don't have a clue that a peer can kill a career through their working to undermine another peer.

Some struggle with bosses, never learning how to manage upward effectively and often failing to communicate their own needs and wants, expecting bosses to read their minds. Many struggle with subordinates and creating effective teams.

I think this all boils down to one fairly simple issue. It is simple in terms of understanding; it is **not** simple in terms of application. People struggle with telling their employees that there is a problem and how it needs to be fixed. It is extremely difficult to confront and deliver basic feedback. This is the most common challenge I have seen and derails more management careers than any other single factor. I have laughingly said that this fact has provided me a fine career in HR management for thirty years now! People struggle with giving other people feedback, especially when that feedback may be perceived as being a bit critical. However, the ability to deliver feedback and help someone work through a problem is a *skill*—it can be learned! When I see managers and leaders build that skill, it then builds their confidence in a great way.

Wright

Let's talk a little about your personal story. You have been able to steadily advance your career in corporate America and now you have a successful business you created from scratch as a consultant, trainer, speaker, and coach. Tell us how this happened and why you think you have been so successful?

Allgeier

I really didn't start out with the goal to become a human resources professional. I did see an opportunity to advance my career at a time when I was frankly desperate for increasing my income and personal stability. I was a single mom of two-year-old twins at the age of twenty-five. I knew that I had to increase my income and my future earnings. Looking back on it, I now realize that I was very quick to volunteer for additional work, additional responsibility, and a chance to learn new skills. I made a decision to try to get myself involved in task forces, committees, and projects that went well beyond my level of knowledge and responsibility at the time.

For example, I remember being asked to lead a project team that was putting together a plan for expanding a Mexican quick service restaurant into new markets. I was exposed to real estate site selection, construction processes, marketing initiatives, and many other aspects of growing a business when there is no brand recognition in place. This had little to do with my Human Resources management role, but it gave me invaluable knowledge about growing a business. I had a role in HR administration at that time, and how in the world I ended up with that responsibility I don't know. However, that work propelled my career at a much faster pace.

I know that I had some outstanding bosses and mentors—amazing people who invested in me, saw potential in me, and who gave me tremendous opportunities. This often came in the form of being willing to give me assignments with fairly high exposure. I probably should not have been presenting to the chairman of the board in certain cases, but they allowed me to do that.

When I had the opportunity to manage others, I have been absolutely blessed with an ability to surround myself with the most talented people imaginable. It is really interesting that I have been able to find people who want to work with me to achieve my vision for various organizations. Today, some of my dearest friends are people who have reported to me through the years. I feel good about maintaining the relationships through different phases.

I also have never stopped being a student. I read about leaders—learning from the lessons others leave us. After consulting managers and leaders for years, I worked very hard at being the very best possible leader I could become. I know I wasn't always successful. I made some bad choices along the way, but I think I was able to learn from them.

Finally, I feel fortunate that I realized it was time to say, "enough is enough." I had achieved far more than I had ever dreamed in my corporate life. As a senior vice president, I realized the final step of my life's career dream. However, I also realized that I needed to make a change for my life to remain meaningful for me. I was able to realize that I was not really enjoying this as much as I once had, and then made a decision to go out on my own, focusing on helping people and organizations develop their human assets.

Wright

You also have achieved success as a leader and manager of others. Clearly you advise and consult organizational leaders in this area. How have your personal experiences as a leader and manager impacted your ability to give solid direction and counsel now?

Allgeier

I really don't think I could have the impact I have now as a consultant or coach without having had direct line management experience. It concerns me that there is a trend that HR professionals are often not experienced managers and leaders themselves. I talk about this quite a lot in the training sessions I do for HR professionals. When the HR "experts" are coaching and consulting line management on issues they have never personally faced, I have real concerns about the quality of their advice and the credibility they possess. I think credibility is best built from doing it, and also making a few mistakes while you are doing it so that you learn what *not* to do. I believe that I learned first hand what mattered most to people, what worked in management, and what does not work. It's this experience and my background in HR that allows me to really impact others now.

Wright

You've had some very insightful or impactful role models throughout your career. Can you summarize the most significant lessons and experiences you have learned through these individuals?

Allgeier

An early lesson came when I was in my twenties. I was reporting to an individual who saw something in my skills and capabilities that I had no clue were there. This was back when I was really struggling to survive—the young single mom. He insisted I develop a fully rounded business understanding, so he supported that by sending me through a multitude of training experiences like finance for non-financial management, marketing for non-marketing professionals, and basically insisted I learn business in all functional business aspects. I realize now that it was amazingly helpful to me.

Then, when transitioning away from this boss, my new manager taught me that differing management styles should be expected and my success would be greatly increased if I could quickly learn to work effectively with those differing styles. This particular boss who taught me this also helped me see I was becoming very one-dimensional in my life—I was totally focused on career, career, career. He was very insistent that I take a step back, take a look at my *total* life, and he really helped me unwind.

I had another boss who was a female professional who was the absolute model of total professionalism. She taught me a lot about image and the fact that details really do matter. She also taught me a great deal about how to gain approval and how to get agreement on ideas and initiatives through effective one-on-one negotiation. And, of course, I mentioned earlier that even when he wasn't involved in a lobby talk, Bob modeled total honesty, integrity, and open communications.

I had another boss who was dynamic, charismatic, and an amazing communicator, but sometimes lacked commitment to people when the pressure was applied. The tough lesson there is that character is not in the *style* someone possesses, it is in the consistent delivery of doing the right thing.

Wright

I am sure you had to work hard, long hours at times to achieve success. How would you advise younger or lesser-experienced individuals about balancing work and the rest of their lives? Did you ever lose your balance and if so, how do you get the balance back?

Allgeier

I think it is a reality that achievement and success really come more from hard work than superior talent or abilities. With basic talent and intellect, hard work is what pushes success for most people.

I did lose balance on occasion. It happened once when I was promoted into a position with much greater responsibility than I had ever experienced. I was in an organization that was going through massive growth. I was also hiring and managing a staff of young, eager people who needed a great deal of my time and attention. I was working unbelievably long hours and at the same time I was married, I had four teenagers at home, and was traveling frequently. I would love to be able to say that I handled it beautifully, but I absolutely did not! Unfortunately, looking back on it, I think I paid a high price because those four teenagers at home didn't have a lot of my attention at that time. Thank goodness they had the attention of my husband, and he was quite capable with them.

In terms of advice to people who are lesser experienced and maybe facing these types of conflicting priorities, I would advise them to develop a clear picture of their own goals. Then, bring the family into the picture. Have them clearly share in and contribute to the family's goals. Get everyone on board. Make a decision—*together*—about what you are and are not willing to sacrifice to achieve those goals. Identify the limits you are willing to set together. And, identify how you will handle it when it gets to be more than you jointly bargained for.

I clearly remember driving down the highway one day, realizing that I had no idea whether I was going to work, or if I was leaving work and heading back home! My work/home-life balance had been lost for some time and it took that driving experience for me to realize it. That was *not* the way to do it!

Wright

I used to go to conferences where they would have all these great business meetings and spouse programs. They would have these programs on how to balance home and career, I am thinking, "You idiots, that is also a male problem! This is the one I want to go to and let my wife go to listen on the one about how to sell widgets. I want to know why my children hate my guts!"

Allgeier

I completely understand.

Wright

Considering your accomplishments, which ones are you most proud of. If you could someday be remembered for something, what would it be?

Allgeier

Professionally, I think I probably am most proud of the fact that I had the wonderful gift and opportunity to manage and lead unbelievably talented professionals. That experience is equipping me with greater credibility in my consulting practice today. I am so proud of those people whom I have had a chance to work with, and I feel very strongly about that.

On the personal side, I am extremely proud of my marriage and my entire family. I am a person of very strong faith, and that faith guides me every single day. Sometimes I have to just pinch myself and ask, "How did I become so fortunate and so blessed?" I think a lot of my blessings have come from God and from no particular action of my own. I think He has a plan here to use me somehow, but I'm not real sure I always know what it is.

Then, in terms of what I would like to be remembered for—I just want to be remembered as someone who worked really hard to help others to become the best that they can possibly be.

Wright

Be nice to put that on your tombstone wouldn't it?

Allgeier

It really, really, really would, I genuinely mean that.

Wright

What a great conversation! I sure appreciate your taking all this time with me today to answer these questions, and I think our readers are going to learn quite a bit, just as I have from our conversation.

Allegier

Thank you. It was a pleasure to talk with you.

Wright

Today we have been talking with Sandy Allegier. She specializes in assisting organizations become better places to work, with a focus on building those critical people skills so needed by leaders at all levels. If you have listened to this entire program or if you have read this chapter, I think she knows what she is talking about.

Thank you so much, Sandy, for being with us today on *Conversations on Success*.

About The Author

Sandy Allgeier is a consultant, trainer, and coach who assists organizations maximize employee capabilities. Sandy began her consulting practice in 2000, with more than twenty-five years of human resource management experience in various business settings. Sandy specializes in assisting organizations increase effectiveness, with a focus on building those critical "people skills" needed by leaders at all levels. With a practical, down-to-earth approach, Sandy shares her knowledge, ideas, and personal experiences to benefit her clients.

Sandra K. Allgeier, SPHR

16121 Plum Creek Trail

Louisville, KY 40299

502-266-0159

www.Sandy@SandyAllgeier.com

Chapter 16

ANDRE FLAX

THE INTERVIEW

David Wright (Wright)

Today we are talking with Andre Flax. Andre brings over seventeen years of face-to-face direct selling. His experience in the direct sales industry has been the motivating force behind his desire to help others become more successful in sales and in their life in general. Andre has been certified in clinical hypnotherapy and is currently pursuing his DCH at American Pacific University.

A student of Neuro Linguistic Programming, Andre is committed to helping people increase their effectiveness in the areas of sales and personal development. He is a member of The American of Society of Training Directors, The American Seminars Leader Association, The National Speakers Association, and International Speakers Network. Andre, welcome to *Conversations on Success*.

Andre Flax (Flax)

Thank you David—thanks for having me!

Wright

You speak about the "seven fundamental principles for achieving success." Would you tell our readers what they are?

Flax

Certainly. The seven principles for success are:

1. Determine what you want.
2. Evaluate what you want against your deepest values.
3. Determine what resources, skills, and knowledge you would need to achieve what you want.
4. Decide how you are going achieve what you want.
5. Be committed to doing the daily, weekly, and monthly disciplines necessary for achieving success.
6. Focus on the outcome you expect when achieving what you want.
7. Consistently re-enforce what you positively believe about yourself and about having what you want.

Wright

Would you give us a brief explanation of the principles?

Flax

The first principle is to determine what you want. Determining what you want requires a little more than writing down a wish list of things you believe will make you happy. In fact if people really looked deep inside themselves, they would find that their deepest desires are directly tied to who they really want to become. What I mean by this is that there is a direct correlation between the things a person wants and their self-image. Our wants are representative of what we think we should or should not have.

Evaluating what you want against your deepest values and beliefs is the second principle. I think this is a critical step in achieving success in life. Most of things people want in life will come in direct conflict with their values and beliefs, and ultimately inhibit the process for having success.

Let me give you an example, most people want to be physically fit and in shape, however most people don't value the process of physical conditioning enough to stay the course on becoming physically fit. So it is important for people to evaluate what they want in comparison with their deepest values and beliefs; otherwise, they will be inhibited from experiencing maximum success in achieving their goals.

The Third principle is to determine what resources, skills, and talent(s) would be needed to achieve what you want. True success is a process; therefore, in order to maximize the level of success to be achieved, people need to know what is required.

The resources are important because sometimes we want to achieve certain things that we may not have the necessary resources for. So first we need to locate or identify what resources we would need in order to help us attain the success we want.

Having the skills and talents needed to achieve a certain goal are also key components in having success. We don't hear much about the need for attaining specialized skills or talent in success material today. However, I think this is why so many people become discouraged about attaining success. Having a positive attitude alone is not enough to guarantee success; you must acquire whatever skills necessary to achieve the success desired.

Principle number four is to decide a strategy for attainting what you want. You must decide how you are going to get where you want to go or how you are going to acquire what you want. This principle is important because it sets in motion your plan of action to achieving what you want. Your strategy is analogous to a vehicle you use to travel from one place to another. You will utilize that vehicle as long as it serves you in getting to where you want to go. If at some point it is no longer useful, you would look to trade it for a newer model. That "vehicle" could represent your current job, it could be deciding to leave your current job and start a business of your own, it could be becoming more involved with volunteer work, or working for a nonprofit, but you must decide on the vehicle. Without the proper vehicle to transport you from were you are to were you want to be, it is almost senseless for you to even consider becoming successful because you need that channel to get you from point A to point B.

The fifth principle is being committed to the daily, weekly, and monthly disciplines to achieving success. This is the fuel needed to move you to success. I believe success is a progressive process, therefore you need to be committed to doing the daily, weekly, and monthly discipline necessary to bring about the success you are looking for. The level of required discipline will differ for each person depending on the goal sought. However, no matter what the goal or desired outcome, the process of discipline cannot be ignored.

Having focus or being totally fixated on the reward(s) of achieving success is principle number six. Having the ability to be so engrossed in the outcome that it gives you your daily motivation will be key to the level of success you will experience. What I mean by this is when we get good at visualizing the desired outcome before it actually happens; we increase the likelihood of achieving it. At the subconscious level we are truly bringing what we want closer and closer each day we visualize it.

The seventh principle is to reinforce the positive beliefs you have about yourself and what you should have in life. This is important because success is a progressive process and a lot of times when challenges come—and they will come—what will have a major effect on how you respond to these challenges will be your belief about yourself and your belief about what you should have in life. If your beliefs are not in line with achieving your highest level of success, you will not succeed.

Wright

How have these principles impacted your life and how have they created success?

Flax

Over the last ten years these principles have been instrumental in my success as a sales manager, trainer, and coach. In my line of work, I am involved with sales people on a daily basis. I have been fortunate to witness the impact these principles have made on the sales people I have trained and coached. As a sales manager, I had to challenge myself to not only reach company sales objectives in markets that were not the most ideal for the products we represented, but to find a way to exceed it. Each year my sales team exceeded company objectives and finished number one. The seven principles I mentioned were directly responsible for our success.

I grew up in a very tough environment in the city of Camden, New Jersey. Everything in my environment suggested that trying to attain success or even better my situation wasn't possible, and it was because of these seven principles that I apply to my life that I was able to create a different life for myself.

At the age of fourteen I got my first job cleaning streets to help support myself. While all my friends were out hanging in the streets playing ball, I was busy working on my future. I knew that if I was going to ever realize any significant change in my life, I needed to do something about it. I was motivated not by the reality of my present situation, I was motivated primarily by the life I saw on television and in movies. I said to myself that there had to be a life outside the life I was living, and so, guided by the seven principles, I began focusing on my education in high school, working throughout high school, and then finding the resources to go to college and to graduate from college.

Following the seven principles gave me the belief that if I just applied myself, believed in what I was doing, and focused on the outcome I wanted, I could achieve success. It was not long before I started seeing more and more success in different areas of my life and as a result I wanted to share these success principles with others.

Wright

In your success talks you state that the level of a person's success is directly impacted by their ability to imagine the desired outcome and pursue it. Would you tell our readers what you mean?

Flax

Imagination is a key component if achieving success. If you look at most successful people today such as Bill Gates, Oprah Winfrey, Bill Cosby, Tiger Woods, Michael Jordan, and Walt Disney, what they all have in common is their ability to imagine the impossible as possible. Imagination is the ability to create with the mind—the goals and outcomes we wish to have. The level of success we attain in life will be directly correlated to our ability to create it in our mind.

Principle number six is all about utilizing your imagination to help direct your efforts to achieving success. I believe it is important that a person who seeks success be able to continually imagine the possibilities and results they desire. You see, the subconscious mind is like a robot and the programs that run the subconscious mind are the thoughts and ideas you feed it through your conscious mind. The more you feed your subconscious with positive possibilities and results, the greater the level of success you will experience. The subconscious mind does not know the difference between a positive or negative thought. The subconscious mind simply executes the instructions fed to it on a continuous basis.

The famous quote by James Allen, "As a man thinks, so is he," is true. We become what we think about or imagine being. So I think it is important for anyone who is seeking success develop a strong imagination and use their imagination to vividly seek want they want and pursue it.

Wright

As a hypnotherapist and a student of Neuro Linguistic Programming, what impact do you think the level of rapport between the conscious and subconscious mind has on a person's success?

Flax

As I mentioned earlier, the subconscious mind is like a robot and your conscious mind acts as the programmer. Together they produce your current state of mind, actions and reactions, as well as your beliefs and values. Our memories and our experiences get stored in our subconscious mind; when we need them, the subconscious mind will bring back that information to serve us in whatever capacity we need.

The conscious mind is constantly filtering information that lines up with our values and beliefs, and deleting information that doesn't. So, when we are able to link the conscious mind with the subconscious mind to produce what we want, we will see tremendous results. By consciously focusing on the things we want, and constantly watching our self-talk, we increase the probability of our success. Remember, what we communicate to ourselves internally actually gets stored in our subconscious mind. Therefore our behavior and our responses are indicative of what we communicate internally to ourselves. The key then is to make sure that the conscious and subconscious mind are in sync—in rapport—with each other working for the same purpose. Again, if we monitor what we say consciously and watch what we think consciously we will train our subconscious mind to deliver to us the things we want.

Wright

What are some of the ways that a person can increase the level of rapport between the conscious and subconscious mind?

Flax

Pay close attention to your self- talk. Eighty percent of our communication is internal. However, what we communicate to our subconscious is directly related to the information we take in on a conscious level. A recent article on information processing said that we are exposed to over 60,000 bits of information each day. The average person will spend fifteen years of his or her life in front of the television. The information you accept and process will ultimately impact the level of your success.

Talk positively to your subconscious. This is best done when you are alone. Talk to your subconscious mind as if you were talking to a friend. The more familiar you become with your subconscious mind the greater the rapport you will build with it. When you consciously give positive suggestions to your subconscious mind you increase the positive experience you have in life. So again, I think it is important to focus on the positive outcomes of what you want versus allowing yourself to get caught up into the negative outcome.

Another way to build rapport is to release negative emotions. Anytime you are seeking to achieve something great in life you will face disappointments. With disappointment come negative emotions. Your ability to quickly release negative emotions will have a major impact on your future success. Remember, the subconscious mind can't determine the difference between positive or negative emotions. So if you communicate to your subconscious mind to store this emotion through repetitive obsessing, whenever you face a disappointment, the stored emotion will materialize to hold you back from moving forward.

Wright

How does a person's belief affect the level of success they can achieve?

Flax

Beliefs are important. I remember hearing motivational speaker Anthony Robbins say that a belief is a feeling of certainty. Beliefs are ideas that when backed up with references of experience gives a feeling of certainty. So, if you have an idea and you have enough references to support the idea it can easily become a belief. Beliefs are important to our level of achievement. I think it is important for people who want to achieve great success to evaluate and judge their beliefs and to make sure that their beliefs are guiding them into the direction of achieving success.

Sometimes we don't believe we can achieve greatness because we believe our success is limited because of our ethnicity, education, age, or size. These beliefs are a hindrance to our achieving great success. In order to achieve greatness we must evaluate our beliefs.

There is a biblical scripture that says belief without action is really not belief ("...faith without works is dead"—James 2:20). If a man says he has belief in something and you don't see the actions behind the belief, his faith or belief is not real. Our faith or beliefs will produce after its kind. If we say we have faith and we believe in a particular thing then our actions are going to be indicative of our beliefs. So whether it is a good belief or a negative belief, our actions will follow. If you have a negative belief about yourself it is going to limit your level success.

Wright

What effect does internal and external communication have on a person's success?

Flax

Our outward communication is a reflection of our internal communication. In certain situation you might not like a person just by the way he or she looks at you and you start an internal dialogue about his or her hair, or size, or the way he or she speaks. That information gets communicated to our subconscious and is translated into our actions. We may think the person does not really know what we are thinking but our body language will communicate exactly how we really feel. How we communicate with others is important to our overall success.

There is a Bible verse that says, "Do unto others as you would have them do unto you" (Matthew 7:12). How you want others to treat you is how you should treat them. How you want someone to speak to you is the same way you should speak to them. So, I think it is important that our internal dialogue matches up with what we want as well as our external dialogue such as how we talk to people. If you want to receive positive feedback you have to give positive feedback, if you communicate negatively to yourself, you are going to produce negative behavior.

Simply put, how we communicate to others and to ourselves will have a major impact on the level of success we experience.

Wright

Explain what you mean when you say that success is in the doing not the trying.

Flax

I usually give an example in some of the seminars that I do. I ask a person to come up and I say I am going to put a pen in your left hand and with your right hand I want you to try to take the pen out of you left hand. What I see people do every time is grab the pen. I then ask, "Did you pass or fail the test?" They always answer, "Yes." I then explain that the task was to *try* to grab the pen and not to grab the pen. You see the word "try" in our language today is another way of saying not to do it. If I had said to the person, "Take the pen out of your left hand with your right hand," he or she would have just reached over and taken the pen; but I said to *try* to take the pen. Try doesn't necessarily mean to take action it means you might or might not take action—it doesn't say actually to do it. I think success is *doing*. I hear people say, "Well I tried it," or "I'm trying." What are you trying? Either you are *doing* it or your *not doing* it. Doing and trying are two separate things. Remember, success is progressive, therefore it is always in motion.

I remember a professor in college once said, " Try is a three-letter word for failure." People tend to try all their lives and never achieve anything. Nike came up with an advertising slogan that said "Just Do It" because it is in the doing that we experience great success—it's not in the trying. Imagine if the slogan said "Just Try It." That slogan doesn't have the same impact as "Just Do It." Doing means that there is a resolve to complete or finish the task or to achieve the goal.

Wright

What impact does modeling another person's success have on the success of another person?

Flax

One of the components of Neuro Linguistic Programming (NLP) is modeling. Modeling the behavior and beliefs of someone who has achieved great success is key to increasing your potential for achieving success for yourself. Success always leaves clues. Modeling is the ability to copy certain attributes and behaviors of successful people so you can experience that same level of success.

Let me give you an example, Michael Jordan is one of the greatest basketball player in the NBA. If I wanted to attain the level of success Mr. Jordan has I would need to find out what he did to become one of the greatest players in the game of basketball. What were his daily, weekly, and monthly disciplines that contributed to his success? By modeling his actions and beliefs, over time I would acquire the same skills and would experience the same level of success.

Even if you don't understand why the person you are modeling does what they do, by modeling the behavior, mannerisms, speech patterns, and the way they dress you will begin to experience the same level of success as the person you are modeling, so modeling is important.

If you are interested in learning more modeling techniques then I highly recommend NLP training. As a student of NLP, I have received tremendous value from the techniques I've learned and I have grown personally and professionally as a result of NLP. Modeling will definitely have a profound effect of the level of success a person has.

Wright

How did you begin speaking on the power of the subconscious mind? How does your research on the topic help you to achieve success?

Flax

I guess it started for me right after college. My first job out of college as a sales person was working for the university raising capital funds. While being trained in sales, I realized that I wasn't experiencing the level of success I wanted. So I purchased the Brian Tracy *"Psychology of Selling"* tapes and began to study and master the information. This led me deeper into the sciences of the subconscious mind.

From that point on I began reading and listening to everything I could get my hands on about the power of subconscious mind and from there I got involved with NLP. It has made a tremendous impact on my understanding of the subconscious mind. It started way back in my sales days and I guess I would say that Brian Tracy's *"Psychology of Selling"* and Earl Nightingale's *"The Strangest Secret"* audio programs were very instrumental in leading me into the science of personal development through the power of the subconscious mind.

Wright

What advice would you give to a person who has tried positive thinking or motivational outlets and has still not achieved the success they desire?

Flax

I think the key is for most people to ask themselves if they doing more on what they know or "trying" what they know. It sounds like semantics but if we are honest with ourselves we will see that many of us set goals without making the decision that no matter what happens we will stay committed to the completion of that goal or desire. You see, "try" allows you to give up early. It allows you to quit when you enter into a place of unfamiliarity. When something becomes uncomfortable to you, "trying" allows you to get out.

Doing makes you committed, doing says there is no way out; doing says, "I can't look back now, there is no way out and there is no other way off this island. I *have* to do it." So my recommendation is to do more of what you know.

Secondly I would advise people to really consider looking at modeling and finding someone who actually has the success they are looking for and tapping into their behavior and the way they think. I would also strongly recommend getting involved in NLP technologies.

Positive motivational information to me is like vitamins—it is like supplements. The real "meat and potatoes" is to understand the power of the mind and how to utilize it to get what you want. The positive materials, positive affirmation, positive thinking, and all of those things are what I call supplements to enhancing the meat and potatoes—the daily regimen of mental conditioning. Studying the subconscious mind and getting involved with NLP will increase success.

People might say, "Well you know, I tried all that positive thinking stuff." Again, my response to them would be to stop trying and start doing the positive thinking stuff and you will see results. In all the years of I've been involved with sales and personal development, this one thing has proven to be true: people who are committed to doing what it takes to achieve success do succeed. It is not in the trying, it is simply doing. So many people say to me, "What if I fail?" My response is there is no failure. Jim Rohn said, " Failure is in an error in judgment repeated over and over again." He also gave the contrast of failure, "Success is a few simple disciplines practiced daily."

If we want to be successful, it is doing the few simple disciplines practiced daily. Success is in the doing. If you want to fail (an error in judgment repeated over and over) then you have to repeat the same errors over and over. This means you are doing the same things over and over, and expecting a different result with consistency. If people are still finding they are not getting the success they want, get away from "trying" and do more of what you already know, start there.

Wright

What a great conversation! Today we have been talking Andre Flax who has been certified in clinical hypnotherapy and is a student of Neuro Linguistic Programming. He is committed to helping people create effectiveness in not only the areas of sales but in their personal lives as well. Andre, thank you so much being with us today on *Conversations on Success*.

Flax

Okay, have a great day! Thanks David!

About The Author

Andre Flax brings over 17 years of face-to-face direct selling. His experience in the direct sales industry has been the motivating force behind his desire to help others become more successful in sales and their life in general. Andre has been certified in Clinical Hypnotherapy and is currently perusing his DCH at American Pacific University. A student of Neuro-Linguistic Programming, Andre is committed to helping people increase their effectiveness in the area of sales and Personal Development. He is a member of ASTD, ASLA and NSA and the International Speakers Network.

Andre M. Flax

DSL Training & Recruiting

189 Windsong Circle

East Brunswick, New Jersey 08816

Phone: 732.698.0859

Chapter 17

LINDA BARRETT

THE INTERVIEW

David Wright (Wright)

As a professional speaker, Linda Barrett is committed to helping others help themselves by showing them how to creatively conquer their challenges, compete more effectively in rapidly changing arenas, and to remain resourceful in the midst of chaos. Her mission is to share strategies for success so that her clients and audience members can accomplish incomparable results.

Linda, welcome to *Conversations on Success.*

Linda Barrett (Barrett)

Thank you David, I'm honored to be a part of this wonderful project.

Wright

You've devoted your life to the pursuit of success and to serving as a resource to others in their pursuit of success. Where did this devotion begin?

Barrett

It began with my father. When I was a very little girl, my dad was the president of our local Jaycees and a Dale Carnegie trained instructor. He and I have always been very close and because we spent so much time together, he taught me a lot, both with his words and by his example. He instilled in me a deep desire to develop my own potential and he constantly reminded my siblings and me that we could "achieve anything we could conceive *and believe*." Today that serves as the core message for every program I provide, so he planted the seeds very early in my life for who I am today and what I do for a living.

Wright

It sounds like your dad had a significant impact on you. Who are some of the other people who influenced your life and your ideas on success?

Barrett

I grew up in a big, close-knit family, so my biggest influences were my parents, grandparents, and other family members. For our purposes today, let me tell you about some of the ways that both my mother and her father influenced my life and my ideas on success.

My mom has always called me "beautiful," a nickname that I of course love! But, more importantly, she taught me that true beauty is something that shines from within. Because of this, I've always worked very hard to cultivate my character and develop the talents God has blessed me with rather than worrying so much about how I look.

With two older brothers to try and keep up with, I was quite a tomboy growing up and never had much interest in the things that typically appeal to little girls. But when I got to college, I learned to delight in my femininity. My new girlfriends taught me how to apply make-up and fix my hair and how to "accessorize" for success. Learning those things was fun, but thanks to my mom, I never got sucked into the obsession that some girls have with their appearance. To me, the way I look on the outside is analogous to the wrapping on a gift. I do like to make the package look attractive but I don't blow my whole budget on it. I'm far more concerned with ensuring that the gift inside has great value. That is an important success tip that my mom taught me and one that I pass on to the young girls in my life.

Wright

Those young girls are lucky to be in your life, Linda, because that's a timely and relevant message.

Barrett

Thank you for saying that, David. Another way my mom influenced my life began with her mother's gift for "tickling the ivories." My grandmother used to play the piano in our living room and fill the house with the most beautiful sounds I'd ever heard. I wanted to be able to do that too, and my mom made that possible for me. From the time I was a young girl until my senior year of college, my mom spent countless dollars and many selfless hours driving me to and from piano lessons and she never missed a recital. She's always been my most consistent cheerleader! To this day she still supports my interest in playing and my ongoing study of piano.

I feel so fortunate because so many people I've met throughout the years have told me they played piano as a kid and now they wish that they had stuck with it. The fact that I *have* stuck with it is completely due to my mom's encouragement and for that I am extremely grateful. Whether I'm just playing the piano at home for my own enjoyment or for friends at hospitals, churches, nursing homes, or for my audiences, playing is one of the richest sources of joy in my life. Having something you love that much in your life is a success in and of itself, so I'm very grateful for that. There are so many other ways that my mom has been a blessing in my life, I could write a whole book just about her. Maybe one day I will do that but for now, let me move on and tell you a little bit about her father who influenced me significantly.

He was a three-star general in the Marine Corps who was considered "a symbol of peace in the Middle East" in the early '50's. As a young man, he pursued a path to the priesthood but then in 1917, he decided to pursue a more patriotic path and joined the United States Marine Corp. He served in both world wars and earned a chest full of medals for bravery in both.

By the end of the second World War, he was the commander of the Third Marine Division. Then, on August 1, 1948, the Joint Chiefs of Staff handed him a commission to help stop wars in the Holy Land. He was detailed to work with Count Folke Bernadotte, United Nations mediator, and the Count's deputy, Dr. Ralph Bunche. Less than two months after my grandfather arrived in the Middle East, Bernadotte was assassinated and Bunche took charge. During the next five years, my grandfather rushed to more than 100 small and large battles from the towering mountains north of Dan to the burning desert south of Beersheba *and stopped all of them!* What made this remarkable was the fact that as chief of staff of the United Nations Truce Supervision Organization for Palestine, he was not allowed to carry any weapons, yet that didn't stop him from crossing battle lines to put an end to the fighting. That earned him the moniker, *"The Marine Who Stops Wars."* In 1950, Bunche won the Nobel Peace Prize. One of the many questions he was asked was how my grandfather was able to do what he did. Bunche said, "The General's success is directly related to the power of his personality. Both sides know they can depend on his impartiality and honesty. They trust their referee. So, when he tells them to stop fighting, they stop!" Thus, according to Dr. Ralph Bunche, the secret to my grandfather's success was the power of his personality and I think anyone who knew him would agree. Kurt Einstein of *Success* magazine said, "Eighty-seven percent of all people fail, not because of capability but because of personality."

I think there's a lesson for all of us in the power of developing our own personalities. The example my grandfather set taught me about the inextricable link between living with honor and the achievement of success. His example inspired me—and many others—to want to pursue a noble path of service to others.

Another lesson he taught by example is the importance of being lighthearted. He used to say that of all the battles he ever fought, the toughest one was the battle he fought to win the heart of Kady Donahoe, my grandmother. He laid siege to her heart for six long years before she finally said, "Yes!" and he said *that's how he learned the art of peaceful negotiation!*

Wright

How delightful. He sounds like a man I would have enjoyed meeting. Linda, many times in a classroom style setting I ask people to write down the top three people who have influenced their lives the most. Besides your family members, who would you say are the top three people who really influenced you down through the years?

Barrett

Outside of my family, the top three people who influenced me most are Mother Teresa, Leonardo da Vinci, and Bill Cosby. What's interesting is that although these three people have dramatically shaped the course of my life, the only one I ever actually met was Mother Teresa and I think that's a good reminder for all of us. Sociologists tell us that even the most introverted individual among us will influence ten thousand other people during his or her lifetime! Most people aren't aware at all of the impact they're having on the lives of others but in fact, I think we all have a responsibility to raise our consciousness and to make an effort to be positive role models for one another. Mother Teresa was keenly aware of this responsibility and in my opinion, she set a wonderful example for others to follow.

My meeting with her was a very brief encounter when she visited my college campus. I was working in the public relations office at the time so I was able to be very involved in the preparations for her visit. I was already an admirer of hers at that point but became even more interested in her life and her beliefs after meeting her.

There are many things about Mother Teresa I admire and strive to emulate but the main thing is the way that she responded to God's true calling. She had already devoted her life to God as a nun at Loreto but she willingly gave up that comfortable existence when she heard the call from God on September 10, 1946, "to love Him in the distressing disguise of the poorest of the poor." She responded wholeheartedly, with complete devotion and passion, giving all the glory to God. What an inspiration! Just think what our world would be like if more of us responded that way when we hear God's call in our own lives!

Wright

That would change the world as we know it, wouldn't it?

Barrett

Absolutely, and certainly for the better. Leonardo da Vinci's influence on me primarily had to do with an epiphany I had a year or two after we'd studied the life of this Renaissance man. I remember sitting in Sister Susan's Physics class one day. We were watching a film about a scientist who had spent the last ten years of her life in a lab working on some obscure formula for something that I can't even recall. What I do recall very vividly is a choice I made that afternoon that shaped my destiny. I was in the eighth grade and I was interested in many different subjects, sports, and hobbies, so to me the thought of foregoing all of them to pursue any one of them was not at all appealing.

What *was* appealing to me was the approach that da Vinci chose in his life. He actively pursued his potential, not in just one area of his life but in all areas of his life. He actively integrated his mind, body, spirit, and soul, and that seemed to me to be a much more compelling path to choose. I think we all have moments in our life that define us and that was definitely a moment that shaped my definition of success for me.

And now for Mr. Cosby. Of the three, he has definitely had the most pervasive influence on my choices in life and on my definition of success. My first memories of Cosby are fond ones from my childhood. My brother Ray and I used to spend hours listening to Cosby albums on the turntable that our Aunt Jeanne (Ray's godmother) sent him for Christmas from California. We thought Cosby was hilarious, so early on he planted the seeds for something I now strongly associate with success, namely laughter and the joy that comes from connecting with others in fun.

He also helped solidify the mental link between jazz and success that now serves as the foundation for my business. My initial appreciation for jazz began in college when I fell in love to the sounds of Nancy Wilson singing her torch songs. The Cosby show furthered my love for jazz, because they frequently had jazz legends on the show as guests. And the Cosby Show itself helped shape my ideas about success. One of my favorite episodes was the one on which they celebrated Heathcliff's parents' fiftieth wedding anniversary. Do you remember that episode?

Wright

Yes, I enjoyed that one as well!

Barrett

Heathcliff (Cliff) made his parents sit at the bottom of the stairs and then his whole family lined up along the staircase and performed Ray Charles' rendition of *Night and Day*. It was fabulous! I always thought it would be fun to do that with my family for my parents' fiftieth! Also, ever since I saw my first Agatha Christie movie, *And Then There Were None,* as a young girl, I've been a huge fan of murder mysteries so when Cosby got his series *"The Cosby Mysteries"* I added that to my own list of "things I'd love to do before I die." Since I've always been crazy about kids, I would definitely consider it a dream come true if I ever got to host a *Kids Say the Darndest Things* type of television show.

My ideas about success have also been influenced by the way Bill Cosby has chosen to live his life off camera and the example he has set with his strong family values and philanthropic pursuits. I really admire Mr. Cosby and my own definition of success *for me,* includes following in as many of his footsteps as possible!

Wright

Certainly not a bad role model to choose. Linda, I understand you're an Outward Bound Alumni; what is that?

Barrett

Well, I suspect that it may have been at least in part, the inspiration for the television show *Survivor* because Outward Bound originated as a survival school for young British seaman who were being torpedoed by German U-boats during World War II. After the war, it evolved into an adventure-based educational program designed to teach people experientially that their only real limits in life are self-imposed. Outward Bound is a classroom without ceilings designed to concomitantly teach self-reliance, leadership, team building, independence, and interdependence. My course was a twenty-four day adventure through the Colorado Rocky Mountains. I consider it to be one of the highlights of my life.

Wright

The organization is ongoing?

Barrett

It is.

Wright

Did Outward Bound teach you anything about success?

Barrett

Outward Bound taught me a lot of things about success and I think one of the most important points that it drove home for me was the idea that I really am capable of far more than I think I am. The course taught us this experientially because every single day we were pushed further and further out of our comfort zones. And just when we thought we couldn't go an inch further, we learned that in fact we had plenty of untapped resources within. All we had to do was be willing to dig a little deeper.

Being immersed in that environment for nearly a month made it easy to internalize the lessons and the beliefs we adopted there, and those beliefs permeated every aspect of our lives long after the course itself ended. It was my Outward Bound experience that really instilled in me an idea I like to pass along to my audience members, i.e., no matter what obstacles appear in your path, *you possess within you all the resources you need to find a way over, under, around, or through them!*

Wright

Is Outward Bound something like a boot camp? What exactly do you do during one of these courses?

Barrett

My course was packed with a wide variety of activities and exciting challenges. One of the highlights for me was our "solo" where we were totally alone and didn't eat anything for *three* days! Living in a full house where meals were never skipped, I had never done either of these things for three hours much less three whole days! That particular experience really played a big role in how I lead my life today because it taught me the value of solitude and how important it is to just be still and listen. There's a quote about this that I love from Ralph Waldo Emerson:

"It is easy in the world to live after the world's opinions; it is easy in solitude to live after your own; but the great man is he who in the midst of the crowd keeps with perfect sweetness the independence of solitude."

Our lives are so hectic these days that I think it's more important than ever to take time each morning to feed our souls and clear our minds of stress and negativity, and to prepare ourselves mentally and spiritually for the day ahead. I think that if you can be the one in your family or in your organization who can remain resourceful in stressful situations, stay calm in the midst of chaos, and bounce back quickly from your inevitable setbacks, then you will have a competitive edge and be an invaluable asset to any group you're associated with. So, that's one lesson that has personally impacted my own success and the message I share with my audiences.

Another highlight of my Outward Bound experience was the half marathon. We had no idea we were going to have to do it. They surprised us with it on the last day. By then, we were all exhausted and ready to go home. We had been jogging each morning, but only a couple of miles and even that was challenging for most of us because of the altitude. Also, I had blisters all over my feet so just putting on my socks and boots was a painful challenge. None of us had ever run thirteen and a half miles before, much less through the Colorado Rockies. Many of us believed they were asking us to do the impossible. But lo and behold, *we all did it!*

When you do something you didn't believe was possible, it has a sort of domino effect on your brain! You start asking yourself what *else* you might be capable of and suddenly your mind opens up to all kinds of new possibilities!

One of the possibilities I considered was, "if I was able to complete a half marathon, *then maybe I could run an entire marathon!*" Not long after that, I did! I ended up running my first marathon with Ben Moore and his group known as, "Moore's Marines." What made that race really fun is that Moore knew Bill Cosby from his Navy days and he regaled us with Cosby stories for 26.2 miles. I was so engaged in his stories I barely even noticed the physical challenges my body was experiencing. Before I knew it, the finish line was in sight and I was able to sprint across it. That was one of the most exhilarating experiences of my life and one I probably wouldn't have had if I hadn't been pushed out of my comfort zone by my Outward Bound instructors. So yes, Outward Bound taught me a lot about success and therefore, I owe a debt of gratitude to my dad and my instructors and to Mr. Cosby. In fact, that reminds me that being grateful and expressing our gratitude to others is another excellent strategy for success.

Wright

Yes, I certainly agree with you on that, Linda. Now, you're known as the "Jazz Speaker." Where did that moniker come from and what does it mean?

Barrett

To explain that, David, I need to take you back to 1987 when I had the good fortune to cross paths with a wonderful keynote speaker named Rosita Perez. Today, Rosita is a retired, highly revered member of the National Speakers Association (NSA). Over the years she won the respect and hearts of many and has been recognized with many prestigious awards including both the Council of Peers Award for Excellence and the coveted Cavett Award, named after the founder of NSA. But on that day in 1987, all I knew, as I sat in the audience with thousands of other people, was that this woman was taking us on an emotional roller coaster ride as she shared her soul and substance with us. One minute we were laughing so hard our sides nearly split and the next minute our eyes were welling up with tears. She had us completely mesmerized! We were all captivated by her stories, her parodies—she played guitar and sang during her presentation—and her willingness to let us in on the lessons of her life.

As I listened to Rosita, I felt as though God was speaking directly to me, revealing His purpose for my life. At the time, *my* plan for my life was to pursue my Ph.D. in Clinical Psychology, to write books, and lecture at Loyola or Johns Hopkins University in Baltimore, Maryland, to marry a man with whom I could share a romance like the one Cliff and Claire enjoyed on the Cosby Show, and raise a big, happy family in a loving, "Huxtable-like" home. But that day, my plans changed! There was no denying what God was calling me to do. So now I deliver programs that are similar in some ways to the one I saw Rosita deliver, but that are also quite different in other ways because my instrument is the piano, my music is jazz, and my stories come from my own life experiences.

As my business evolved, I found that I needed to be able to describe in a nutshell what I do. Essentially, I am a speaker who uses jazz as both a medium and a metaphor for success to motivate, educate, and entertain my audiences. *"The Jazz Speaker"* captures the essence of what I do, so it stuck.

Wright

I remember when I was in college I went to see one of my heroes, Count Basie. He had a great, great, singer with him who was also one of the greatest jazz singers who ever lived. He is also one of my heroes and I was so glad when Bill Cosby invited him on the show to be his wife's father, the great Joe Williams. It was really, really good. So we share that. I didn't know there were a lot of women around who loved jazz music. I'm glad you do.

Barrett

Me too. Jazz has enriched my life in countless ways.

Wright

Marian McPartland who plays on public radio is still going at it great. She just has some of the most interesting conversations with some of the greatest jazz pianists in the world. So what does jazz have to do with success?

Barrett

There are actually many parallels, too many to share in our conversation today, David and so many in fact that I am writing a book on that very subject. One example is that in order to succeed in today's increasingly competitive marketplace, you and I have got to cultivate the ability to improvise creative solutions. We can no longer rely on the solutions that were effective in the leisurely pace of the past because they simply are not up to the rapid-fire challenges of the present. We must build new neural networks to rise to the new challenges we face. Jazz improvisation offers me an excellent vehicle for teaching people how to be able to do that.

Wright

Great. We'll look forward to reading your book to learn more about that! So what strategies have you found most helpful in overcoming the challenges you've faced in your life?

Barrett

Throughout the years, David, I have discovered several strategies that have really helped me with my quest to conquer the challenges in my own life. One of my all time favorite strategies originated with my mom. She is an avid reader and I wanted to adopt her good reading habits. I was always coming across new things I wanted to learn more about but my reading speed was simply never fast enough to keep up with my interests.

Then I read an article Bill Cosby wrote about speed-reading and I had some immediate success using the strategies he suggested. That motivated me to learn more about how to improve my reading abilities, so I enrolled in a speed-reading course. Initially it helped a lot because I diligently did all the exercises the teacher gave us to do. Over time, however, I got busy with other things and before I knew it, I had slipped back into my old habits of reading.

Wright

I remember many years ago I took that Evelyn Wood Reading Dynamics course, and increased my reading speed from about 250 words to about 1200 and my retention was way up there. Then I found that as I didn't use it later on I just lost it.

Barrett

Exactly David, that's a very common experience for people who take that course. Another experience I had that is very common for traditional speed-readers is that like you, I enjoyed an immediate boost in my reading speed but over time, as my speed continued to increase, I noticed that my comprehension started to decrease. Then I slowed down, in order to retain my comprehension, which of course, defeated the whole purpose!

Then I read a book about Neuro-Linguistic Programming (NLP), a technology developed by John Grinder, a professor of linguistics, and one of his brightest students, a computer programmer named Richard Bandler. One of the presuppositions of John and Richard's new science of human performance was the idea that if anyone could do anything exquisitely well, then their results could be reproduced by anyone else who was willing to learn how to model the exquisite achiever. It stood to reason that NLP could offer me the solutions I was seeking. I became a Master Practitioner and took a number of other related courses, all of which gave me new exciting tools for success.

Through those courses I was introduced to one of my all time favorite strategies I referred to a few moments ago. It's called "The PhotoReading Whole Mind System" and it is amazing!

Wright

How does this differ from traditional speed-reading? What is "whole mind"? Are you talking about learning to apply it across the board?

Barrett

The PhotoReading Whole Mind System is a revolutionary new way to approach the written word. It's a process that engages the whole mind in order to glean the meaning of text. Some people like to refer to PhotoReading as the "Ferrari" of reading courses because dramatically increasing your reading speed is one of the many benefits that PhotoReaders enjoy, but the benefits of PhotoReading go way beyond speed. It offers a completely different approach to absorbing new material, allowing you to accomplish results that wouldn't be possible with regular reading or traditional speed-reading techniques, and it offers solutions to the common challenges encountered in traditional speed-reading courses.

A fellow NLP enthusiast who trained with Bandler and Grinder developed PhotoReading. His name is Paul Scheele and he is a prolific author and internationally acclaimed expert in the field of human performance. Back in 1985, a client asked him to develop a course to help his executives keep up with their reading demands so he incorporated what he knew from NLP along with several other exciting technologies, including pre-conscious processing and accelerated learning.

Wright

Is this a self-help course or do you have to be taught?

Barrett

There are several different ways to learn the process. Paul wrote an excellent book titled *PhotoReading,* explaining the entire process; it's a delightful read. For example, when you open the book, the first thing you're greeted with is Paul's tips for maximizing your time and experience. He explains that if you've only got twenty-five minutes, you're to read the paragraphs indicated by a cartoon character icon of Albert Einstein riding a bicycle. If you've got an additional thirty minutes, then you also read the paragraphs that are indicated by a cartoon character icon of Albert Einstein jogging. If you have yet another forty-five to ninety minutes, then you go back and read the paragraphs that are indicated by a cartoon character icon of Albert Einstein with a light bulb over his head. As I said, it's a delightful read!

If after reading the book, you still want more, you can get Paul's personal learning course, which includes a workbook and CD's that enable you to learn at your own pace at home. Or, if you are like me and love the environment created at live events, that's an option as well. Paul has a network of PhotoReading instructors he has licensed to teach the course all over the world.

Wright

And you're licensed to do that?

Barrett

Yes, I am and I believe everyone should take the course! I am so enamored with PhotoReading that I look for every possible opportunity to educate others about it because it offers so many exciting benefits. For example, one of the byproducts of PhotoReading that has been invaluable to me is a process called "direct learning," because these days, even if you stay with the same company for a long time, your roles and responsibilities are likely to change constantly. As a result of this, the ability to acquire new skills very rapidly would give you a competitive edge, and direct learning makes that possible. Paul has also authored an extensive library of thoroughly researched, exquisitely written personal learning courses that offer additional strategies for success.

Wright

What a rich resource for me and our readers, Linda. Thank you for sharing that. So tell me something that has been driving me crazy ever since I received your materials. What is a "thought somersault?"

Barrett

This is an idea I came up with after observing something my mother did years ago. It happened shortly after the tenth anniversary *of her thirty-ninth birthday!* For years, she'd gotten away with her "little white lie" because she looked so young for her age, but on her forty-ninth birthday, it occurred to her that in a few short months, my oldest brother, Tim, was going to turn twenty-five and she was going to have a credibility issue. We joked about it on her birthday and then forgot about it.

A few months later while our whole family was out celebrating Tim's twenty-fifth birthday, a woman my mom knew stopped at our table to say hello. None of us had ever met her so my mom introduced us. She said, "This is my husband, Jack, and these are his children from his first marriage!" We all got a good chuckle over that clever line and later when I reflected on it, I realized that what she had done was a somersault in her head. She took a thought and turned it around in her mind until she was able to put a more positive spin on it.

In music there is something called a "turnaround technique." It's a short chord progression musicians use to keep a tune in play and that's exactly what a thought somersault can do for you to keep you in play in the song of life. It's a technique you can use to turn your thoughts around when you find yourself indulging in unresourceful, negative emotions or are tempted to invest time and energy feeling sorry for yourself.

One lesson that I've learned repeatedly from my own experiences as well as from observation of others is that it is not the challenges or the changes we face but rather the choices we make that really matter. What we tell ourselves in our head about the challenging situations we all face is what dictates success or the lack thereof.

There are lots of different ways that people can somersault the thought for themselves; we can also do it for others. My father was excellent at somersaulting thoughts for me when I was a little girl. Whenever I would face any sort of challenge, he had the most wonderful way of completely turning my thoughts around about it until I was able to gain a more positive perspective on the situation. Mother Teresa was excellent at this, too. For example, in an interview, she once said, "I know God would never give me more than I can handle...I just wish He didn't trust me so much!"

Wright

I think I remember seeing that quote somewhere. She was certainly an inspiration. While you were speaking about your father implementing thought somersaulting, I was thinking more about the conversation itself. I've got a forty-three-year-old daughter and a forty-one-year-old son. I've also got a sixteen-year-old daughter. Times have changed so much that you have to make appointments with them now. With the computer and television, and school and homework, and things like that it's not like it used to be. I'm like all the old folks my age who wish it were like it was in the past; unfortunately the past will never be back. I miss those conversations and I try to make time for them but it is difficult.

Barrett

I hear you, David, and you are definitely not alone! More and more, I'm finding that one of the biggest challenges my friends, colleagues, and audience members are facing has to do with the increasing prevalence of multi-generational households and workforces.

One example of this occurred last year when "Ivan the Terrible" threatened to sink New Orleans even further below sea level! I recently relocated here from Annapolis, Maryland, so I've never been here during a bad hurricane. My neighbor, Tony, knows that, so on Monday morning of the week Ivan was supposed to hit, he rang my doorbell. He was a Green Beret and now serves as the Vice-President of the Special Forces Association so he has access to military intelligence. He had heard this might be the worst hurricane ever to hit New Orleans so he encouraged me to get out of town quickly if I could. I had several appointments lined up and a lot of work to do so after he left, I turned on the weather channel and there was no mention of severe weather so I kept it on but went about my business. It wasn't until later that night that the weather channel started mentioning that a bad storm was brewing. By the next morning, they reported that there was a definite cause for concern and encouraged anyone who *could* leave to do so as quickly as possible.

Well, apparently Tony had told his parents the same thing he told me on Monday morning but, like me, they waited until Tuesday to heed his warnings! By then, hotels within a 100-mile radius of New Orleans were already booked to capacity so finding a place to go was becoming a big challenge. Tony told them to call his wife at work because she wanted to help them find a place to stay. He asked his mom to call him as soon as she and his father got to the hotel safely. By mid-afternoon, he still hadn't heard from his mother and was getting worried, so he called her cell phone and she answered.

He said, "Mom, where are you?"

She said, "Your father and I just pulled into the parking lot of a Kroger's grocery store. We're trying to find the hotel but we're lost so we stopped here for directions."

Tony said, "What hotel are you looking for?"

His mom replied, "Sandy told us to go the "dot com hotel."

Immediately he realized what you've probably already guessed, David! What Sandy had suggested was that her mother-in-law go to hotels.com! Her intent was for them to check availability on the Internet while she made some calls to see what she could find.

This type of miscommunication is not at all unusual in households and offices all across America because you have seniors, baby boomers, generation Y, and generation X all living and working together with their dramatically different generational values, knowledge bases, interests, experiences, beliefs, etc. That has created a whole host of new communication gaps. As a result, nearly every time I speak these days, I devote at least a portion of the program to addressing these common communication challenges. Here again jazz is an excellent vehicle for communicating the idea of creating harmony as a strategy for orchestrating success.

Wright

Well, what an interesting conversation. You are a delight and I've learned a lot here today. I think maybe when people write their list of the three people they would like to have dinner and conversation with, you're probably going to be on a lot of folks' lists.

Barrett

Well, what a sweet thing to say, David. I hope your prediction comes true because I would be delighted "to be on a lot of folks' lists."

Wright

Today we have been talking with Linda Barrett who is president and CEO of the Barrett Resource Group, Inc., a national speaking, training and motivational entertainment firm that focuses on teaching people how to perform to their potential.

Thank you so much Linda for being with us today on *Conversations on Success*.

Barrett

Thank you so much David. It was really a privilege and a pleasure to have this conversation on success with you!

As the President and CEO of The Barrett Resource Group, Inc., Linda Barrett serves as a resource for success. The dual, lifelong interests that have driven her success are human potential and music. Nationally known as "The Jazz Speaker," Linda combines her passion for helping people in pursuit of peak performance with her passion for playing jazz piano to create custom, content-rich programs for meetings, conventions, retreats, awards banquets, and fundraisers. Taking the lead from role models like Victor Borge and Bill Cosby, Linda gets audience members to laugh as they learn her practical strategies for success.

Linda Barrett

The Barrett Resource Group, Inc.

1000 W. Esplanade Avenue

Suite 102 PMB 150

Kenner, LA 70065

New Orleans Office: 504.468.8716

Maryland Office: 410.812.2689

Email: LindaBarrett@JazzSpeaker.com

www.JazzSpeaker.com